LITERACY
AND
EMPOWERMENT

Literacy
and
EMPOWERMENT

The Meaning Makers

PATRICK L. COURTS

Series in Language and Ideology
edited by DONALDO MACEDO

Bergin & Garvey
New York • Westport, Connecticut • London

Library of Congress Cataloging-in-Publication Data

Courts, Patrick L.
  Literacy and empowerment : the meaning makers / Patrick L. Courts.
    p.   cm. — (Language and ideology series)
  Includes bibliographical references and index.
  ISBN 0-89789-260-7 (alk. paper). — ISBN 0-89789-261-5 (pbk. :
alk. paper)
  1. Language arts—United States—Evaluation. 2. Literacy—United
States. 3. Sociolinguistics—United States. 4. Self-actualization
(Psychology)   I. Title. II. Series.
LB1576.C745   1991
302.2'244—dc20   91-2267

British Library Cataloguing in Publication Data is available.

Library of Congress Catalog Card Number: 91-2267
ISBN: 0-89789-260-7
       0-89789-261-5 (pbk.)

First published in 1991

Bergin & Garvey, One Madison Avenue, New York, NY 10010
An imprint of Greenwood Publishing Group, Inc.

Printed in the United States of America

The paper used in this book complies with the
Permanent Paper Standard issued by the National
Information Standards Organization (Z39.48-1984).

10 9 8 7 6 5 4 3 2 1

Copyright Acknowledgments

The author and publisher are grateful for permission to reprint from the following
sources:

Nicole Ambrosetti. "Reading a book is best . . . " is used with permission.

John Ashbery. Excerpt from "What Is Poetry" From *Selected Poems* by John Ashbery.
Copyright © 1985 by John Ashbery. Reprinted by permission of the publisher, Viking
Penguin, a division of Penguin Books USA Inc.

Excerpt from *Alice in Wonderland* by Lewis Carroll, edited by Donald J. Gray, published by W. W. Norton & Co. (1971), is reprinted with permission.

Excerpt from *Catch-22* by Joseph Heller, copyright © 1955, 1961, 1989 by Joseph
Heller, is reprinted by permission of Simon & Schuster, Inc.

Excerpt from "There Was a Child Went Forth" by Walt Whitman, *Complete Poetry
and Selected Prose*, Riverside Edition, copyright © 1959 by Houghton Mifflin Company.
Used with permission.

Excerpts from "Mature Literacy and Resurrections: The Birth of the Reader" by
Patrick L. Courts, in *Whole Language: Explorations and Applications*, edited by Robert
W. Blake (1990), and "Reading, Writing, and Impenetrability" by Patrick Courts,
in *Reading, Writing and Interpreting Literature: Pedagogy, positions and research*, edited
by Robert W. Blake (1989), are used by permission of the publisher, New York State
English Council.

Excerpts from "Literacy, Cultural Literacy, and Trivial Pursuit" by Patrick L. Courts,
in *Pennsylvania English* (Fall/Winter 1989), are used by permission of the publisher.

Contents

Foreword

Donaldo Macedo

Patrick Courts's *Literacy and Empowerment* not only advances the present theoretical debate over literacy, it also examines how "the process of knowing and coming to know has been preempted by a system that forgets to carefully question and examine its own presuppositions; scholarship and thinking have been co-opted by the *business* of research"—research which is "owned by the military-industrial complex." Courts unmasks the illiteracy of literacy approaches designed to produce readers who become victims of the present development of neatly prepackaged reading and writing programs which are presented as the solution to difficulties students experience in reading and writing.

Courts mounts an articulate attack on traditional approaches to literacy which have been deeply ingrained in a positivistic method of inquiry. These approaches abstract methodological issues from their ideological contexts and consequently ignore the relationship between the sociopolitical structures of a society and the act of reading. In fact, the exclusion of social and political dimensions from the practice of reading gives rise to an ideology of cultural reproduction, one that views readers as "objects." Furthermore, these traditional approaches to literacy have failed to provide a theoretical model for empowering historical agents with the logic of individual and collective self-determination. While traditional approaches to literacy may differ in their basic assumption about the reading process, they all share one common feature: They all ignore the role of language as a major force in the construction of human subjectivities. In other words, they ignore the way language may either confirm or deny the life histories and experiences of the people who use it.

In this superb volume, Courts offers an approach to a pedagogy of literacy that centers on the role of language in the construction of everyday meaning. His approach is structured around M.A.K. Halliday's premise that language develops primarily through social interactions which shape the linguistic structures of the individual and shape his or her cultural world. According to Halliday, language occurs in contexts, but meaning is never saturated by the contexts in which it is constructed. Consequently, meanings as they emerge from the process of knowledge construction are always partial. Courts laments the fact that the dominant language of schools and colleges is situational (context dependent) and that sociolinguistic interaction in the school does not break the pattern of situationally dependent language; that is, most reading and writing courses do little to interrupt or explicitly contest the reproduction of language practices which are forged within an instrumental, cause-and-effect logic. According to Courts, students need facility with what he calls, after Halliday and others, "exploratory-expressive" language. I would add that beyond "exploratory-expressive" language, students need to appropriate a critical language that will enable them to understand the ways in which different discourses encode different world views. The semantic value of specific lexical items belonging to a different discourse differs radically, in some cases, from the reading derived from the standard dominant language of the curriculum.

The major issue is that students' own linguistic code reflects not only their reality, but also their lived experiences in a given historical moment. For instance, in the case of Black English, terms that encapsulate the drug culture, discrimination, daily alienation, and the struggle to survive the substandard and inhumane conditions of ghettos, constitute a discourse black Americans find no difficulty in using. In fact, it is through a critical understanding of this raw and sometimes cruel reality that black students can begin to unveil the obfuscation that characterizes their daily existence inside and outside the schools. Their language is, therefore, a powerful tool demystifying the distorted reality prepackaged for them by the dominant curriculum.

Although Courts does not directly address the issue of linguistic minorities, an issue to which I will return later, he convincingly argues that "schools in general, including colleges and universities, have become stewards to the language of getting things done rather than the language of exploration and expression of self and other." As he points out,

the crisis of literacy in our colleges is especially urgent: While educators debate student-centeredness and experiential approaches to teaching, and literary critics and philosophers argue the sense and nonsense of deconstruction versus New Criticism, students are *being told* the meaning of *Romeo and Juliet*, memorizing it, and regurgitating it.

Literacy and Empowerment constitutes an impassioned and articulate attack on reading and writing classes based on workbooks and grammar lessons,

lessons which force students to "bark at print" or fill in the blanks. Students in such classes are too busy reading to learn to read. They are also too busy writing to write—by engaging in grudgingly banal exercises such as practicing correct punctuation and drafting business letters. Books used in most classrooms are, Courts points out, too often in the service of commercially prepared ditto sheets and workbooks. Courts's account suggests that most university programs do not take advantage of the language experiences that the majority of students have had before they reach the university. Teachers become the victims of their own professionalization when they delegitimize the experiences that students bring with them into the classroom.

Literacy and Empowerment is fundamentally a book about the nature of meaning and truth and the role of language; it is a book bent on exploring how meaning comes to be known and shared. It follows the basic and important assumption that language is at the center of human development and literacy is all about the possibility of meaning making, communication, and the active construction of relationships. Schools, therefore, should be places where students are invited to practice the possibility of meaning making. Instead, schools too often practice superficial decoding experiences decontextualized from the real-life experiences and affective investment which students make in everyday social life, experiences that attempt to prove reality through the surface structure of language. Courts describes the present predicament as one in which earlier models of literacy have been replaced by literacy for economic advancement and personal advantage in the marketplace. This utilitarian approach produces readers who meet the basic reading requirements of contemporary society. Such an approach emphasizes the mechanical learning of reading skills while sacrificing the critical analysis of the social and political order that generates the need for reading in the first place. This position, in fact, has led to the development of "functional literates" groomed primarily to meet the requirements of our ever more complex technological society.

Courts argues that cultural literacy has to mean something to students and must not exist simply as a list of items to be learned. Human beings don't grasp information (even if it is wrapped in the mantle of our cultural heritage); they make meaning. That is, the world or the text does not sit out there in the social world waiting to be discovered and grasped. Reading is more than decoding but rather involves the creating of systems of intelligibility, or schemata, that individuals use to create meaning. In short, Courts argues for what he calls a "literate cultural literacy." Such a literacy invites students to read both outside and inside realities (both the world and the word, in Paulo Freire's terms) and to become better and more confident meaning makers.

What is important to Courts is the extent to which students invest in the process of constructing meaning. Courts sees the process of meaning making as something that should fundamentally inform the entire spectrum of reading, writing, speaking, and listening activities that are employed in schools. Courts's study is an articulate and compelling criticism of forms of public education that all too frequently fragment meaning and encapsulate the role of education in bureaucratic and technological concerns. It is an attack on both content-based and skills-based programs, claiming that both approaches come perilously close to meaninglessness. Either students are forced to approach knowledge as a cluster of fragmented skills based on a behavioral model of learning (like a form of ideological drill that produces artifacts for the approval of sanctioned experts), or else they try to cover so much content that the exercise becomes almost meaningless. Ironically, too much emphasis on mastering facts can lead to a content-neutral curriculum. Courts finds such an emphasis "perverse, almost psychotic," particularly as this emphasis approaches content "as fragments of unrelated information," usually in preparation for multiple-choice exams. In this way mainstream schooling augments its discretionary power, turning students into what Henry Giroux calls "clerks of the empire."

Courts's study is primarily concerned with the teaching of middle-class or upper-middle-class students, those unburdened by racial discrimination and poverty, students who have done well in elementary and high school settings and are now populating the university lecture halls and seminar rooms. If schools are failing these students, the situation by implication does not bode well for those students less economically, socially, and politically advantaged. It is toward the linguistic minority students that I would like to turn my discussion now.

The pedagogical and political implications in literacy programs for linguistic minority students are far-reaching and yet largely ignored. These reading programs often contradict a fundamental principle of reading, namely that students learn to read faster and with better comprehension when taught in their native tongue. The immediate recognition of familiar words and experiences enhances the development of a positive self-concept in children who may be insecure about the status of their language and culture. For this reason, and to be consistent with the plan to construct a democratic society free from vestiges of oppression, a minority literacy program should be based on the rationale that such a program must be rooted in the cultural capital of subordinate groups and have as its point of departure their own language.

Educators must develop radical pedagogical structures which provide students with the opportunity to use their own reality as a basis for literacy. This includes, obviously, the language they bring to the classroom. To do otherwise is to deny minority students the rights that lie at the core of the notion of an emancipatory literacy. The failure to base a literacy program on the minority students' language means that oppositional forces can neutralize the efforts of educators and political leaders to achieve decolonization of schooling. It is of tantamount importance that the incorporation of the minority language as the primary language of instruction in literacy be given top priority. By using their own language minority students will be able to reconstruct their history and their culture.

I want to argue that the minority language has to be understood within the theoretical framework that generates it. Put another way, the ultimate meaning and value of the minority language is not to be found by determining how systematic and rule-governed it is. We know that already. Its real meaning has to be understood through the assumptions that govern it, and it has to be understood via the social, political, and ideological relations to which it points. Generally speaking, the issue of effectiveness and validity often hides the true role of language in the maintenance of the values and interests of the dominant class. In other words, the issue of effectiveness and validity becomes a mask that obfuscates questions about the social, political, and ideological order within which the minority language exists.

If an emancipatory and critical literacy program is to be developed in the United States for minority students in which they become "subjects" rather than "objects," educators must understand the productive quality of language. James Donald puts it this way:

I take language to be *productive* rather than *reflective* of social reality. This means calling into question the assumption that we, as speaking subjects, simply use language to organize and express our ideas and experiences. On the contrary, language is one of the most important social practices through which we come to experience ourselves as subjects. . . . My point here is that once we get beyond the idea of language as no more than a medium of communication, as a tool equally and neutrally available to all parties in cultural exchanges, then we can begin to examine language both as a practice of signification and also as a *site* for cultural struggle and as a *mechanism* which produces antagonistic relations between different social groups. (Donald, 1985)

It is to the antagonistic relationship between the minority and dominant speakers that I want to turn now. The antagonistic nature of the minority language has never been fully explored. In order to discuss more clearly this issue of antagonism, I will use Donald's distinction between *oppressed* language and *repressed* language. Using Donald's categories, the "negative" way of posing the minority language question is to view it in terms of *oppression*— that is, seeing the minority language as "lacking" the dominant standard features which usually serve as a point of reference for the minority language. By far the most common questions concerning the minority language in the United States are posed from the *oppression* perspective. The alternative view of the minority language is that it is *repressed* in the standard dominant language. In this view, minority language as a repressed language could, if spoken, challenge the privileged standard linguistic dominance. Educators have failed to recognize the "positive" promise and antagonistic nature of the minority language. It is precisely on these dimensions that educators must demystify the standard dominant language and the old assumptions about its inherent superiority. Educators must develop an emancipatory and critical literacy program informed by a radical pedagogy so that the minority language will cease to provide its speakers the experience of subordination and, moreover, may be brandished as a weapon of resistance to the dominance of the dominant standard language of the curriculum.

To be implemented, a critical and emancipatory literacy program needs to move away from traditional approaches which emphasize the acquisition of mechanical skills while divorcing reading from its ideological and historical contexts. To accomplish this literacy goal will require a pedagogy more explicitly grounded in a politics of liberation such as those developed by Paulo Freire, Henry A. Giroux, Peter McLaren, and Jim Gee, among others. However, if used in conjunction with certain strands of critical and feminist pedagogy, Courts's account can greatly enhance our understanding of not only how language functions to construct forms of context-dependent knowledge but also how teachers can employ pedagogical strategies to enhance the formation of such knowledge. Many teachers who profess to work from a radical or critical position lack the requisite pedagogical practices for transforming their program into meaning-making events; it is precisely for this reason that *Literacy as Empowerment* is so important.

Courts's book is a grounded review of linguistic, literary, and literacy theory leading up to the more radical formulations. While making no claim to situate his work within the tradition of critical literacy, Courts offers observations that not only are hospitable to approaches developed within the critical tradition, but also serve as an important entree to texts defined within liberationist political projects. What is so valuable about Courts's work is that it is concretely embedded in an ongoing attempt to reform literacy practices within the academy. In this timely volume Courts offers teachers a myriad of inventive approaches to cultural literacy that include the personal essay, writing exams, annotated bibliographies, research papers, student journals, reader notes, and peer editing, among others. These approaches are designed to help students gain some insight into the social construction of knowledge and the effects of such knowledge when it is used in the service of particular social, political, or ideological interests.

As Henry A. Giroux (1990) illustrates, language has the power of truth even though it is founded on social conventions that are the result of uneven struggles over the primacy and legitimacy of certain discourses. The fall from normative linguistic grammaticality that we often see in inner-city school settings does not represent a failure of groups marginalized and exploited on the basis of linguistic difference and economic disenfranchisement but rather brings into relief the political differences always present when textual borders are crossed by readers differentiated on the basis of race, class, and gender. Domains of signification are not simply systems of arbitrary differences but have been developed within social and linguistic practices that are cross-cut by relations of power and as such need to be analyzed historically with respect to the particular genres, rhetorical tropes, and system of intelligibility they assume (McLaren, forthcoming).

Along with critical educational theorists such as Giroux, Freire, and McLaren, Courts recognizes the contingency and partiality constitutive of the process of meaning making. For instance, Courts's position on language and literacy acknowledges the "gap" that exists in the construction of knowledge that would allow language to serve as more than simply a prison-house, but also as a vehicle for self-transformation. This is most clearly articulated in Courts's emphasis on the rule-generated structures through which individuals project the world, and is emphasized in his employment of Derrida's concept of *dehiscence*—the gap that allows and necessitates the further construction of subjectivity through language, even in the face of an always/already disappearing present.

Courts notes that even though we cannot fully know or explain contexts, sociolinguistic interactions, and/or the degrees to which these shape our "schemata," we do exist within certain contexts at certain times, and we are always both inside and outside such contexts at the same time. And even though we can never specify everything about the contexts which create us within language, we can know enough to reinvent ourselves through forms of meaning making that enable us to examine and shape the conditions and presuppositions that structure our world. Language in this sense becomes, for Courts, "the assertion of our present, the recognition of being alive, and the (re)creation of our origin. Even if it is fully possible to achieve." Consequently, Courts wishes to see language function heuristically as a vehicle for creating imaginative alternatives to present conditions of possibility and responsibility for self- and social transformation. In this sense, Courts's volume is very much about the construction of subjectivity, identity, and agency through language, and the possibilities for students to create new, more imaginative and critical forms of agency.

Literacy and Empowerment is about helping students to develop the power to "actualize literacy," teaching students to use language in order to create the possibility of meaning, and helping students move beyond the arbitrary, situational motives that exist when reading and writing are engaged in primarily for a grade or for personal advancement in the area of social competition. This volume will help teachers move beyond the authorial ideologies surrounding literacy in order to make connections in and across student experiences so that readers are as much in control of the text as they are controlled by it. Courts refers to the process of control and of moving beyond rehearsal of the literal facts of a text as the development of the "actual reader." While the development of "actual readers" hardly guarantees liberation, it certainly is a prerequisite for liberation, a pedagogical and political prerequisite that the history of our time demands.

Acknowledgments

I have received so much assistance in the creation of this book that it is difficult to know where to begin. My deepest gratitude goes to Minda Rae Amiran for her invaluable editorial assistance with the manuscript while it was in process and for introducing me to the issue of assessment. Thanks to George Sebouhian, who was one of the first to read and generously comment on the manuscript and whose challenging intellect keeps so many of us intellectually honest and charged. I thank Jeanette McVicker, whose commentary on the manuscript made me feel that it was potentially helpful to college teachers and who reminded me that I needed to return to the world of Foucault as I examined the nature of power in our society and in the educational system.

I also want to express my gratitude to Michael Halstead, who did his best to help me avoid gross errors in the sociological areas, and to Kathleen McInerney, who helped keep me abreast of new developments in the areas of pedagogy and reading theory. And I happily include Rose Sebouhian, one of the finest high school teachers I know; she brought me "inside" the alternative high school (School to Employment Program, or S.T.E.P) she created, and she helped me believe that the book might be of value to high school teachers. Any list like this must include Stephen Tchudi, who was my mentor more than twenty years ago and who kindly provided me with copious, constructive editorial advice while the manuscript was in process.

There are others to thank: Robert Deming, who tried to make me a neo-Marxist and failed (who made me read wonderful articles that I never would have read, who helped me think new ideas); and all those undergraduate students who read, commented on, and discussed parts of the manuscript— often providing the best (and most unabashedly direct) reader feedback.

Thanks to Penelope Deakin for all her assistance in the Writing across the Curriculum Workshops, for years of encouragement and powerful conversation about teaching and writing and tutors—and for the wine.

I am also thankful to Robert Blake, editor of the NYSEC monograph series: His encouragement helped me more than he can know. In addition, I am grateful to Joanne Foeller, whose assistance in the initial typing and production of the manuscript went far beyond what one might reasonably expect; and I appreciate the fact that Richard Goodman makes such a service available to us at the State College at Fredonia. Another note of thanks to Roberta Corcoran-Andrasik for her assistance with the index and to Richard Hart for his research assistance.

Of course, my thanks to "the kids": to Patrick, Kim, and Ingrid, who always help me keep this "stuff" in perspective, whether I like it or not, and who in many ways are the reasons why I care so much about meaning makers; and to six-year-old Nicole Ambrosetti, who reminded me that "Books don't realy know there meaning until you read them." Finally, a special note of gratitude to Karen Mills-Courts, who introduced me to Heidegger and Derrida (destruction and deconstruction) and then helped me to understand this new world. It is she who speaks roses in deep winter, she who makes my meanings worth making.

Introduction

Reading a book is best not just because it's good . . . but because the book does not know its story. This will tell you why. One day a girl went to the library. It heard someone crying. Then she found it out. It was a book. She said, Why are you crying? Because I want someone to read me so I know my story. So the girl read it and so they were happy. because of this that is why you have to read a book. and the book will be . . . HAPPY!!!

Nicole Ambrosetti, age six

This is a book about literacy—not functional literacy or the ability to read a job application and fill in the blanks, but genuine literacy, the kind of literacy that empowers the individual to make meaning of the world of oral and written language in which we are all immersed. This is a book for students, for teachers, and for anyone who cares whether our society is populated by followers or by leaders. And it is a book for people who care about kids. It is a book about a very conservative revolution—the revolution that will occur as people become genuinely literate readers, writers, speakers, listeners, and viewers.

Almost none of the kids I hung around with while I was growing up on the South Side of Chicago read much of anything. We were a large group, always enough for a baseball game if the girls in the crowd would participate, seldom less than twenty of us together on those muggy summer nights that make cities part of what they are. We were mostly white and middle–middle class. Some went to Catholic schools and others to public schools. None of us dropped out. We grew up too early for drugs, but just in time for alcohol. Most of us stayed within the bounds of the law and middle-class morality, but a few ended up in jail. Almost everyone drove too fast. Some of us went to college, but most did not.

Everyone I knew was able to read, but almost no one read much of anything, especially not books. Even I—who would later become an English major in college, teach English in some of the Chicago public schools, and go on to earn a doctorate in English—didn't really start reading much until I was in eleventh grade, and I didn't read voraciously until I was about eighteen and worked the second shift in a steel warehouse. In fact, I still remember going to the public library when I was a kid. My mother insisted that I go every two weeks and take out some books because, like most of our parents, she wanted me to read. And I remember taking the books back each two weeks, untouched, unopened, and unread. I was a busy kid and had little time for reading. Anyway, I was one of the best "readers" in school, where reading was primarily defined by the oral performance of "reading" a paragraph as the teacher went up and down the rows "teaching" each of us to read as we took our turns reading some inexhaustibly boring silliness about some kid who lost her red boot because she hadn't put it where her mommy told her to put it. This may have been hot stuff somewhere, but not on the South Side of Chicago. In school, reading also meant filling in blanks in workbooks, which I must have done well but which I never understood at all. And reading meant sounding out words printed below pictures or listed in phonics paradigms. It didn't bother me much because I could do it—even before I got to school I could do it, so for me it was a relatively un-intense way of getting approval. For a few other kids, however, it was incredibly painful as year after year they took their turns proving that, whatever we were doing, it wasn't working for them.

High school brought changes because we were finally given stuff to read that had some content. I was still too busy to let it overwhelm me, but I didn't mind it, and I even enjoyed some of the novels we were required to read. Even so, I didn't get too carried away with the idea of reading until I got that second-shift job in the steel warehouse. Partly, I suppose, it was because there is just not much to do except read when you work second shift. But it was more than just having the time with no one around, more than being wide awake at 1 A.M. with nothing else to do than listen to some sultry deejay's voice. Perhaps it was in this relative isolation that reading suggested the possibility of visiting boundless infinities; perhaps it was the public secrets that were mine alone as I entered the worlds of *U.S. News and World Report* and the lives of Faulkner's characters. Perhaps it was because I wasn't doing it for school, but because it made sense to me, in my living and being. Whatever it was—and that is partly what this book is about—it stuck and stuck good. Whatever I was doing, I knew it made sense—more sense than anything I had ever done before.

Even though I grew up in the city, I really grew up in "the neighborhood." And I have always thought that city folks are at least as provincial as rural folks, because we seldom left that neighborhood, and when we did, we felt uncomfortable, knowing that we were not where we belonged. In the safety and familiarity of the neighborhood, however, we genuinely belonged. Everyone in the neighborhood had nicknames. I still remember that one late night, after we had seen Hitchcock's *Psycho* at the drive-in, a few of us stayed out late telling each other scary stories until I wasn't sure I wanted to walk home alone. Just two of us were left when Crow asked me why I liked to read, what I got out of it. It wasn't meant as a challenge or an insult; this group was much too tight for that kind of silliness. But I was only a teenager at the time and even though I knew he wanted a real answer—he really wondered why I did it—I wasn't sure how to explain. I think I said it had a lot to do with why we all stayed out so late and continued to tell stories that night, but I didn't give him much of an answer.

Later, of course, I would be able to hold forth on the subject. Now I know that reading did and does the same thing for me that good rock and roll or Mozart or Miles Davis does for me. I know it has do with political and personal empowerment; it gives me the power to transform myself, to move inside and outside of minds and worlds that exist by virtue of the printed text. Sometimes it makes me angry, other times happy, often puzzled. Sometimes tired and frustrated, or guilty, or energized. Sometimes it makes me feel both alone and embraced, all in a single moment. But I am still not sure that Crow would have understood what I meant. Not because he was stupid, mind you. Far from it. But because for some reason Crow had never felt what it means to read, to really read. For him it was not empowerment. It was what schools and teachers forced you to do in order to give you tests, in order to give you grades, in order to fill up time that adults had mandated, and because it was "good for you." Like brussels sprouts, or something you hated but they made you do it. When someone made you do it, you tried to find ways to avoid it, and if you couldn't avoid it, you just tried to get it over with.

Just as only a few from that neighborhood learned to enjoy brussels sprouts, even fewer learned to love reading and be empowered through it.

It is important to note, however, that all these kids could read. None of them had trouble passing multiple-choice tests. They could read and write. They could fill out job applications. Those who chose to could get into college (and many did, although most of them eventually quit because they hadn't the foggiest notion of why they were there in the first place). They were not illiterate.

I also remember Bear, another kid from the neighborhood. He was intelligent, headed for a white-collar job and eventual "success," a college graduate—he always did about *B* work in school. While I was an undergraduate preparing to become an English teacher, he told me that he had always like English in school, even in college. When I asked him what it was he liked best about it, he said, "Grammar, because it's so damned easy.

You just learn a few rules and how to diagram and you got the whole thing beat. Besides that, I'm a good speller. So I got it knocked." When I asked him what books he had read that he liked, he said, "None. I never finished a book in or out of school. But you didn't really have to read the stuff to do good on the tests because all you had to do was memorize the answers they told you to memorize and find them on the [multiple-choice] tests." Even I had some trouble believing this, because Bear was plenty smart. So I asked him again, "You mean to tell me you never read a whole book?" My challenge caused him to remember: "Oh, yeah. I read a book about Houdini one time. It was pretty good. He could get out of anything."

So there it was. Crow wasn't at all sure what it was I got out of reading, for he had certainly never gotten anything joyful or fulfilling out of it. For Bear, English was easy because he was a good speller and had learned the rules of grammar (he had learned how to do Reed-Kellogg diagrams). Crow disliked English and Bear liked it. Neither one read much of anything and both avoided writing whenever possible. Go figure.

But that was quite a while ago, in the late 1950s and early 1960s. And it seems that lately we've run into a *real* problem in literacy. I have even heard that the nation is at risk. I have heard it called a crisis. Mostly, it seems to me, the focus is on the fact that some people (somewhere between four and twenty-five million people—I love statistical precision) are illiterate. I think this label refers to people who can barely function in the most basic occupations and are therefore unable to participate in the exciting economic growth of the last decade, the economic growth that has most of our young people working at Wendy's, McDonald's, or Burger King. But given that we have college graduates working in many of these "service areas" (isn't language wonderful?), I am just not sure what the word *illiterate* means when it is used to describe this broad range of human beings. I mean, maybe six million people are unable to read at all. What characterizes the other twenty million?

Of course, we all know of some people who cannot read at all or who read very poorly. And that is a tragedy. I agree with Bruno Bettelheim and Karen Zelan, who say in *On Learning to Read: The Child's Fascination with Meaning*: "The ability to read is of such singular importance to a child's life in school that his experience in learning it more often than not seals the fate, once and for all, of his academic career" (1981: 5). I think it is tremendously important that people be able to read, but not just because of its importance in their academic careers. Rather, it is important because it is part of the linguistic center of what it means to be human beings; it is why the second part of the title of Bettelheim and Zelan's book is so important. Literacy is about *meaning*. Literate people are *meaning makers*. Literacy involves more than reading: It involves language in all of its functions—as it is spoken, heard, written, read, visualized, signed, thought. While someone's notion of basic literacy may be satisfied by people who can decode signs and fill out job applications, no one's notion of mature literacy can rest there or be lulled into self-righteous inertia because we are presently focusing on such illiteracy in the media and in a few special programs.

There is much that I want to get straight in this introduction. That is why I have described my own experience and the experience of many of my friends. This book is not about illiteracy as it is so often discussed. This is a book about *literacy*, about what mature literacy means, why so few people feel the empowerment of language and its many uses, how some of the "very best" schools can be failing some of the most "successful" students. It is about a malignancy that has crept into the teaching of reading and writing, an *ill* that has contaminated literacy. It is about the possibility of being a successful student in a good school, getting a college degree accompanied by a high grade-point average, and still being "ill-literate."

Its gestation began when Crow asked that question and I was unable to give him a sensible, powerful answer, because I wanted Crow to like to read as much as I did. This book is not about people who cannot read at all— people who have been almost entirely locked out of our socioeconomic system because of their skin color, where they were born, or their earning power. This book is about people who can read well, by many standards (especially as their scores are reported through the large testing corporations; especially as the criteria for these standards are based on multiple-choice tests that have little or nothing to do with mature literacy). This book is about kids who do well in our high schools and colleges, people who finish high school and go on to good jobs with good salaries, people who finish college and go on to other good jobs with better salaries. It is about the kids I grew up with and the kids I teach now. It is about the present state of literacy and the literate. As such, this book also explores the current state of the art in linguistic theory, with particular emphasis on psycho-and sociolinguistics, cognitive psychology, and philosophy. While it directly criticizes what is going on in our schools and colleges, it also offers some directions that we might take to remedy a serious situation.

To some extent, it is a direct attack on what we have settled for, as a society, as teachers and parents, and as students. But that is the negative side—attacks are relatively easy to make. Much more importantly, this book argues for perceiving language and language-related activities from some radically new points of view. It argues against the present systematic and systematized approach to language activities in schools and colleges. But the argument is not so much against systematization as it is against the obsessive commitment our schools and administrators have to programmed activities, programmed texts, and the revered programmed workbook with all its little blanks waiting to be filled in. It argues against viewing students as big blanks who have to be filled up with information so that they can pour out their knowledge into the little blanks in the workbooks. It argues against the logic that vests the power and control of public education in the unexamined corporate hands of commercial textbook publishers and that most powerful group, the test makers—the ones who create the standardized multiple-choice tests, decide which answers are correct, and report the percentiles and scores and averages that control the lives of our youth. This book examines the results of a system that allows its curriculum to be controlled by corporations whose major purpose is to make money by selling their textbooks, workbooks, and tests to public schools with little regard for the educational needs of the students. It examines the nature of a system whose logic derives from the profit motive of outsiders rather than the knowledge and experience of professional insiders (the teachers) and the needs of the learners (the students).

Finally, it argues for the empowerment of teachers and students. It is a call to arms for the most conservative of educational revolutions, for nothing could be more conservative than to return the act of meaning making to those who are directly and most responsible for making meaning: the students, the teachers, us—the people.

First, a note about the organization of this book—a note that I believe is highly significant and at least partially indicative of the kinds of problems on which this book focuses. I begin with a few relevant anecdotes. Some years ago, I began creating a course for English majors who intended to teach in the secondary schools. The course was to focus on psycholinguistics and reading—the psychological, linguistic, and cognitive processes that appear to be at the center of the reading process. I wanted to create a course that, albeit almost entirely theoretical, would give my students the power to create sensible methods of teaching reading and writing as they moved into the teaching profession. When I was nearly done creating the course—which was based on the works of Ken and Yetta Goodman, Frank Smith, and Stephen Tchudi, among others—I found myself discussing it with a colleague from another college. Since he was in an education department and was interested in reading, I particularly wanted to hear his views of the course and to see what suggestions he might have for improving it. Instead, apparently surprised at my naiveté, he warned me that "Education majors can't handle that kind of stuff. It's too hard! Give them methods. That's all they want anyway." He went on to explain that, while I might "get away" with that "stuff" in a graduate course for experienced teachers, they would probably hate it too.

The wildest thing about this anecdote is that it is true. It made me angry at the time and it still does. It makes my students angry when I tell it to them. I hope it makes you angry.

The second experience occurred more recently. Various friends of mine had been reading the manuscript for this book and giving me help and advice for revisions. One reader, a person in a doctoral program in another state, asked if I intended both high school and college teachers to be a part of the audience for the book. I said, "Yes." Another reader asked me the same

question, and the conversations that followed were important enough for me
to summarize them here. Unlike the educator who told me that teachers are
intellectually unable to handle difficult ideas, both of these readers knew
very well that this was not the case. Indeed, one is a high school teacher.

Their concerns were twofold: (1) Some teachers who might benefit by
much of the book might be turned off by the first chapter; its theoretical
nature might cause them to think that this was just another college professor
trying to sound self-important or write about stuff that had little to do with
the realities of teaching; and (2) Since college teachers generally cared so
little about effective teaching, they wouldn't read a book like this at all.

Their comments certainly gave me pause to think. On top of this, some
of my other readers disagreed that this was really a problem. I had a classic
writer's dilemma: I had chosen good readers to peer-edit my manuscript,
and I was getting conflicting feedback. But I had spent a long time writing
this, the semester was about to begin, and I had an awful lot to do just
teaching my own students. I have tenure. I don't need a publication. My
wife and kids love me. I have good health, good friends. Who needs this
kind of grief?

But, we agreed, that is partly what introductions are for—to deal with
these kinds of problems. And so, with these anecdotes behind me, let me
return to my comments about the organization of the book. The first chapter
remains theoretical: I cannot make my arguments for change, for the implementation of meaningful language activities, without laying some ground-
work. If I do, I simply produce another methods text whose appeal (even
when the methods are perfectly good) extends only to those who wish to
plug in an activity here or there in order to get through a blue Monday or a
bleak Friday. Furthermore, the first chapter's theoretical underlayment is
intended as more than a subfloor that inconspicuously provides a smooth
surface on which to place an elegant carpet and fine furniture. Of course,
this initial chapter is intended to offer firm and clear support for what follows,
but it operates more like the theme in a symphony as it wends its way,
sometimes more conspicuously than others, through the orchestration of the
text. It provides the center for the entire piece, presenting the possibility
of a unified whole rather than a series of vaguely related notes.

Less metaphorically speaking, teaching methods based on nothing more
than their apparent appeal to students generally amount to little more than
tricks. Anyone can come up with flashy methods that will get them through
a class period, but approaches to effective teaching—the ability to create
sequences of methods over a period of time that genuinely contribute to the
students' learning—are generated by theoretical structures. And the creation
of approaches based on generative theoretical structures, the implementation
of methods, should produce a dynamic interrelationship with the theoretical
structures that causes both to change and grow through experience and
reflection. Indeed, one might easily argue that much of what passes for teach-

ing and learning in our schools is based on an unexamined and insidious
system of circular logic entrenched in a tradition of methods: We teach this
way because this is how people learn; we teach phonics so students can
sound out words and read aloud; students read aloud because this gives them
practice at phonics and reading; students do this activity in order to succeed
at the multiple-choice test that evaluates their success at the activity; we
don't do that in sixth grade because they do it in seventh grade, but we do
this in order to prepare them for doing that. Why? Because!

All too often, methods of teaching are prescribed by people whose major
relationship with the education of our students is a commercial one. You
don't *use* their methods, you *buy* their curriculum (and their textbooks, and
their workbooks, and their filmstrips . . .). You don't teach your students,
you teach the program. And you must do so because "so much money" has
gone into this program that it must be good (why else would we have put
so much money into it?). But the ultimate reasons for creating the program—
the kids themselves and what we want them to learn—seem to go by the
board.

I do not know how to scream in print, but if I could I would scream this:
Teachers are intelligent, creative professionals! (And those who are not, are not
teachers!) While all of us get ideas for methods from other teachers, without
some firm theoretical position we have no way of evaluating the sense of a
given method (beyond its appeal to the students) and no way of sequencing
other methods in relationship to any single method. Furthermore, most of
what I call for in this book requires that teachers and students work hard.
Without a good reason for doing so, I cannot imagine why teachers would
implement such changes. Chapters 2, 3, and 4 describe a scenario and build
a case for a conservative revolution. I am not simply suggesting the implementation of certain changes; I am arguing that we must reject certain time-
honored and well-entrenched elements of our educational system.

But just because the first chapter comes first doesn't mean you have to
read it first. If you would rather measure the sense of the book by reading
the methodological approaches I suggest, finding out whether or not they
have anything to do with the real kids who populate your classrooms, then
read the last two chapters first. But if you do this, I hope you'll measure the
sense of the method by returning to the earlier chapters and reading the
reasons underlying the methods.

Perhaps more importantly, I criticize both teachers and schools in this
book. But I believe I never show the contempt for teachers or students that
was suggested by the professor who felt that they could not understand or
care about complex ideas. I have known and taught many high school and
college students and many people who teach in high schools and colleges.
I have known and taught fools, idiots, and occasionally some people who
deserve contempt. But the overwhelming majority of the students and teachers I have worked with, at all levels, have taught me how fortunate I am to

be a teacher and what richness and depth characterize the meaning-making abilities of all human beings. With very few exceptions, I have found both high school and college teachers to be intelligent, interested, and, often, overworked professionals who care deeply about their work and their students. My greatest concern regarding this book is not that it is too difficult for some teachers or that some may not care enough about teaching to bother with it. My greatest concern is that I would waste their (your) time.

Consequently, whatever meanings you make herein, it is my fondest hope that you find some value in them for yourself and your students.

One last note: This book really began many years ago, sometime around 1969 when I was in graduate school and Stephen Tchudi was my mentor. He introduced me to the work of James Moffett, John Dixon, Patrick Creber, and others, not to mention his own genuinely creative approaches to the language processes of students. Under his tutelage I revisited the work of Jean Piaget, discovered Lev Vygotsky, sorted through the sense and nonsense of Neil Postman and Charles Weingartner, and carefully examined the ideas of Kenneth and Yetta Goodman and Frank Smith. Later, because of this beginning, I would wander into the world that James Britton creates in *Language and Learning* (1970), and would discover an affinity for the works of Ernst Cassirer, Judith Langer, Noam Chomsky, William Labov, and others too numerous to mention. Still later, I would begin my own classroom experiments with reader-response activities in the classroom, read in the areas of subjective criticism and reader-response theory. And most recently, over the past few years and with the help of my best friend and wife—who patiently explained, over and over, the importance of philosophers like Heidegger and Derrida—I slowly began to understand the significance of philosophy in the study of language and literature and teaching.

What has struck me most powerfully through these intellectual and experiential sojourns, and what has never ceased to delight and amaze me, is this: It all connects. All these writers and theorists are working on the same problems and issues. Each in his or her own way has been examining the nature and origins and functions of language in human beings. Each has been examining the process of making meaning and the role that language plays in that process. Thus, this book is really about the fact that language is the possibility of making meaning, a possibility that we all possess by virtue of our humanness. That is all that language is; but as such, it is everything.

Teaching is about helping our students and ourselves realize that possibility. Reading, writing, speaking, listening, visualizing—genuine literacy has a single primary purpose: meaning making.

LITERACY
AND
EMPOWERMENT

Language and Literacy

> What is needed to meet the crisis of literacy is a critical literacy that frames reading and writing in terms of moral and political decision-making. Literacy in this view is not linked to learning to read advertisements and becoming better consumers, or escaping into the pages of romance novels or spy thrillers; critical literacy links language competency to acquiring analytical skills which empower individuals to challenge the status quo.
>
> Peter McLaren, *Life in Schools*

Over the past decade or two, and most recently as part of the "Reagan agenda," literacy has become a major, national concern. Publications have emerged as varied in intent and quality as the article "Why Johnny Can't Write" in *Newsweek* (December 8, 1975), the book *Becoming a Nation of Readers* (Anderson et al. 1985), and the journal *College English*, to name just a few. Most of the popular media, of course, have focused on the illiteracy rampant in some areas, suggesting that between four and twenty-five million Americans are essentially unable to read and write beyond a minimal "functional" level (Purves 1990: 2). (However, in and of themselves, statistics with a twenty-million-person variance represent no small degree of media hype and confusion, at best—and at worst, deceptive manipulation.) Regardless of the accuracy and (ab)use of statistics, almost no one would argue that *adult literacy* is adequate, although many would argue about the definition of the term itself and what is meant when we say that an individual is literate.

First, by way of clarification, I offer the following examples. When asked by a television reporter, "If you get evicted, where do you go?" a migrant worker replied, "Nowhere. We don't got no other where to go." These are the people we make television specials about, but about whom we do little else. I am distinctly not addressing the disgraceful complexities that create the conditions surrounding this woman and her counterparts in our society; there is no room on the day shift for them. But I would draw attention to this: At the very least, her language speaks clearly and immediately to the reality of her situation. Finally, regarding this example, while basic literacy is indeed very important, it is highly questionable whether or not it is a condition that would significantly affect the lives of people caught in the kind of socioeconomic traps that characterize the life of this migrant worker. Or, to put it differently, not all bag ladies are illiterate.

This next quote is from a sports announcer, a college graduate. He may illustrate a larger group of people—the people who are literate in only the most superficial sense of the word, the people who believe that being literate means being able to say very little at great length with great rhetorical complexity. He says, "The development of the play should be such that it transpires in the end zone so that Cleveland creates the opportunity for seven points." (As nearly as I could tell, he meant that Cleveland would try to score on the next play.)

By way of beginning, then, I offer some distinctions about literacy. I am not suggesting that literacy is best defined by a dictionary of words, dates, names, and events such as the one proffered by E. D. Hirsch, Jr. in his recent book, *Cultural Literacy*. The very presumption that anyone knows what "every American needs to know" speaks for itself. But, more importantly, the underlying theoretical assumption that the problem of literacy might best be addressed through a "shared vocabulary," even in the admittedly complex sense suggested by Hirsch, ignores the complexities of language and learning evidenced in both empirical research and philosophical-theoretical discussions characterizing psycho- and sociolinguistics, cognitive *science*, the philosophy of language, and literary theory. In short, even the most sophisticated, nontrivial version of Trivial Pursuit represents neither a legitimate nor an effective approach to the problem of literacy.

I reiterate: There is nothing inherently wrong with Hirsch's list, except that it barely scratches the surface and represents, at best, the beginning of a list that is infinitely long and that must be continually expanded. The problem is that it centers itself in a body of knowledge, a list of terms. More specifically—and directly counter to Hirsch's argument that current problems in education are to be placed firmly on the shoulders of John Dewey, Rousseau, and content-free curricula—the literacy problem is not first or only a product of what people do or do not know, as much as it is a problem of what people are able to do with what they know. Print literacy (and probably all literacy) is best defined as a *meaning-making* process rather than a simple coding or decoding of meanings already presented as givens. It has not been an overemphasis on meaning-making processes that has caused the literacy problem, but an overemphasis on fragmented contents, an overemphasis on bits and pieces of knowledge with little focus on relationships among the fragments. This obsession with fragmented knowledge mutually reinforces an almost religious belief in and devotion to so-called objective, standardized, nationally normed, machine-graded, multiple-choice, "make-your-best-guess," decode, identify, fill-in-the-circle-with-a-number–2-pencil tests that purport to measure everything from literacy to critical thinking.

Furthermore, that such tests produce scores that correlate highly with success in college (a fact often used to defend their validity) is a comment on (1) the nature of high school curricula that prepare students to take the tests, (2) the monolithic corporate structure that produces and grades the tests (and various books, workbooks, and even courses designed to enhance one's performance on such tests), and (3) the college curricula that lend credence to high scores on the tests by awarding high grades and college degrees to people who have become masters at *identifying* "correct" answers. Indeed, when former White House spokesman Pat Buchanan said that it is the job of schools not to teach students "to think" but "to teach them to think correctly" (CNN, "Crossfire," January 17, 1988), he seemed unaware of how disturbingly well the job was already being done. One is reminded of Bob Dylan's ironic suggestion in "Subterranean Homesick Blues" that, after all is said and done, elementary school, high school, and college often seem to accomplish little more than helping the learner get off the night shift and join the status of working days in a clean shirt.

It is my position that schools are failing to educate students in any enabling sense, that many of the apparently literate students who graduate from our high schools and colleges are genuinely illiterate, lacking a sense of personal and intellectual responsibility and/or power as readers/writers, as listeners/speakers, and, it follows, as thinkers.

The definition of *literacy* intended throughout this discussion is broad and complex, but I think it represents what most people associated with genuine learning intend when they use the word in describing a goal for education and an intellectual state or set of abilities that they wish to have characterize a college graduate. Furthermore, this literacy involves more than print literacy or the ability to read a text; it involves the ability to use one's innate linguistic ability to both create and "read" (make meaning of and through) the surface structures, whether they be oral or graphemic. Literacy, in any important sense, must extend well beyond decoding skills or the ability to "bark at print" through the application of phonics (Wardaugh 1969); it must extend far beyond the formulaic exercise of writing a well-wrought, vacuous paragraph whose major reason for existence is to prove that the writer can write a paragraph. (In and of itself, this is a highly questionable skill, to say the least—when was the last time someone told you to "go over there and write a paragraph"?)

In short, literacy, like language (innate linguistic ability) in general, invokes a generative, active intellect creating and interacting with reality, and it means much more than learning how to read a recipe or fill out a job-application form (Ronat 1979: 75).

The word *literacy*, then, suggests a state of being and a set of capabilities through which the literate individual is able to utilize the *interior world of self to act upon and interact with the exterior structures of the world* around him in order to make sense of self and other. Print literacy implies the ability to make sense of the world through the processes of reading and writing; oral literacy implies the ability to make sense of the world through speaking and listening. Media literacy implies the ability to make sense of the world through a dynamic mixture of visual-audial and sometimes tactile media. In all these instances, literacy suggests an (intra- and inter-) active, creative process of coming to know self and other; at no time does it suggest a primarily receptive process through which one simply "receives" or "is given" knowledge.

THE PROBLEM

In his "Editor's Introduction" to *Language, Schooling, and Society*, Stephen Tchudi writes:

Seminar participants saw the greatest barriers to progress coming from outside the teaching profession. James Moffett raised the question of whether or not society truly wants the schools to create students who are *literate in the fullest and best sense* [italics added]. More than one study group suggested that society seems to prefer students who clearly can function at a minimum skills level—who can say, read and obey commands—but does not crave to have them raised to higher levels of skill, where their literacy might disrupt the political *status quo* through articulate criticism. (Tchudi 1985: 7)

In his address to the groups attending the International Federation of Teachers of English Conference that generated *Language, Schooling, and Society*, James Moffett asks:

If greater knowledge leads to better action, why are most schools going backwards, retrenching into materials and methods long since tried and found untrue? What are the obstacles that thwart the best efforts to improve discursive learning and that flout the knowledge accumulated by research? (Tchudi 1985: 89)

While I essentially agree that the greatest barriers to literacy education (probably all education) come from "outside the profession," I also believe that teachers at all levels have been terribly lax about taking on their proper roles of leadership and responsibility by not refusing to implement some of the sillier policies that have been foisted upon them and their students. By and large, however, I found myself in close agreement with the central positions taken at the conference. Consequently, this book explores Tchudi's important assertions and suggests some answers to Moffett's queries. The focus is distinctly not on basic literacy or methods of teaching very young children to read and write, although these topics are not entirely ignored. Rather, the purpose here is to examine literacy "in the fullest and best sense"—the literacy of our high school and college graduates. The aim is to explore the theoretical underpinnings of that literacy and to suggest actions to alleviate the problem.

While much of the initial part of the discussion will focus on the nature of language as linguistic ability, its development, and the roles it plays in the human condition, the linguistic, sociological, philosophical, and educational implications of the initial discussion will focus on the questions that follow. Why is it that students—young adults in high school and college, highly motivated students who wish to and do succeed at doing well in school—seem to learn so little there, especially in subjects outside their private interests or declared majors? Why, in the midst of the most exciting discussion of the semester (from the teacher's point of view, at least), does a student ask (for the whole class), "Is this going to be on the test?" or "Do we have to remember this?" Why do many college graduates, English teachers included, achieve a relatively minimal degree of literacy, especially in the sense of being active, generative intellects creating and engaging the world? Finally, what do teachers need to learn about themselves, their students, and schools in order to radically change and improve this unacceptable situation?

In order to answer these questions, the educational system—elementary through graduate school—will be considered as a text that is populated by administrators, students, and teachers at the same time that it is created and read by students, teachers, and administrators. This occurs at the same time that both the text and those who populate it are part of a larger (con)text: society and the institutions that comprise society. Any such undertaking— the attempt to uncover genuine causes and to suggest reasonable approaches to improving the situation—invites one of two responses: simplistic or complex.

The simplistic response reflects five accusing attitudes:

1. *Kids Today!* Kids don't much care about learning; they need to mature enough to share the adult's desire for learning; they are too centered in a desire for immediate gratification. Therefore, no matter what we do, it never seems to work very well.

2. *The Damn Teachers*! Teachers are poorly trained; all they care about are their own little areas of interest; teachers get too much money; teachers are responsible for too many different things; teachers don't care about real learning.

3. *Society Won't....* Not enough money is spent on education. The local

community, or the state, or the federal government has too little (or too much) control over the curriculum. Schools of education have devolved into a contentless monopoly; teachers' unions interfere with constructive change.

4. *Kids Don't Know Anything.* Using Hirsch's logic, the "content-neutral curriculum" derived from Rousseau and Dewey has caused the problem.

5. *If Only Parents Would....* Parents don't discipline their kids the way they used to; women should be at home taking care of the kids; they don't raise their kids with the right morals and values.

More directly, the simplistic response points to some of the major and real problems and says, "These are the problems!" as though the problems in general are the causes of *the* problem!

The complex response begins with questions rather than accusations. It asks: What is the nature of the problem(s)? What causes it (them)? Can it (they) be rectified and if so, how?

In discussing the answers to the complex response, language as an innate ability to make meaning will be the focus. This focus is not chosen simply because literacy or the lack of it constitutes the major problem in schools today, but because language is the system of meaning making by which we create ourselves, our society, our problems, our solutions, our realities. Language is the system through which we teach and learn; it is at the center of being (if, indeed, there is a center). Probably beginning the moment a human being is born, a chain of linguistic and cultural events precedes and contributes to shaping that individual's degree of literacy. Like a physical chain, this chain of events can be broken or disrupted, recast, but then the disruption itself becomes part of that chain. Consequently, any discussion of linguistic competence, language development, and/or literacy must necessarily begin at the beginning in order to examine the ways in which the chain is forged in our society. Therefore, this discussion begins with an examination of the nature of language, meaning, and linguistic interaction. It borrows freely from the worlds of linguistics, psychology, sociology, philosophy, and education. Before examining the specific nature of language activities in the schools—and the ways in which these language activities shape the kinds and degrees of literacy that characterize American students as they enter, move through, and graduate from college—it establishes a theoretical ground. Finally, it offers some direction for approaching the problem of literacy. Consequently, although it may appear a far remove from the literacy level of the average college graduate, any full picture of the problem demands that the discussion start at the beginning (as best we can describe it) of language learning.

What is language, and how do human beings learn it? It is surprising to find that two such simple questions should produce so much research, writing, and—sometimes—conflict. But in fact, the nature of language and the human capacity to develop language form two of the most puzzling and important issues in defining what it means to be human. Whether one examines (1) the work of Saussure, Chomsky, Piaget, Halliday, and others who (regardless of important differences and theoretical subtleties) define language as a rule-governed system of meaning making and communication, or (2) the work of a philosopher like Derrida who might define it as "writing" (in a very special and carefully elaborated sense) or as a "possibility" for making meaning and being (but a possibility that unravels in its process of being)—regardless of how one deals with these complex and important disagreements (issues that will be addressed later in this book), the following generalizations about language learning appear to have a reasonable degree of descriptive validity.

THE NATURE OF LANGUAGE

For our purposes here, language is not simply a system of phonemes; it is not simply a set of surface structures (sounds or written marks of some kind). While these external, surface representations of language are enormously important and may not be disregarded, neither the oral surface structures (sounds) nor written surface structures (marks) are sufficient to define language. For our purposes, *language is the possibility of making meaning of and in the world*. Oral and written surface structures are external signifiers of this meaning-making act, and these surface structures are generated by language, which is itself a rule-governed structure of meaning making. But it is the nature of language to be self-contradictory because the rule-governed structure is like an unstable chemical element—constantly acting and reacting, constantly changing from what it was to what it was not. Evincing itself in the process of deterioration, always moving toward absence in the attempt to establish presence, language instantly and infinitely unravels what it ravels as it ravels.

As such, language defines the very fragile nature of being human and of meaning itself. It is this fragility, the inherent and constant changing (deconstruction and construction), that makes it so essential to the definition of being human and to explaining why all humans in all cultures learn it. It may even explain why there is so much of it at the level of surface structures. For example, even a moment's consciousness of the sheer amount of language that surrounds us every minute of every day—the language of colleagues and acquaintances, the language of radios and televisions and newspapers—is staggering. So, if language as the possibility of making meaning determines our humanness, perhaps we employ the surface structures to assure ourselves that we are not alone in the world. Perhaps this is partly why we learn it so well, so completely, and so quickly.

The problem, of course, with the last sentence is in the word *learn* insofar as it suggests that language is something to be learned or mastered or acquired. While some might wish to describe it this way, focusing on surface structures of sound or print, and others might wish to focus on it as being

composed of definable grammatical, syntactical, or semantic rules, the constant changing of language militates against treating it as an object. Treating
language as an object ignores its very nature. Clearly, any definition stating
that language is a possibility for making meaning, a possibility or potential
that is (apparently) an essential element in any definition of *human being*,
removes it from any objective category. Language development, then, is
the process of realizing the possibility. Language, therefore, is a meaning-
making system in a constant state of change, metamorphosing as it develops,
being subjected to new meanings as it comes into being (Chomsky 1972:
95).

Of course, there is also a commonsense way of talking about language.
(But note that the only way to talk about language is through language, and
thus we are immediately caught in the problem of using the thing itself to
define itself and of using the thing itself to analyze the nature of the thing
whose nature we are employing.) As long as one brackets the complex implications of the previous definition of language, the theoretical and empirical
work of sociolinguistics and psycholinguistics affords some momentarily
firmer ground for a discussion of language learning.

LANGUAGE DEVELOPMENT

Providing that they are not severely brain-damaged and that they are in
contact with other human beings, all humans in all cultures learn their native
language by approximately the age of five. In traditional terms, this does
not mean that they actually generate sophisticated, standard structures in
the language, that they are able to understand everything that is said to
them, or that they can read everything in print. (Nor does it necessarily
mean, by the way, that they could not create language in the event that
they were absolutely deprived of all other human contact.) For Saussure, it
means that they have developed *langue*—that is, they have developed (or
acquired, intuited, learned, or mastered) the rules of language that allow
them to generate the surface structures of their native language (Saussure's
parole). In other terms, they have developed language *competence*, although
their language *performance* (surface structure demonstrations either oral or in
print) will not demonstrate the full range of the competence. Chomsky offers
an important distinction that will simply be mentioned here. Instead of
suggesting that language is something outside the human being, he insists
that one is born with it; it is in the very nature of human beings, and one
need not acquire what one already has (Chomsky 1975: 61; Ronat 1979: 63–
68). (For more elaboration and distinctions of Chomsky's view as opposed
to a view like Piaget's, for example—that language is part of a biological
development that moves through biological stages—see Piattelli-Palmarini).

While psycholinguists theorize the interior structure of language in an
attempt to articulate the rules that govern the production of language or

(forgetting the implications of the word *govern* for the moment) the rules (grammar) that might account for the generation of the surface structure of language, sociolinguists firmly plant themselves in the world, examining language within social situations from a sociological perspective of linguistic interaction. This is important because a linguist like Chomsky does not see communication as the central or most important aspect of language, whereas a sociolinguist is primarily concerned with language as a system of communication and how it develops within and further shapes social situations (Ronat 1979: 83–85).

A SOCIOLINGUISTIC ACCOUNT

Many studies have documented the development of the surface structures of language in the infant (Andersen 1990; MacNamara 1982; Ferguson and Slobin 1973; Brown 1973). For the purposes of this discussion, however, a single primary focus should suffice.

In a fascinating account of language development, the sociological linguist M. A. K. Halliday documents the language development of Nigel beginning at the age of nine months, recording changes over one-and-one-half-month periods (so that NL2 = Nigel Language at ten and one-half to twelve months) (Halliday 1975). Given his sociological orientation, it is not surprising or unreasonable that Halliday defines language in terms of social interaction and in terms of the functions of language in those situations. While this introduces certain problems into any discussion of language as an interior process defining humanness and allowing the "possibility of meaning" (a problem that will be examined later), it also affords empirical insight into the development of oral language in a human being. Although his focus is almost entirely on the development of oral language (Halliday 1978: 37, 51, 55, 57), Halliday affirms that "linguistic processes" are the essential means "whereby a human organism turns into a social being" (Halliday 1978: 12). Declaring himself momentarily disinterested in discussing origins of language within the human being, he is "emphatically not a behaviourist," sees the "nativist" versus "environmentalist" argument to be one of recasting nature-nurture "in a new guise," and clearly declares that his focus on social behavior includes an assumption of some innate capacity in the human organism (Halliday 1978: 54).

Halliday begins documenting Nigel Language at the nine-month stage because, in his terms, this is the point at which Nigel achieves his "breakthrough into language." But by this he does not mean that Nigel suddenly begins to communicate in his mother tongue. Instead, it is at this age that Nigel appears to be producing his own private language. The sounds the child produces are generally not identifiable imitations of the surface structures of adult language. Rather, they appear to be created by the child with no identifiable external point of origin (Halliday 1975: 62).

It is important to note that any statement such as the one just made clearly centers the interpretive power of the adult who is deciding and interpreting that what Nigel exhibits at the age of nine months is language and that what he exhibited prior to this was not language. That such a study can be conducted in no other way is no criticism, but this fact raises the importance of surface structures (i.e., sounds the child makes) to the center of attention, potentially removing attention from whatever inside the human being allows and/or generates such sounds.

Halliday is not unaware of the problem. He points out that most studies of language development begin too late in the child's development (normally around the eighteen-month stage). "The child may have a well-developed semantic system long before he begins to combine words, in fact long before he has any words at all, if by 'words' we mean lexical elements taken over from the adult language." At the same time, he cautions that, while children may engage in communication "at the age of a few weeks or even days," this is not yet language in any sense of identifiable patterns of surface structures (Halliday 1975: 61–62). He also notes the essentially interpretive process involved in citing the child's social use of language, emphasizing that "any educated adult" is likely to impose "some kind of theory" in order to explain the meaning of what appears to be the beginnings of the surface structures of language (Halliday 1975: 40).

Beginning, then, at NL1 (Nigel Language at nine to ten and one-half months) Halliday splits the development into three phases: Phase I marks the beginnings of the private but recognizable language discussed previously and lasts until about sixteen and one-half months; Phase II marks the beginning use of adult vocabulary and begins to end around the eighteenth month; and Phase III marks the beginnings of "adult language," when the vocabulary develops rapidly and both the forms and functions of adult language are recognizable in their initial stages. Halliday further describes the "functions" of language as they develop over the three phases: "Instrumental," or "I want"; "Regulatory," or "do as I tell you"; "Interactional," or "me and you"; "Personal," or "here I come"; "Heuristic," or "tell me why"; "Imaginative," or "let's pretend"; and "Informative," or "I've got something to tell you" (Halliday 1975: 37). The developmental sequence that emerges is:

(1) that the first four functions clearly precede the rest, and (2) that all others precede the informative. The informative function does not appear until nearly the end of Phase II, round about NL9 (21 to 22 ½ months); but this was not entirely unexpected, since the use of language to convey information is clearly a derivative function, one which presupposes various special conditions including, for one thing, the concept of dialogue. (Halliday 1975: 40)

For the time being, the primary significance of Halliday's account of language development in Nigel (Halliday 1975) and his discussion of language as a social semiotic, firmly and absolutely entrenched in social interactions (Halliday 1978), is this: It is clearly demonstrable that linguistic surface structures begin to appear as early as nine months and that these private aspects of language quickly develop into standard, recognizable surface structures of the mother tongue. Furthermore, and most significant, as early as NL6 (around seventeen months), Halliday notes the development of the mathetic function of language (preceded by a purely pragmatic function). This is "language enabling the child to learn about his social and material environment, serving him in the construction of reality. This function is realized, in the first instance, through the child's observing, recalling and predicting the objects and events which impinge on his perceptions" (Halliday 1975: 75). This observation is particularly important to several points that will follow later in the discussion: For example, (1) human beings use language both in the creation of and interaction with "reality" (Goodman 1978); and (2) the ability to "predict" (an important aspect of cognitive learning theory) evidences itself in linguistic surface structures very early in human development (Smith 1982: 60–63).

That this is not simply a behavioral process in which the learner responds to the linguistic stimulus of the environment, eventually mastering the proper responses and thereby acquiring language, is little argued. Ever since Chomsky's review of Skinner's linguistic position (Chomsky 1958: 124–58) and the enormously important work that he and others have carried out in the areas of linguistics and cognitive psychology, few would argue what is an essential point about language learning and language use: Language is more than the possibility of communicating; it is the possibility that allows the creation of meaning and the creation of communication. Moreover, insofar as it is a possibility, it is absolutely not a guarantee of the creation of or communication of meaning.

The following summary of initial language development, couched in somewhat more human terms than what has preceded it, may help here. Again, remembering that any talk of a deep structure of language or of language as rule-governed demands the bracketing of a system that constructs and deconstructs itself in any given moment of being, it is worth investigating the kinds of structures that are used to describe the possibility we are calling language.

What seems clear about the process is this. Beginning at birth, children are surrounded by and immersed in the language of the immediate community—normally the community of home and family. Since the child is born with the *possibility* of making and sharing meaning and not the *fact* of the ability to do so, it is at first necessary for the caretakers—mother, father, brother, grandmother, and others—to make meaning for the infant.

[The] culture shapes our behaviour patterns, and a great deal of our behaviour is mediated through language. The child learns his mother tongue in the context of behavioural settings where the norms of the culture are acted out and enunciated for him, settings of parental control, instruction, personal interaction and the like; and, reciprocally, he is "socialized" into the value systems and behaviour patterns of the culture through the use of language at the same time as he is learning it. (Halliday 1975: 23)

Thus it is that many parents keep up a running dialogue for the infant, sometimes taking responsibility for both parts of the conversation because the infant has not yet mastered the standard surface structures of oral or written language. The parents literally "read" the infant's needs, desires, intent, purposes, and meanings. When the infant cries, the parent comes to the child, speaking: "Does baby want to eat? Oh, I bet this little baby is hungry and wants her bottle right now. Yes, see, that's exactly what baby wanted." Unless, of course, baby isn't hungry, the parent has misread, and more crying, rejection of the bottle, and various unmistakable odors cause the parent to say, "Oh, how could daddy have made such a mistake? You want to be changed, don't you? There now, that's better, isn't it?" With a little luck, the parent eventually reads the text correctly and the child quiets down. But without a little luck—and any parent knows this situation—it is next to impossible to figure out what it is the infant means. The infant has not yet mastered the possibility well enough to communicate, and the parent is forced into a guessing game of eliminating the most obvious possibilities one at a time. And this is not the only time that miscommunication will lead to a lack of sleep for all parties. (Of course, without all this frustration and confusion, kids would be slow to learn how to swear, so even this serves a clear social purpose.)

This particular stage passes speedily as the child begins to learn to employ surface structures of the language to assist in the sharing of meaning. And things become even clearer to the child the first time she "says" something vaguely suggesting a "real" word because everyone in the house starts screaming and yelling and being "so proud" of whatever it is baby just did. As Halliday suggests, these surface structures of language operate entirely within a social situation, an interaction that generally reinforces success immediately and clearly. Of course it takes time, but the first utterances of "wa-wa" almost always lead to the parental response of "Does baby want water? Would you like your cup filled with water? Here, I'll fill your cup with some nice cold water from the faucet and you can have a drink." Again, it may be that the elliptical utterance of "wa-wa" was not a request for a drink. It may be that the child just wanted to splash some water around or throw it on the floor, but at least the parent is no longer guessing in a vacuum. More importantly, even in the earliest linguistic interactions with the child, the parent is illustrating and demonstrating the surfaces structures of language and the rules that appear to govern those surface structures. In each interaction the parent models the syntax, lexicography, morphemes, and phonemes of the language. In each case the parent makes clear that, whatever else it is, this language stuff helps you get what you want and adults think it is very important. Shortly after these initial efforts, language seems to explode into the repertoire of the child. Discarding many private surface structures that she may have created, the child adopts the surface structures of the adult community.

Certainly, what is most obvious about this process is the rate at which language development occurs and the joyfully obsessive commitment that characterizes its development in the human being. Having found that the world can be named and that they have the ability to do the naming, children begin an almost nonstop appropriation of whatever linguistic surface structures surround them; having learned that surface structures of language facilitate the exploration of self and other (expression and communication), they quickly become facile users of the dialect of their linguistic community.

As Chomsky and others have noted, however, such language development in the human being is not explained by behavioral learning theory. What the child appears to learn is a set of generative rules, a system of pluralizing, producing adverbs from nouns, negating, querying, naming. The learner produces surface structures she has never heard before. And this process is marked, generally, by a nearly obsessive use of language—a constant, almost nonstop process of asking and naming, of external (and internal) monologue and dialogue. Once the possibility of language becomes an operative fact in the human being's life, it becomes enormously significant. Almost immediately it becomes the tool for gaining some control over the world. In the process of naming that which had no name, in the process of learning that there are names, the human begins to feel power. But the fact remains that neither empirical experimentation and observation nor symbolic logic solves the problems or answers many of the questions surrounding the nature of language. There is still significant disagreement among linguists, psychologists, and sociologists about what language is, what is or is not innate, how meaning and syntax are related, not to mention how language is acquired or how it develops (Gardner 1985: 207–22).

Although Halliday does not wrestle with the nature and/or origin of language in the human being (neither one is really within the province of the sociolinguist), his assertion that language is essentially social, that it develops in terms of "shared meanings and shared contexts" (Halliday 1978: 141), is important and deserves careful consideration and qualification. Insofar as he intentionally focuses on surface structures of language and their role in social interactions, Halliday is correct when he says, "In order for language to be a means of learning, it is essential for the child to be able to encode in language, through words and structures, his experience of processes of the external world and of the people and things that participate in them" (Halliday 1978: 21). While this appears to be inarguable from a commonsense point of view, it does not necessarily follow that an isolated individual would not realize language and move from the "possibility of" to the "making of" meaning, regardless of the social environment or lack thereof. Of course, the individual's surface structures (if they existed) would almost certainly be radically new and different, perhaps not even recognizable to us. This is especially obvious if one accepts Chomsky's theory that language is an innate characteristic of human beings and therefore not dependent on social interaction. But, most importantly, this distinction serves as a reminder to avoid confusing surface structures and sociolinguistics with language and psycholinguistics.

In addition, even in his discussion of text and context, certain important problems arise. Halliday defines text as

the language people produce and react to, what they say and write, and read and listen to, in the course of daily life. . . . The term covers both speech and writing, and is quite neutral as regards style and content: it may be language in action, conversation, telephone talk, debate, dramatic dialogue, narrative fiction, poetry, prayer, inscriptions, public notices, legal proceedings, communing with animals, intimate monologue or anything else. (Halliday 1975: 123)

While he appears to recognize that the text "is an indeterminate concept," he also says that a "situation [is] a determinant of text." Or, more fully:

[The linguistic] system is a meaning potential, which is actualized in the form of text; a text is an instance of social meaning in a particular context of situation. We shall therefore expect to find the situation embodied or enshrined in the text, not piecemeal, but in a way which reflects the systematic relation between the semantic structure and social environment.

The situation, then, appears "constitutive of the text" (Halliday 1978: 141).

Obviously, much of what Halliday suggests has all the appearance of "truth" in the reality of many human beings. However, a most significant point in Halliday's study is this: At a very early age (nine months in Nigel's case), human beings begin to evidence, externally, their language development. Since it appears undeniable that meaning making necessarily precedes the external evidencing of meaning making—that is, surface structures of language simply *evidence* meaning making, they do not *comprise* it—then it is equally undeniable that the child has been "languaging," realizing the possibility of making meaning, well in advance of the appearance of any recognizable surface structure. (The word *appearance* is important in the preceding sentence because it is only the adult's interpretation that places a given surface structure [sound] in the realm of linguistic surface structures prior to the age of nine months.) The great likelihood (ask any parent) is that the child has begun the process of meaning making at least as early as birth. The speed and intensity that characterize the development only emphasize the importance of language and languaging.

Clearly, much of our language learning takes place within situations that are part and parcel of social interactions, and the meanings that are a part of such interactions "*are* the social system: the social system is itself interpretable as a semiotic system" (Halliday 1975: 141). Moreover, that these sociolinguistic interactions may themselves be rule-governed or structured is an hypothesis in need of examination. It moves the discussion in the important direction of speech-act theory, necessitating a brief sojourn in and examination of this theory, including both criticisms and qualifications.

SPEECH-ACT THEORY

In his well-known book *How to Do Things with Words*, a collection of "The William James Lectures delivered at Harvard University in 1955," J. L. Austin examines "performative" utterances wherein "the issuing of the utterance is the performing of an action" as illustrated by "*contractual* ('I bet') or *declaratory* ('I declare war')" utterances (Austin 1975: 7). In his examination of performatives, he makes the following distinctions: *locutionary* acts are "the act of saying something"; *illocutionary* acts represent the "performance of an act *in* saying something as opposed to performance of an act *of* saying something"; and *perlocutionary acts* "often, or even normally, produce certain consequential effects upon the feelings, thoughts, or actions of the audience, or of the speaker, or of other persons: and it may be done with the design, intention, or purpose of producing them" (Austin 1975: 94–101).

Austin's focus is on the linguistic conditions that surround such performatives and the elements that cause them to operate either successfully or unsuccessfully as linguistic interactions. He emphasizes that "the words must be spoken 'seriously' so as to be taken 'seriously' " (1975: 9). Also, he asserts that if the speaker inwardly, consciously, does not seriously intend the utterance, the utterance is made in "bad faith." Thus, in the act of promising something, "it is appropriate that the person uttering the promise should have a certain intention, viz. here to keep his word" (1975: 11). Articulating his "doctrine of Infelicities," he points out that in addition to "unhappy" performatives that are marred by bad faith, the utterance may also "misfire because the procedure invoked is *not accepted*" (1975: 14–27). In either case Austin appears to be focusing on the importance of a conscious intent on the parts of both speakers and hearers.

Moving from the important work of Austin, we should examine that of his student John Searle, who produced *Speech Acts* in 1969. Searle's work is significant because he studies speech acts in order to examine the rules that govern meaning within given linguistic interactions. He hypothesizes that

speaking a language is performing speech acts, acts such as making statements, giving commands, asking questions, making promises and so on; and more abstractly, acts such as referring and predicating; and, secondly, *that these acts are in general made possible by and are performed in accordance with certain rules for the use of linguistic elements* [italics added]. (Searle 1969: 16)

Searle considers speech acts to be "the basic or minimal units of linguistic communication," insisting that it is "an analytic truth about language that whatever can be meant can be said" (1969: 16–17). Closely agreeing with Austin in many respects, Searle uses the word *defective* to describe speech acts that Austin might have termed unhappy or infelicitous, noting, importantly, that not all the defects that might intervene within a given speech act necessarily "vitiate the act in its entirety" (1969: 54).

What is most significant about Searle's work is his attempt to cite the conditions under or through which meaning occurs and is shared by individuals within given linguistic interactions. The following extract expresses his position:

The speech act or acts performed in the utterance of a sentence are in general a function of the meaning of the sentence. The meaning of a sentence does not in all cases uniquely determine what speech act is performed in a given utterance of the sentence, for a speaker may mean more than what he actually says, but it is always in principle possible for him to say exactly what he means. Therefore, it is in principle possible for every speech act one performs or could perform to be uniquely determined by a given sentence (or set of sentences), given the assumptions that the speaker is speaking literally and that the context is appropriate. And for these reasons a study of the meaning of sentences is not in principle distinct from a study of speech acts. . . . Since every meaningful sentence in virtue of its meaning can be used to perform a particular speech act (or range of speech acts), and since every possible speech act can in principle be given an exact formulation in a sentence or sentences (assuming an appropriate context of utterance), the study of the meanings of sentences and the study of speech acts are not two independent studies but one study from two different points of view. (Searle 1969: 18)

The promise, then, is significant. The study of speech acts should unlock some of the mysteries surrounding the nature of meaning as it occurs in and through language. But as might be expected in such a difficult undertaking, the problems are enormous.

Consider, for example, Searle's statement about speakers, hearers, and intention: For the speaker, "saying something and meaning it are closely connected with intending to produce certain effects on the hearer," whereas for the hearer, "understanding the speaker's utterance is closely connected with recognizing his intentions." And "in the case of literal utterances," it is the shared language that bridges the gap between speaker and hearer (Searle 1969: 48). Implicit in the statement is the assertion that intention is fully present and conscious in the speaker and that the speaker is fully conscious of this presence. Not only can what be meant be said, but the speaker knows what is meant. Furthermore, it is implicit that the hearer, in such a case, is also fully conscious and present. But what is most problematical is that he is fully conscious of the speaker's intention.

That Searle may be correct, that these are the conditions under which meaning might be fully shared by people within a linguistic interaction, seems to me to be self-evident. But it is equally evident that these conditions would seldom exist, and, when they did, would be mutually unknowable by those involved. By emphasizing (full) consciousness of intention on the parts of both speakers and hearers, Searle has made an important move away from an empirical focus on the surface structure of language as he moves toward an examination of the role of language in the social semiotic of interest to Halliday. But he has also, without examination, posited the possibility of full presence and full awareness of intention among speakers and hearers. This criticism does not even begin to confront the problems brought into the field of play by his use of words like *literal, serious,* and/or *common language.*

DECONSTRUCTING SPEECH ACTS

The problems of speech-act theory have been thoroughly examined in a series of articles beginning with Jacques Derrida's "Signature Event Context" (1977), Searle's reply to Derrida in "Reiterating the Differences: A Reply to Derrida" (1977), and the playfully serious reply to Searle's "Reply" by Derrida in "LIMITED INC abc . . . " (1977). In his "Reply," Searle restates his position and, in effect, restates the problem. Insisting that "*actual* speech acts" are "capable of communicating from speakers to hearers an infinite number of new things," he goes on to state that

hearers are able to understand this infinite number of possible communications *simply by recognizing the intentions of the speakers* in the performance of the speech acts. Now given that both speaker and hearer are finite, what is it that gives their speech acts this limitless capacity for communication? The answer is that the speaker and hearers are *masters of the sets of rules* we call *the rules of language,* and these rules are recursive. They allow for the repeated application of the same rule. . . . An iterability of the application of syntactical rules . . . *spoken or written* . . . is the *necessary presupposition* of the forms which that intentionality takes [italics added]. (Searle 1977: 208)

I provide all the italics here in order to underscore the problems inherent in the language being used. That the "presupposition" and "rules" go unexamined is the least of the problem. By far a more complex problem is created by the word *actual* (what is *not* an actual speech act?), and the startling suggestion that recognizing intention (even one's own) is simple.

But my own remarks describing some of the problems with speech-act theory pale in comparison to the both entertaining and "serious" response that Derrida provides to Searle's reply. Most important, however, is the fact that Derrida's response is not simply a playful deconstruction of Searle's position—and it is especially not a willful misunderstanding of either Austin or Searle. Instead, coupled with "Signature Event Context," it clarifies and examines the problems any of us face when we study language and meaning. It is not my intention here (at least as far as I can tell) to reproduce the deconstruction of speech-act theory performed by Derrida; rather, I intend to move between the interplay of "Signature Event Context" and "LIMITED INC abc . . . " to present another analysis of the problems speech-act theory brings into focus in order to describe and delineate more fully the problem of meaning.

In short, I am freely grafting Derrida onto this text (and one can be relatively sure that he never intended it be grafted any more than he might have anticipated this particular context!).

In "Signature Event Context," Derrida correctly points out that "Austin's analyses at all times require a value of *context*, and even of a context exhaustively determined, in theory or teleologically" (1977: 187). He also states that an avoidance of Austin's "infelicities" demands

consciousness, the conscious presence of the intention of the speaking subject in the totality of his speech act. As a result, performative communication becomes once more the communication of an intentional meaning, even if the meaning has no referent in the form of a thing or of a prior or exterior state of things. The conscious presence of speakers or receivers participating in the accomplishment of a performative, their conscious and intentional presence in the totality of the operation, implies teleologically that no *residue* [*reste*] escapes the present totalization." (1977: 187)

This last quotation reveals a great deal. Derrida is not saying that contexts do not exist and, therefore, that any theory depending on a notion of context must necessarily be wrong. Rather, as he writes in the beginning of "Signature," he intends to "demonstrate why a context is never absolutely determinable, or rather, why its determination can never be entirely certain or saturated (1977: 174). Indeed, the words "entirely certain or saturated" are essential here and they make uncommonly good common sense.

Speaking generally for the moment, consider any given context and the contexts of individuals within that context. Is the context determined by the space in which the event is occurring—a physically determined context? Or is that (perhaps) determinable context radically compromised by the various psychological contexts of the various participants? Clearly, much depends on the mutual determination of intention among participants, but even if (when) this is possible, the individual contexts must remain significantly varied by virtue of the inherent differences in experience, knowledge, and concerns of the various individuals.

As Derrida points out in "LIMITED," the very speech act in which he is involved as author of the article defies any clear determination of context, as has the "chain" of speech acts that have preceded the moment of writing. Beginning by noting the apparent participants in his own speech act, he mentions himself ("Who, me?"), Austin (who is dead), Searle's Austin (the one whom Searle accuses Derrida of misunderstanding), Searle (whom he has never met), and Sarl (the corporate author of the "Reply" as constructed by Derrida). He highlights the crux of the problem in any attempt to absolutely determine context. In Derrida's speech act ("LIMITED"), nothing is predetermined and neither convention nor ritual freeze meaning, intent, or origin. In each case, in each speech act, the absence of the signifiers is elemental and essential; each act allows (if not actually encourages) another act, moving both context and meaning into the boundlessness of deconstruction. Comparing the situation to "set theory," Derrida writes that "this concerns the essentially *indeterminable* character of such an analysis. . . . [Each analysis is] *partial*. It will always be lacking the completeness of a set" ("LIMITED" 1977: 165, 174).

Just as he does not exclude the importance of context, indeterminable as it may be, he most certainly does not exclude the importance of or fact of intentionality. The problem, he explains, is that he sees no possibility for intention ever to be fully present in any speech act for either the speaker/writer and/or the hearer/reader. While he agrees with Sarl's statement that " 'there is no getting away from intentionality, because a *meaningful sentence is just a standing possibility of the corresponding* (intentional) speech act' ", in his opinion Sarl chooses to

[place] undue and artificial emphasis on *-ful*, . . . [because] there cannot be a "sentence" that is fully and actually meaningful and hence (or because) there can be no "corresponding (intentional) speech act" that would be fulfilled, fully present, *active* and *actual*. The value of the act (used so generally and analyzed so little in the theory of speech acts), like that of event, should be submitted to systematic questioning. (Derrida, "LIMITED" 1977: 195)

In other words (words that are at least momentarily my own), intention is an important fact of any event or speech act, but because it cannot ever be fully present, the possibility of *mis-* (*mis*takes, *mis*-understandings, *mis*-statements, *mis*-interpretations)—the possibility of partial, incomplete, and un-*ful*-filled speech acts is always/already an integral part of the moment of the speech act. It is not so much that *full* understanding is impossible as it is that even in the moment of its occurrence it would be in the process of deteriorating and never fully present or knowable as fully present. In short, the uncommon sense of a speech act, any linguistic event, is that the rules postulated by Searle (or by any other rule-governed theory of language) do not protect the event from *mis*-firing. And the degree of the *mis-*, the degree to which participants in linguistic events (*mis*)understand one another, is directly correlative to the degree that they guess and/or intuit their own and the other's intentions. The problem, of course, is that, even if there is a moment of mutual understanding, it is always/already escaping, leaving us at best with a trace of the moment:

The category of intention will not disappear; it will have its place, but from that place it will no longer be able to govern the entire scene and system of utterance. . . . [The] intention animating the utterance will never be through and through present to itself and to its content. The iteration structuring it a priori introduces into it a dehiscence and a cleft [*brisure*] which are essential. (Derrida, "Signature" 1977: 192)

The term *dehiscence* draws its metaphorical value "from the realm of botany," in which it marks "emphatically that the divided opening, in the growth of a plant, is also what, in a *positive* sense, makes production, reproduction, development possible" (Derrida, "LIMITED" 1977: 197). This notion of dehiscence, the statement of a "*positive* sense" asserting the possibility of "production, reproduction, development" seems to me to be a much disregarded notion in discussion of deconstruction in general and one that will become particularly important to my discussion later on.

But for the moment I offer the following observation: If one accepts the commonsense position presented by Searle in *Speech Acts*—that linguistic interactions function according to conventional(ized) rules allowing both speaker and hearer to "understand"—one must also accept the fact that this might occur only in the most ritualistic of linguistic moments, where the language itself barely matters because the moment has been entirely pre-defined by legal, religious, or cultural ritual (swearing on a Bible in a court of law, reciting marriage vows, christening a ship).

Thus, the more actual or normal the speech act (given the problems of context and intention, to mention only a few of the problems inherent in linguistically stating and sharing meaning), the more possibilities exist for the speech act to misfire. Using Searle's "Reply" as an example of Searle's own *mis*understanding, Derrida states the problem as follows:

Let us suppose, for a moment, that this is true, simply true. I would like to pose, then, the following question: if a misunderstanding (for example, of Austin's theses) is possible, if a *mis*- in general ("mistake," "misunderstanding," "misinterpretation," "mis-statement," to mention only those included in Sarl's list of accusations, from the first paragraph on) is possible, what does that imply concerning the structure of speech acts in general? And in particular, what does this possibility imply for Austin's, Sarl's or for "my own" speech acts, since, for an instant at least, in a passing phrase, this latter case is apparently not excluded entirely ("it is possible that I may have misinterpreted him as profoundly as I believe he has misinterpreted Austin")? (Derrida, "LIMITED" 1977: 171)

RECONSTRUCTIONS?

In this intricate discussion of context, reconsider the kind of project outlined by Halliday. If the child is engaged in a speech act with the adult, what are the degrees of context and intention that are shared and conscious? Any adult would have to agree that he is creating the child's context, and as problematic as such an assertion is, it does not even begin to approach the problem associated with the child's mutual role in the consciousness of intention and context. In terms of development, one might put forth a theory of context development similar to that of language development, but that raises so many problems that it is hardly worth pursuing. (Just for example, are we ready to argue that, just as there are language universals, there is a sociological grammar of context universals?) I would suggest a simple solution—one that, by virtue of being relatively simple, is almost necessarily wrong. Chomsky has said that one of the problems with behavioral psychology is that it "excels in its experimental techniques, but it has not properly defined its object of inquiry. . . . Thus it has excellent tools . . . but nothing very much to study with them" (Ronat 1979: 46). Perhaps, however, contexts (not intentions) are best described in terms of behavioral science. Certainly, stimulus-response-reinforcement models lend themselves to such a project, but one is still left with a "so what?" because such a model, by virtue of its commitment to avoiding the very existence of intention, commits itself to studying the least important surface structures possible to observe. What good, one might ask, is the description of a context that has little or nothing to do with the thoughts, intentions, or consciousnesses of those involved?

More important, while we may be unable to describe a saturated or determined context—and while full consciousness (let alone mutually shared consciousness) of intention may be impossible—contexts and intentions do exist. That they may be significantly similar or surprisingly different for those involved, at any given moment, suggests that the *mis-* of misunderstanding may be redundant.

In short, even if language is rule-governed and even if the rules are describable, stating one's own meaning is difficult; knowing one's own meaning is momentary and marked by a (de)constructive spiraling; and sharing (fully communicating) one's own meaning with someone else is fraught with degrees of unlikelihood. Of course, this is also what makes it so much fun, and "Being in the world" with other human beings is what makes it so necessary. To no small extent, rather than indicating the impossibility of meaning anything by or to anyone, the words *difficult, momentary*, and *fraught* in the last sentence are intended to invoke Derrida's *dehiscence*. Each word suggests the possibility, not the impossibility, of knowing, stating, and even sharing meaning.

COGNITIVE SCIENCE—ANOTHER VIEW

Cognitive psychologists offer a variety of views and terms that assist in the metaphorizing of this "structure." Some cognitive psychologists would say that human beings interact with the world around them and create conceptual schemata based on these interactions. As each experience is internalized and schematized, it becomes part of a network of experience and concepts and forms a web of meaning or a theory of the world in the head. Some psychologists suggest that these schemata are composed of categories and hierarchies within the categories. For example, there might be a category for "things you can sit on" in which most of us put chairs and couches. This category might fit into another for home furnishings, which in turn might fit into a broad category for "things humans have created to make themselves more comfortable and/or to make their surroundings more beautiful." This theoretical, schematic network is particularly significant when it is used to explain how people relate one experience to another, create sets of expectations based on these schemata, and literally theorize that what will happen next is related to what has happened and is likely to fit into a set of predictable patterns based on what has happened previously.

Of course, the problems are innumerable. The chair that was categorized with home furnishings could be categorized with "things you can hit someone with" or "things to pile your clothes on" or "things to stand on when you change a light bulb." Several questions arise immediately: Are schemata formed individually, asserting some sort of radical relativism? Or are they universals, genetically coded in all human beings? Are they essentially culture-bound and imposed, being derived from the environment? Or are they somehow a mixture of all of the above? In his exceptional study of the "state of cognitive science," *The Mind's New Science,* Howard Gardner does a remarkable job of examining such questions and the positions outlined by various theorists. What becomes primarily clear in this research is that nothing is particularly clear. A major study of color perception, for example (by Marr, in Gardner 1985: 349), appears to support an argument for perceptual universals, but it does not remove the likelihood that perceptions of meaning, or concepts—that which is not physically perceivable—are culture-bound and/or individually relative.

If the nature of perception itself is complex and much argued, all the more so is the nature of schematizing and/or categorizing. Gardner writes:

In confronting questions of categorization, we have moved into distinctly human terrain, involving both language and reasoning capacities. Few would quarrel with the claim that this area is less advanced than the study of perception; indeed, as Geertz suggests, the possibility remains that the most crucial questions about categorization may continue to elude cognitive-scientific methods. Perhaps cognitive science as a field will prove unequal to the task of explicating the genesis, nature, and use of our more complex and evocative concepts and categories. (Gardner 1985: 359)

As is evident in much of the current research in cognition, complex studies based on computers designed to model the processes of the human mind (studies of artificial intelligence, or AI), albeit important, revealing, and fascinating, are not immediately (or ever?) likely to unlock the mysteries (Gardner 1985: 387). Current research simply does not support the notions of clearly defined categories or of the human being as a "logical thinker" (Gardner 1985: 340–80). Indeed, if anything,

Human thought emerges as messy, intuitive, subject to subjective representations— not as pure and immaculate calculation. These processes may ultimately be modeled by a computer, but the end result will bear little resemblance to that view of cognition canonically lurking in computationally inspired accounts. (Gardner 1985: 386)

Clearly, if anything at all can be said to be clear, the concepts of schematizing and categorizing leave us with some pretty difficult questions, and most of the questions depend on an explanation of language that appears not to be forthcoming. For example, there is the problem of one individual's schemata versus the schemata of others. If they think the chair is a priceless antique and you think it is something to stand on, problems are likely to arise. There is also the obvious problem of terms in the previous paragraph. Where do these categories come from in the first place? Are they universals that we are all born with, waiting to be filled in through experience? Are they entirely dependent on environment and culture; that is, are schemata entirely the result of behavioral conditioning? And what does it mean to "internalize" experience in the first place? If everything out there is genuinely out there but the individual cognitively acts on what is out there, creating webs of meanings, networks of schemata, how does one do this? To a large degree, these schemata must be products of the possibility of meaning—they are language dependent. This is another (important) way of talking about deep structure or some internal system of making meaning.

One of the most problematic things about these schemata, aside from the impossible question of their origination, is this: If they are individually created and based on individual experience, how do they escape the problems associated with radical relativism? More directly, if people are involved in the process of creating meaning and this involves the creation of schemata or categories into and through which all experience is processed, how do people manage to create the same associational webs, the same schemata? Of course, the answer is that we do not know that people do create the same webs; it is impossible to know, and this was all just a metaphor in the first place. As a metaphor, however, it reveals that individuals in a given situation need not be making the same sense of that situation, often are not making the same sense of it, and unless some overt act reveals the mismatch of interpretation and/or meaning making, no one knows that different meanings have been made, different schemata created and/or employed. If nothing else, this suggests that we cannot put too much faith in surface structures of any kind. If people can (and are likely to) read a situation with various degrees of difference, how much more likely are there to be confusions over meaning when they are using the surface structures of language to share a meaning?

These last paragraphs appear to leave us with nothing clear-cut and certain, and to some extent that is true. Certainly, Gardner's goal appears far distant—that cognitive science will ultimately "provide a cogent scientific account of how human beings achieve their most remarkable symbolic products: how we come to compose symphonies, write poems, invent machines (including computers), or construct theories (including cognitive-scientific ones)" (Gardner 1985: 391). But if such a goal is even to be approximated, then we must continue to theorize; and we need language, in both the external and internal senses, in order to do so. Consequently, regardless of the messiness of human thinking, and recognizing the complexity of concepts and terms like *categorizing, schematizing, thinking, perceiving,* and *languaging,* I will continue to employ the terms throughout this discussion. I ask that the reader remember that whatever realities these terms suggest, the terms are metaphors at best. They "say" what is not in order to suggest what may be. Perhaps all writing, even so-called scientific writing and scholarly writing, is best described as the process of telling a lie in order to suggest a truth that cannot be said. But then, in truth, what else can linguistic surface structures be but metaphors?

CONCLUSION

In an upper-level undergraduate course I teach on psycholinguistics and the reading process, I ask students to write annotated bibliographies on books and articles as they read in the area. Recently, one of my students pointed out: "Every study I read ends by saying that 'we can't be sure about this [the implications or findings]. More research is necessary.' " Sometimes, for the students, it seems as though nothing concluded with suggested action, and this frustrates them. "Why am I reading all this stuff—studying and taking tests—if all I'm going to discover is that 'we don't yet know, for sure'?" The question is a fair one.

The students do not know that their questions have been preceded by an era of "easy answers," all of which offer (or, most often, sell) the textbook or program or workbook or method that will solve the problem. Nor can they necessarily know that, often, much of what is offered as good methodology for classroom teachers bears little or no relationship to either empirical or theoretical scholarship. The result, characteristic of the split between many teachers and many scholars, is that each denigrates the other—the teacher pointing to the scholar's irrelevance and the scholar pointing to the teacher's anti-intellectualism. It is unquestionably true that additional research is necessary, so much that the future of yet-unborn cognitive scientists and sociolinguists appears guaranteed: Given what has been revealed so far, one can only guess that the empiricists will be able to continue for an in(de)finite period of time. And, of course, unless they are outlawed, theorists will continue indefinitely to theorize, suggesting new directions of empirical research for the young and the motivated, and itemizing the faults of those who came before.

That is what we academics do. That is also the point of this summary synthesis of the research and theory in the areas of language, meaning, and cognition.

If we recognize how little we know about the origin and/or nature of language, we may become more honest in some of our classroom activities and approaches to teaching. At the very least, we may become more sensitive to the confusion we all experience in terms of fullness of consciousness and intention, especially when it is applied to someone besides ourselves. A step farther might be to recognize that "my syllabus, my course, my lecture, my text, my test, my thesis, my . . . " may, at best, only approximate that of "my" students. Most importantly, we might try to recognize that the theory of language suggested here absolutely and clearly defines the academy as it operates outside the classroom. Only in the classroom does any academic worth his salt dare to claim absolute certainty about truth; most academics worth anything other than salt know better than to claim it there, in the classroom. But if one looks to the world of academic publishing, one immediately sees that the enterprise itself testifies (in a biblical sense) to the changing nature of meaning and truth and to the role language plays in these changes.

Put more simply, we will run out of trees and paper long before we run out of the "language" that all of us delight in employing and exhibiting whenever anyone will allow it. Much like the infant who has discovered the surface structures of the local community and who engages in the nonstop production of those structures and the lifelong exploration of the community, we evidence the deconstructive nature of language by our commitment to producing more and more of it in order to (re)state what we see to be meaningful—at every opportunity. Even if we believe that we have recognized someone else's context and intention, we find ourselves obsessed by the need to "mean more"—to speak/write more. We are always saying "in addition" or "in other words," unless we are saying "to the contrary" or "on the other hand." We are always supplementing because we intuitively recognize that what Derrida says is true: Everything in language is a matter of *supplement.*

But I said this has something to do with teaching—with us and our students. Here it is: Those of us who teach should have our students engage in the production of language in order to produce surface structures that might allow the approximation of meaning, the knowing of meaning, the sharing of meaning, and finally, the examination of meaning. If we choose to ignore the dehiscence, that is most certainly up to us. But the growth will take place with or without us, for the most part, and we might seriously consider what we can do to facilitate it instead of inhibiting or ignoring it.

Or we can give multiple-choice tests and let the machine grade them. We can give lectures to multitudes. But let's not call it teaching.

As was said earlier, humans of all cultures learn the underlying structures of their language (or begin to implement the possibility of meaning making and sharing) by the age of five and often much earlier. In most industrialized countries, certainly here in the United States, this is just about the time they are sent to school. Prior to this, unless they have been in nursery schools, most of their language interaction has been social and has been directed by their own immediate needs and purposes and the needs and purposes of those around them—normally family and friends. It has also been noted that during these first five years humans learn more than they will ever again learn in so short a period of time. It is more than ironic that as this period ends, school begins.

What happens with language in school? Up to this point language has been at the center of the individual's human development, and the individual has done an excellent job of implementing the possibility of meaning making and communicating. No wonder, then, that kids are a little surprised when they get to school and find out that they now need to "study" language. In fact, they don't really study it as much as they practice it, and the "it" that they practice often bears little relationship to real language in any sense of the word.

Prior to school, human beings are immersed in the process of languaging: They use language to create meaning, to create and control their world, to name their realities, to fulfill their needs, to love and be loved, to play, to be alive. But when they get to school, they start practicing it. Of course, they don't practice language in terms of the possibility of meaning making and meaning sharing (at least not for the most part). Instead they practice surface structures. At best, they may practice writing sentences and, some-times, even paragraphs. They practice reading. They immerse themselves in workbooks that ask them irrelevant questions about irrelevant topics. (Question: "Who sat on the cat's mat?" Fill-in-the-blank answer: "The rat.")

While they practice in some pretty strange ways, the purposes and results of this practice should be disturbing to everyone because it is here that the problems decried throughout education and society begin. It is ironic and sad that what begins in the early grades is repeated, in various modes, throughout the schooling experience by the very teachers who, at the same time, decry the results of such silliness.

In short, the first thing many schools appear to do is consciously, formally, "forget" how people learned language in the first place. Immediate emphasis is given to one of several concerns and agendas, depending on the school, but most seem bent on avoiding the sensible, real, interactive uses of language that preceded school and that worked so well in the individuals' learning processes. What follows is an examination of the language activities that typify much of what goes on in the average person's schooling.

2

An Historical Perspective: or, How We Got from Here to There

I thank God there are no free schools or printing, and I hope we shall not have these hundred years, for learning has brought disobedience, and heresy, and sects into the world, and printing has divulged them, and libels against the best Government. God keep us from both.
Governor Sir William Berkeley, *An Official Report on Virginia* (1671)

Having already established the problems of context, I will limit the context for this discussion of literacy to England and North America. I will be concerned primarily with English-speaking peoples, and I will begin with the medieval period in England. Literacy, in almost any sense of the word, is a relatively recent concept when applied to anyone other than a selected elite of aristocrats and/or church people. Indeed, as Michael Clanchy notes, "at least three quarters of all books printed before 1500 and most books printed in the next century were written by medieval or ancient authors" (Clanchy, in Resnick 1983: 8). Readers and writers primarily comprised the clergy and/or very select groups of specially educated people. Early emphases on public literacy were somewhat limited and almost always associated with religion first and legal/economic issues second.

In the nontraditional sense of the word, writing preexisted everything as the universe awaited the becoming of the meaning makers. Once they arrived, the sun was read as God; volcanoes articulated the words of God; animal tracks were read; the messages encoded on painted and tattooed bodies were read; the heavens, the earth, water and fire were read. Indeed, literacy of this sort was widespread. But in the traditional sense of the word, writing "first developed in the near East for the purpose of government" and was inextricably tied to "utilitarian functions" (Stock 1983: 32). Slowly, writing moved beyond the utilitarian function, becoming a means of recording and ordering reality. At first, as might be expected, writing and literacy were viewed with suspicion and even hostility because print appeared threatening to "oral societies," which were often characterized by "isolated communities with a strong network of kinship and group solidarity" (Stock 1983: 15–16).

While twentieth-century industrial societies like our own clearly contain smaller communities within larger communities—even some that maintain unique signs and customs of a particular ethnic, religious, or racial group— genuine isolation is difficult to achieve or maintain. Even when it is powerfully imposed through inherent strains of classism and racism (as in parts of the Soviet Union, in the ghettoes of North America, or through explicit governmental policies of a country like South Africa), print and electronic media accompanied by the enormous physical mobility of the populations of industrialized nations show us to be significantly different from medieval communities. Indeed, groups that attempt to maintain an isolated identity of their own operate within a constant tension created by the communities that surround them and impinge on their boundaries (Amish communities or Indian reservations, for example).

On the other hand, this apparent impossibility is challenged by some writers who believe that modern societies maintain isolated communities resulting from societal strains of racism or other powerful systems of stereotyping and segregating. Some of these writers suggest that these communities are "residually oral" cultures where "oral modes of expression permeate thinking. [The people] come from homes where speech is more widespread than reading or writing" (D'Angelo in Bailey and Foscheim 1983: 104). Of course, even in highly print-oriented cultures (perhaps we are really talking about social classes here), one would be hard put to imagine a home or group in which print (reading and writing) was more prevalent than oral language (speaking and listening). On the other hand, there may be an element of truth in the commonsense assertion that some communities, most typically middle- and upper-class communities, place a higher premium on print literacy than do poorer, more segregated communities.

Such generalizations are fraught with problems, and before they are accepted, even as gross generalizations, they must be subjected to careful examination and qualification. Since these particular issues will be examined more fully as we move into a discussion of contemporary notions of literacy, I note only one significant distinction at this point. While such comparisons of oral cultures (over periods of hundreds of years and from societies as different as our own and those of medieval England) may suggest certain similarities, they also present the necessity for careful distinctions—not the least of which is the fact that such a comparison ignores the roles of television and radio as they invade even the most isolated, segregated communities in our culture. Almost everything in our contemporary society is recorded in print, on audio or video tape, or on compact disc. With little discrimination, editing, or conscious selectivity, speeches, conferences, interactions of all sorts (varying as widely as from the *Congressional Record* to interviews with people living in a flood zone) are recorded and "read" by incredibly diverse groups of individuals worldwide. If literacy is related to more than print media, it is difficult to imagine a community that is not immersed in reading and writing.

But as Brian Stock points out, this was not the case prior to the printing press, partly and obviously because it could not possibly be so until the technology was invented to allow such obsessive and widespread recording of the various realities that make up the modern world. The medievalists, for example, "recorded only what they felt deserved to survive, and this inevitably included bits and pieces of the ancient heritage" (Stock 1983: 31). Through such selective recording, he suggests, they created order—a classical heritage of order on which they might fondly look back from their position of immediate chaos. Thus, even at these very early stages, and even though it involved a very small group of highly select individuals, literacy allowed an ordering of reality (and therefore the creation of a reality). Most important, Stock posits a psycholinguistic development of enormous significance: "The mind acquired the capacity through the use of language to structure the raw data of the senses, so written statements began to act as reference points of giving meaning to everyday human relations" (Stock 1983: 59).

In stark contrast to the medieval world, however, is our own. Even if we are busy creating realities through our various technologies, the fact that we appear to do so obsessively, maniacally writing and reading everything, may suggest that we are creating chaos from chaos in order to examine chaos. But that is getting far ahead of the immediate (hi)story.

In Elizabethan England, learning to read was urged as part of one's road to salvation. In New England in the late 1600s, literacy was presented as "the key to the success and survival of a reformed Christian Culture" with reading and writing argued to be necessary as a defense against barbarianism and embarrassment, and as tools for commercial success. (This is not unlike many arguments associated with literacy in the twentieth century.) In *The Court and Country* (London, 1618), Nicholas Breton quotes a yeoman who sounds almost weary of the whole issue:

This is all we go to school for: to read common prayers at church and set down common prices at market, write a letter and make a bond, set down the day of our births, our marriage day, and make our wills when we are sick for the disposing of our goods when we are dead. These are the chief matters that we meddle with and we find enough to trouble our head withal. (Dunham and Pargellis 1968: 468)

Still, even when literacy is defined in relatively simplistic terms—being able to decode the Bible and basic legal documents, being able to sign one's own name—we find that it was not particularly widespread. According to David Cressy, "50% or more of the population was illiterate" (Cressy in Resnick 1983: 40). Furthermore, while some men of the cloth stressed the importance of literacy so the flock might read the Bible, it was also clear that it was not necessary for salvation. Richard Steele asserts this in his sermons: "Though you cannot read a letter in the book, you can by true assurance read your name in the Book of Life, your scholarship will serve . . . if you cannot write a word, yet see you transcribe a fair copy of a godly righteous and sober life, and you have done well" (*The Husbandman's Calling*, 1533, cited by Cressy in Resnick 1983: 27).

Over the course of a few hundred years characterized by increasing democratization, urbanization, and industrial revolution, the world began to change. A brief, generalized list of changes occurring in the nineteenth and twentieth centuries evidences some of the major differences affecting the need for and nature of literacy in the modern world. "Public" schooling became a major force in both England and America as the emphasis on and need for literacy increased as a result of child labor laws, systems of funding public education, laws requiring children to attend school until they were at least sixteen years of age, changes in the job market, increasingly complex technologies, and a host of cultural, social, and political changes. There is little need to document the different rhetorics that surround the emphasis on literacy in this country as we moved from a melting pot to a progressive socioeducational system, and then to a post-Sputnik educational system devoted to developing various literacies in the service of personal, economic, nationalistic, and militaristic needs. During the past decade, unprecedented emphasis has been put on the need for public literacy, although primarily on print literacy—the time-honored first two R's (reading and writing)—and the main emphasis is on a relatively unsophisticated kind of literacy. By and large, "literacy for salvation" has been replaced by "literacy for economic advancement and personal growth."

At its lowest level, the emphasis has been on doing something about those in our society who are nonliterate or illiterate. This includes people who cannot read or write at all and those who do so at such an elemental level, so inadequately, that they are unable to function socially and economically. Only recently (during the last forty years or so) has much attention been paid to the literacy levels of high school graduates, and only in the last decade has the literacy of college students been much discussed. The writing-across-the-curriculum movements of the last ten years are one visible result of such a focus, as are the discussions throughout academia over the last twenty years regarding the literacy components of general college programs. That the agenda involves something more than simple coding and decoding skills is obvious in the range of books from *Becoming a Nation of Readers* (Anderson et al. 1985) to *Cultural Literacy* (Hirsch 1987).

In the introduction to *Become a Nation of Readers*, we read that "Reading is a basic life skill. It is a cornerstone for a child's success in school and, indeed, throughout life. Without the ability to read *well*, opportunities for *personal fulfillment* and job success inevitably will be lost" (Anderson et al. 1985: 1). In the preface to *Cultural Literacy*, Hirsch writes:

> The anthropological view stresses the universal fact that a human group must have effective communications to function effectively, that effective communications require a shared culture, and that shared culture requires transmission of specific information to children. Literacy . . . is no autonomous, empty skill but depends upon literate culture. Like any other aspect of acculturation, literacy requires the early and continued transmission of specific information. . . . Only by accumulating shared symbols, and the shared information that the symbols represent, can we learn to communicate effectively with one another in our national community. (Hirsch 1987: xvii)

Given Hirsch's stature as a literary critic and the recent public response to his book *Cultural Literacy*—a response that has moved the book into national bestseller status and has won Hirsch the honor of being interviewed on national television—his ideas deserve examination.

E. D. HIRSCH, JR., AND *CULTURAL LITERACY*

The book is a mélange of ideas, criticism, and suggestions focusing on the current crisis in education, which Hirsch curiously places on the shoulders of Rousseau and John Dewey in particular and "romantic formalism" in general. In support of his thesis he cites (and largely leaves underdeveloped) an impressive and important array of topics: the abominable intellectual chaos and lack of shared information among presumably literate Americans, the content-neutral curricula of our schools, the psycholinguistic nature of the reading process, dangers of bilingualism and multilingualism in America, cognitive schema theory, and so on. Finally, he presents the beginnings of a solution represented by a phenomenal sixty-two page, double-column list of words, terms, names, sayings, and dates that comprise what the book cover had already told us is the "Thinking American's List."

By my own rough count, the list provides about five thousand items that we thinking Americans need to know.

From a humorous perspective, this is certainly not asking too much of either the individual learner or the schools that teach the learner. Consider these facts. Between the ages of five and eighteen, the average American spends about 2,300 days in school (my figures are rough; I've tried to adjust for days off and sick days). Given that each of these school days involves

approximately four hours of instruction (adjust these figures for school announcements, paper passing, bell ringing, and general settling-in activities),
the average American spends about 9,200 hours in what is often described
as a teaching-learning situation. This means that any curriculum that simply
taught a word, date, name, famous saying, or something on Hirsch's list in
each hour slot during the school day would be able to teach and review
everything on the list by the time the student graduated from high school.
I suppose we might go on to more specialized lists for the college curriculum,
but I leave that to someone else's book.

Humor aside, Hirsch makes some important points. I do not intend to
suggest that his central theses are wrong. First, without some semblance of
a shared cultural heritage, communication of almost any kind is bound to
suffer. More directly, readers/writers with radically different cultural heritages are likely to produce readings/writings that seriously misfire. But careful
distinctions need to be made between terms like *cultural heritage*, *schemata*,
and *background information* if we are to avoid the kind of confusion that leads
to lists of what every American should know. The schemata that Hirsch
mentions are, metaphorically speaking, complex interweavings of concepts
and facts—everything one has experienced. They do, in a sense, contain
information; but, more important, they create the network that facilitates
the process of meaning making through the creative interrelating of concepts
and information. In and of itself, information of any kind is not particularly
important. Information (all experience) becomes important as one makes
sense of it, as one relates it to other (bodies of) information and concepts,
as one creates and revises schemata.

The background information that is necessary, or at least helpful, when
a reader engages works that have been produced in the distant past—the
information necessary to allow a reader to engage in a dialogue with absent
writers—is the information that teachers must provide within the teaching-
learning process *as it is directly related to* that which is being experienced,
discussed, read, and written about at a given time in a given classroom. In
short, schema theory does not suggest that schemata are just there, waiting
to be filled in. To whatever extent they are "there" (where?) at all, they are
in the constant process of (de)constructing.

In terms of real, live students, we might consider two possible groups. First
are those who are likely to come to us with cultural heritages that differ in
important ways from those embraced by the mainstream of the culture. These
students have been prevented through race, economics, sex, or social status
from sharing in the general culture. They may not only lack the background
information that one might deem necessary for engaging in a dialogue with
authors of the past; they may actually differ cognitively from those who have
been raised within the mass culture. (Of course, this suggestion is not entirely
new and is supported by the experiences individuals have had on standard "intelligence" tests with their built-in biases.) But throughout this discussion we

have focused on students who are part of the mainstream, students who are succeeding in school. This second group must also be considered.

The second group generally comes to our classrooms with a shared cultural heritage. It is a heritage made up of shopping malls, rock and roll, Dungeons and Dragons, video games, soap operas, Walkmans, Little League—most of the trappings that make up the cultural heritage of middle-class adult society.

Furthermore, only someone completely out of touch with American schools would deny the fact that a shared heritage of any sort has become less and less something one can count on in a classroom. For many of our college students, history appears to have begun primarily with the birth of Christ, and, except for the curious geographical fact that it appears to have occurred in Bethlehem, just about all other history occurs primarily in North America and has happened rather recently. Knowledge of Christ does not generally suggest a knowledge of the Bible, the 1960s happened a long time ago when there were also hippies, and television has always existed (Assessment Committee 1989). Of course, while criticizing the historical-cultural knowledge of many of our students, it is equally important to recognize that many of them know more about science and technology (unfortunately, one must emphasize technology here) than many of their adult role models—and that many of the adult role models appear to have an equally confused and limited sense of culture and history.

One might well argue, along with Hirsch, that general ignorance of one's own heritage has reached crisis proportions. I experience this distressing realization in a classroom filled with college sophomores, juniors, and seniors when they reveal that they haven't the slightest idea of what is in the Bill of Rights or the Constitution. Not that they haven't memorized certain parts (some have had to in order to pass a test, of course), but they do not understand the meaning. These are the kids who are literate, who are doing well in college. One might note that they certainly do not constitute the threat to government that the governor of Virginia worried about at the opening of this chapter. But in fact, this is only to say that the problems cited by Hirsch are more widespread and have been around much longer than his theory about romantic formalism explains. Most of these students were "taught" the Bill of Rights and the Constitution in high school. So what is going on?

Like their parents and theirs before them, these students find much of what occurs in school to be irrelevant to their immediate lives, but not because they have radically different schemata. Rather, they are not engaged in the process of making meaning of the background information schools seem always to be giving them in order that they might use it for some future project. Whether the cultural heritage be reduced to a massive list of items or be itemized through a sequential or spiraling curriculum—as long as the cultural heritage simply is something that we believe people should

know because it may come in handy some day—we will be frustrated and
the students will ignore us. Until the Bill of Rights means something to
them personally, it can only mean nothing.

Hirsch makes another significant point when he indicates that our schools
have suffered seriously from an inordinate emphasis on "skills-models" of
learning (Hirsch 1987: 112–13). This emphasis is based on behavioral models
that fragment learning into discrete skills to be practiced, mastered, and
utilized as building blocks for the next set of skills. Indeed, the model is
still dutifully implemented in many English classes in America.

In any discussion of skills models or cultural heritage models of learning,
it is particularly interesting to review some of the observations made by John
Dixon in *Growth through English* (1975), the book he wrote to summarize and
develop some of the powerfully insightful positions articulated at the Anglo-
American Conference on the Teaching of English (The Dartmouth Conference) in 1966. One of the most important books written about the teaching
of language and literature during the past twenty-five years, it is notable in
that it begins by exploring the "models" of teaching and learning that have
characterized the teaching of English. Dixon cites the skills model first, the
cultural heritage model second, and the personal growth model third. Noting
that the skills model was most suited to an era in which "initial literacy"
was in great demand, he identifies its clear limitations: So often used in the
literal sense when applied to teaching and learning, the word *skill* poorly
describes the array of complex factors involved in language, literature, and
learning. He also points out that skills models emphasize drills and tend to
make the means become the end, ignoring the learner's imagination and
creative learning abilities, which generally causes boredom and frustration
for all concerned (Dixon 1975: 1–2). In his discussion of the "cultural heritage
model," he points to its central tendency to stress "culture as a *given*" and
"to ignore culture as the pupil knows it, a network of attitudes to experience
and personal evaluations that he develops in a living response to his family
and neighborhood" (Dixon 1975: 3).

Dixon and the overwhelming majority of those who participated in this
important conference favor the personal growth model; but before we discuss
this model, an immediate qualification is necessary. Nowhere in his book
or in the related writings of which I am aware does anyone suggest the
simplistic, romantic notion that learners should simply be left to grow on
their own. Nor does anyone suggest that the model neglect the intellect in
favor of an overemphasis on feelings. Perhaps most significant and most
consistently misunderstood and/or ignored is the fact that the personal growth
model does not deny the existence of or need for skills any more than it
denigrates the composite of works and thoughts that come together to create
our cultural heritage.

Quite simply, the personal growth model honors the other models by
emphasizing their interaction within the personal growth of the learner as

she moves among and through the events of the past and present into the future. What seems generally ignored in discussions of "process oriented" approaches like the personal growth model articulated at Dartmouth (and powerfully rearticulated and extended at the November 1984 International Federation for the Teaching of English Seminar at Michigan State University) is this: The personal growth model emphasizes intelligent, substantive, important uses of language—across the entire spectrum of reading, writing, listening, and speaking—more than does any other model of teaching. By emphasizing understanding rather than memorization and substantive articulations rather than formulaic exercises, this model launches a direct attack on the content-free curriculum that Hirsch so correctly criticizes (Tchudi 1985). Where lifeless skills and antique ideas had once held center stage, the personal growth model insists on breathing life back into the curriculum by inviting the learner to use (rather than simply practice) skills in the process of making meaning of the past as a pathway to the future.

If such suspicious goals derive from the works of Rousseau and Dewey, they are much honored in the blaming.

Indeed, when examining attacks on the educational system, it is always wise to analyze carefully the parts of the attacks that suggest a golden age when things were considerably different and/or better. I am personally un-aware of a time when most people in our own or any other culture were, in general, more literate, more sensitive to and knowledgeable about their own or anyone else's culture, and significantly less chauvinistic or ethnocentric. As the initial discussion of the history of literacy notes, small, elite groups have historically existed—literate groups who shared and mandated the wit and wisdom of the era. Of course, we still have such groups. But if we are going to hell in a basket, it is the same basket that people have been riding in for years, and the trip is mercilessly slow.

Hirsch correctly decries the "fragmented" curriculum that typifies much of American education. But when he suggests that the initial problem growing out of the "romantic formalism" propounded by the followers of Rousseau and Dewey was continued in the 1960s and 1970s as an "extreme yet logical extension of the romantic formalism that has been the dominant theory taught in our schools of education over the past fifty years" (Hirsch 1987: 125), the assertion must be questioned. This interesting but unfounded assertion en-tirely ignores the powerful behavioral emphases in American schools of ed-ucation and psychology, just as it ignores the various state departments of education that have, over the last twenty years and continuing right up to the present, allowed standardized testing to become the monopolistic money-making proposition that it is today. Starting as early as the 1950s, American students and teachers have been subjected to curricula driven by commercial publishing companies, teacher education programs driven by taxonomies of competencies, and attendant systems of evaluation for the competencies of both teachers and students (note the math and language competency tests in New York State), "value-added" emphases in education that powerfully re-emphasize standardized tests, and so on. In short, one has to search long and hard to find any widespread implementation of the romantic formalism that has caused all the problems.

The cultural heritage model of education proffered by Hirsch is not a new idea, and it certainly has some aspects to recommend it. Both Samuel Johnson, who wished to honor "that which has been longest known and best understood," and Matthew Arnold well represent such a time-honored esthetic. But any assertion of a cultural heritage—especially when it becomes central to an educational system, philosophy, or curriculum—always has and probably always will result in a frozen and more restricted canon of truths based on the already entrenched canon from which it derives. For physical evidence one need simply review the required readings for college courses as the titles are stacked carefully in campus bookstores throughout the United States. Indeed, contrary to what is often cited as an argument for the cultural heritage model (e.g., "These days you find courses in black or women's literature holding the same status as traditional courses in the Restoration. Oh my!"), one finds that the literary canon has held up quite well. Deconstructionists can do what they will, but they have had little significant effect on the curricula of "the academy." And when they do appear to be anywhere near having an effect, they are soundly renounced as intellectual heathens who speak and write in the tongues of devils.

But what is most surprising is this: Hirsch is a well-known, much-published literary critic. As such he is, presumably, fully knowledgeable of the stimulating and engaging controversies that presently abound in poststructural, philosophical, literary, and linguistic theory (Culler 1982). Yet he apparently chooses to disregard the implications of contemporary theory; this call for a cultural literacy based on a nationally shared vocabulary ignores the fascinating controversies about the nature of language and meaning, the nature of the reading process, and, in fact, the possibility of anything even approaching Hirsch's concept of cultural literacy. To the extent that contemporary literary theorists (including a broad range of philosophers and psychologists) share a common ground, it is in their attempts to discuss the "problem of meaning": (1) *whether it exists* (In the contextually boundless world of oppositions and reversals of deconstruction, once inserted into the machine of language, and in a world characterized entirely by the instability of constant, infinite change and motion, how can we discuss meaning?); (2) *how it came into existence* (If it exists, who made it? He who made the lamb?); (3) *where it resides* (Within texts existing in boundless contexts? Within human beings—reader/writer/speaker/listener? Within signs [and what is a sign that it may be read, by whom, and how did it acquire meaning?]?); (4) *how it is identified* (Communally, when communities agree on a meaning? In terms of describable speech acts? Through the application of paradigms like those of Marxists, feminists, Freudians, or through the application of all of the above, leading to countless, infinite, equally defensible, equally valid meanings in the midst of no definition of validity or meaning?)?

Finally, more directly related to the reading process itself, Hirsch creates the possibilities for serious confusions and misunderstandings. At the beginning of chapter 2, Hirsch cites Robert Glaser's comments from the foreword of *Becoming a Nation of Readers* in order to indicate how far we have come in understanding the reading process, not to mention approaches to and methods for teaching reading, but he does not cite the statement at the end of the introduction pointing out that "new knowledge about reading and schooling... answers some questions... but it leaves others unanswered and sometimes furnishes conflicting answers" (Anderson et al. 1985: 4). Furthermore, as is so often the case in discussions of reading and literacy, he fails to make some enormously important distinctions. Hirsch does not distinguish between the processes involved in initial reading activities and the processes involved in helping those who can already read become better (more literate) readers; he does not recognize that many young people come to school already able to read and clearly predisposed toward the activity as opposed to others for whom the activity seems completely foreign; he does not indicate that our "new and improved" methods of teaching reading continue to fail miserably with those who are unable to read (the logic is intentionally circular here—research sometimes seems to suggest that our methods work very well for those who learn to read but not for those who don't—and one might wish to question the effectiveness of such methods); and he cites standardized tests like the verbal SATs (Hirsch 1987: 4) as though they had some validity in terms of testing literacy (not to mention the confusion that presently exists over the nature and validity of tests used to determine "grade levels" in reading [Klare in Pearson 1984: 681–744]).

In short, Hirsch appears to suggest that we understand how people learn to read and what it is they do when they are actually reading.

But attacks like this are relatively easy to mount, and they do no one much good except insofar as they clarify confusions and/or misinformation. While there is much that I find objectionable in his book, it raises a major issue that must be addressed. Whether it be Hirsch or the ghost of John Dewey, no one connected with education at any level, from elementary school through graduate school, is satisfied with the current state of literacy, cultural or otherwise.

In what follows, I want to characterize what I see to be a major problem in the area of literacy and a major obstacle to the opening of any minds in any way. First, I begin with what I see to be a major flaw and a significant personal bias on Hirsch's part: Throughout his book, when he refers to reading and learning, he posits the "text" (not just literary texts, of course) as the repository of information. He emphasizes the need for a "universally shared national vocabulary," the necessity to identify the "specific knowledge that children need to learn in school," (Hirsch 1987: 19), and he says that "To be truly literate, citizens must be able *to grasp* the meaning of any piece of writing addressed to the general reader" (italics added) (Hirsch 1987: 26, 12).

I have two major objections to the bases and implications of these positions. First, as should already be clear, no one can reasonably suggest that there is any widespread agreement about where meaning comes from, how it is made, and how it is shared. As human beings learn language, they hear, understand, and produce sentences that they have never before heard or seen; as they learn to read, human beings make sense of sentences they have never before seen. As they write, they write sentences that have never before been written. In short, human beings are not simply *graspers* of information, they are meaning *makers*. Presented with a text, the mature reader interacts with it, or acts upon it, or engages in a transaction with it, or submits to it, penetrates and is penetrated by it. The description of the reading process, what happens when reader meets text, is much debated and variously labeled, but few engaged in the debate describe the process as one of *grasping*.

Hirsch's focus on a shared vocabulary introduces serious problems. While he surely does not mean vocabulary in any simplistic sense of the word— and assuming that he is talking about the conceptual schemata that might accompany the items in his list—his disclaimers at the beginning of chapter 6 are not particularly convincing (especially given the publication of *The Dictionary of Cultural Literacy*, Hirsch, Kett, and Trefil 1988). Indeed, when one notes that he appears willing to allow standardized tests, like some specially revised version of the verbal SATs, to measure the success of the project, even those who agree with the concept of a shared vocabulary must certainly shudder. Even with a highly defined list such as the one provided by Hirsch and his colleagues, the verbal SATs represent a simplistic, naive, and potentially destructive (certainly counterproductive) measure of literacy that should be abolished rather than revised. Any such faith in standardized testing, especially standardized testing of anything as complex as literacy, must surely be viewed as more formally romantic than even Rousseau's ideas.

Thus, in the act of attacking Dewey's progressive experimentalism, Hirsch presents his own brand of hopeless romanticism: By specifying the information each thinking American should know, by itemizing a vocabulary we will share across all linguistic, ethnic, local, and state boundaries, and by centering a single, standard English, we will come together as one nation, presumably under God. Such a promise appears like an ethnocentric version of the beatific vision intended to lead to a genuinely united United States of America and is as naive as it is distressing to contemplate.

Unfortunately, as we have already established in the discussion of cognitive science, the individual background knowledge that Hirsch correctly identifies as so important to the reading/learning process is far more complex than any notion of shared vocabulary can ever begin to suggest. Neither the world nor the text sits in space waiting for the learner to grasp it. While Hirsch clearly understands that reading involves much more than the simple decoding of words and sentences, he does not emphasize the complexity involved in the reading process. Readers do not simply come to a text (or any experience), internalize that which is outside them (incorporate that which is "other"), and thereby grasp new knowledge. Even learning theorists who are committed to cognitive theorizing (and I include myself among them) understand fully that schemata are theoretical structures. As has been noted earlier, terms like *schema, categories,* and *hierarchies* are metaphors for describing that which we cannot describe and which we certainly do not fully understand. They are all we have to describe the apparently rich, flexible, and changing associational web that we call mind. Quite simply, we must rely on these metaphorical structures in order to discuss what may go on in the human mind as it meets and makes its worlds. As human beings read their world, they appear (metaphorically speaking) to create networks of schemata and categories and hierarchies within categories. These cognitive structures, unstable and dynamic, are the repository (sometimes called long-term memory) of the background or nonvisual information Hirsch mentions in chapter 2 of his book. Human beings do not simply receive or grasp the meaning that is out there; they create meaning as they "read" what is out there. And insofar as individuals create meaning, any notion of a shared vocabulary becomes considerably more complex than Hirsch suggests.

But as Christopher Norris points out in *Contest of Faculties,* after deconstruction,

if structuralism has indeed been rendered problematic by these later developments, it has not been superseded or its enterprise quietly laid to rest. According to Derrida, a certain "spontaneous structuralism" has always been philosophy's most characteristic mark and gesture. That is to say, philosophy has rested its claims upon the appeal to such regulative notions as reason, method and "structure" itself—concepts whose purely *metaphorical* nature it has not been able to recognize, since this would entail the dissolution of philosophy, the unthinkable step "beyond" logocentric tradition. "Structure is perceived through the incidence of menace, at the moment when imminent danger concentrates our vision on the keystone of an institution, the stone which encapsulates both the possibility and the fragility of its existence." Yet Derrida is equally insistent that deconstruction must work from *within* this edifice of concepts, seeking to shake (or "solicit") its structure, rather than thinking to bring it down at a single, apocalyptic stroke. There is no passing "beyond" structuralism except by a constant and vigilant awareness that the structuralist enterprise is deeply complicit with the whole prehistory of philosophic reason. And—as Derrida shows in his essay on Foucault, "Cogito and the History of Madness"—there is no way of breaking with philosophic reason that doesn't at the last use strategies borrowed from that same ubiquitous tradition." (Norris 1985: 222–23, quoting Derrida 1978: 160, 6, 31–63)

Finally, it is this "incidence of menace," always pointing to "both the possibility and the fragility of its [structure's] existence," that generates and

necessitates the constant process of meaning-making activities through language in the face of the immediate, spiraling deconstruction (dissemination)
of that very meaning.

So, if all is not to be lost, if a constructive possibility exists, it exists only
insofar as human beings engage in the frustrating and exciting possibilities
inherent in language—the possibility of making meaning. That this may
then allow the possibility of sharing meaning, while hardly provable, seems
highly desirable. Perhaps it is a case in which the thinking may make it so.

This may be a situation in which the good and the bad news are identical:
We are constantly in the process of constructing and creating our world
through language because it is constantly in the process of being destructed
or deconstructed through language. Language is our possibility for being in
the world, but only insofar as we simultaneously use language to destroy
and create that world.

If we wish to improve our own literacy levels and those of our students,
we must recognize that any genuinely literate "cultural literacy" may not be
based primarily on a vocabulary list that will be subjected to evaluation
through the monolithic, money-making, life-controlling testing agencies that
have been dictating educational curricula and evaluation of student learning
over the past many decades. That people have to think, speak, read, and
write about something, as opposed to simply babbling on about nothing, is
undeniable. That we must have some sense of mutual agreement on the
specific contents of given disciplines and areas of study is equally undeniable.
But we have long known all this, and a new list just will not do when genuine
reform is necessary. What we must begin to emphasize in education is not
simply what students know, but what they are able to do with what they
know. The case against a fixed cultural literacy and shared meaning is un-
deniably serious. But whatever *all* is, it is not fully lost.

HOW SCHOOLS SHAPE LITERACY: CONTENT-FREE CURRICULA

As can be expected of as fine a writer and thinker as Hirsch, many of his
criticisms are important and to the point. One might argue that students are,
at least in part, experiencing a "content-neutral" education, although any
insistence that "romantic formalism" caused all the problems seems down-
right unfounded. Anyone who knows public education at all knows its in-
credible ability to resist change of any sort. In citing the flaws inherent in the
implementation of the progressive movement, Hirsch owes his audience the
courtesy of citing the reactions against the movement that were generated
by the launching of Sputnik. One is truly puzzled that Admiral Rickover
comes in for none of the blame! Perhaps the problems Hirsch finds are really
the direct result of an overemphasis on fragmented bits of information ded-

icated to a bureaucratic-technological race to beat the commies who (speaking of created and changing realities) used to want to bury us (Khrushchev and Kennedy), but who now want to be our cultural, intellectual, and economic friends (Gorbachev and Bush). Perhaps many courses today are so jam-packed with content—each little piece of information vying for its rightful place of equal importance among all the other little facts—that the content necessarily becomes neutral and meaningless. One might simply look at an introductory physics text or accounting text, find out what is covered in the fifteen weeks (or ten or twenty, depending on the bureaucratic logic of the given institution), in order to find that lack of content is hardly the problem—or at least not the only problem.

On the other hand, one might also examine the skills-based programs that are so popular in many schools and some colleges and universities in order to verify much of what Hirsch so rightly criticizes. More than a few educational programs boast about the fine, highly sequenced system of text-books, workbooks, teacher guides, commercially prepared fill-in-the-blank handouts, and essentially "teacher-proof" materials that characterize the educational enterprise. In these schools students are busy filling in blanks, circling correct answers, practicing grammar, usage, punctuation, and computation. In these schools content appears essentially peripheral to the activities the students are engaged in, but the activities are essentially meaningless in and of themselves. This is because they are based primarily on a behavioral model of learning that emphasizes the practice and reinforcement of fragmented skills related to almost no human activity that occurs in the real world (except, perhaps, the skills necessary for working in some sort of assembly-line endeavor or identifying "correct" answers on a standardized exam).

I am reminded of the time I spoke to a group of faculty and students at a private college, a small, relatively elite military academy. When the meeting was opened to audience discussion, one student in the audience rose, in full dress uniform and sword by his side, to tell me that if his high school teachers had really done their jobs he would not have had to spend his summer in "grammar camp" before being admitted to the college. I suspect that he suffered from a content-free education. I further suspect that spending a summer in grammar camp involves studying a lot of grammar (well, mostly usage, I imagine, don't you?), but I doubt that it helped this young man do anything other than get himself admitted to the military academy. On the other hand, he didn't want to learn grammar or usage, but he did need to get admitted to the academy because, as he told me later over a game of pool, he couldn't inherit his father's business unless he got a college degree.

The problem of a content-free education also brings to mind an earlier reference to comments made by Pat Buchanan on the CNN show "Crossfire" (January 17, 1988). While debating the importance and fairness of the recent Supreme Court decision regarding the rights of student editors of school newspapers (i.e., they don't really have any rights; they have privileges that are given and may be taken away by the adults in charge), Buchanan pointed out that the purpose of education is not to teach students to think for themselves, but rather "to think correctly." So, in a sense, between Hirsch, ex–secretary of education Bennett, and Buchanan, we have the new curriculum (or at least the guiding philosophy): Specify what it is they need to learn, teach it to them, and then teach them to think correctly about it. (I suspect that this last sentence is unfair to Hirsch, who almost certainly does not intend such fascist simplicity. I do not think it is unfair to either Bennett or Buchanan.)

I don't know, of course, what schools Hirsch has been visiting or what students he has been talking to. Most of the schools I am either personally familiar with or have read about would hardly consider themselves to be offering a content-free education to their students. And yet, as regards the larger picture, I find myself as disturbed as Hirsch over what I see going on in education. Unlike Hirsch, I see the problem to be directly related to a perverse, almost psychotic emphasis on content, particularly on content as fragments of unrelated information. I also see the problem directly reflected in the obsessive commitment American education has to testing everyone's knowledge (not to mention their critical thinking, their values, and so on). I see the problem most clearly evidenced in our commitment to having students evidence their mastery of any given content area through the use of standardized tests.

This brings me back, via an admittedly long and winding road, to the question of literacy in the schools. Just as Hirsch emphasizes the importance of "grasping" information in order to develop a shared vocabulary, so also does our educational system define learning as a process by which you learn the right answers. It is both unfortunate and ironic that many schools have already begun to implement Buchanan's solution.

That students of any age may feel as weary as Breton's sixteenth-century yeoman remains recognizable by most parents whose children are still in school (including college). Clearly, we continue to "meddle" and "find enough to trouble our head withal," but the "chief matters" have shifted. Just as Hirsch declines to supply generous amounts of statistical data evidencing the existence of a literacy problem in the United States, so also will it be avoided here, for the most part. The statistics are so confused that they barely matter. That there is a problem—that not enough people in our society are fully literate—is neither argued nor arguable. The significant questions are these: (1) How is literacy defined in our schools and how might it be described—or, what are the literacy levels of high school graduates who are going on to college and what characterizes the literacy level of a college graduate? (2) How are these literacy levels shaped? (3) If they are inadequate, in what ways are they inadequate? (4) What can be done about it?

Let us begin with the first question. When we talk about the mature literacy of the average high school graduate who is going on to college (not just the average high school graduate), what exactly are we talking about?

The National Assessment of Educational Progress reports in 1980 (Applebee, Langer, and Mullis 1981) and 1986 (Kirsch and Jungeblut 1987) confirm what both high school and college teachers throughout the nation suspect. Most recently, an unpublished assessment study conducted at the State University of New York at Fredonia reaffirmed and illuminated the situation (Assessment Committee 1989).

Most entering freshmen are able to read introductory texts and write relatively correct English, but they do both inadequately. Student writing might be characterized as basically correct in terms of grammar and usage; overly formal and wordy or elliptically personal; either highly overgeneralized and lacking in supportive/explanatory detail, or highly detailed, but fragmented and lacking overall cohesiveness. Often, as writers attempt to sound like a political spokesperson or the sports announcer mentioned previously, they produce writing that lacks any personal voice and/or commitment. As readers, students are generally able to find and memorize key ideas, particularly with the help of lectures and study guides; they are often unable, however, to see relationships among ideas within a text, relationships between a text and a lecture, and of course, relationships among ideas presented in different courses and different texts.

If their writing is characterized by a slavish dedication to form rather than content—a dedication unfortunately uninformed by the ability to employ complex forms and styles—their reading is characterized by an oppressive commitment to detail and memorization in service to future regurgitation. This often results in massive confusion of both detail and concept. Their papers are often fragmented, indicating a nearly physical struggle to "get something down on paper" and resulting in words that look as though they had been carved into the paper through the force exerted on the pen; or their papers look like elfin script, as though the pen had glided effortlessly over the paper while making marks devoid of thought, energy, or time. In their reading, a similar process takes place: In their devoted attempt to carefully underline all the important ideas and significant facts in the textbook, they color the whole text yellow with magic marker, leaving almost no word unilluminated and thus illuminating nothing—everything is important or it wouldn't be in the text; or they treat the book with the respect often given the finest, most delicate antiques—trying to avoid any possibility of spoilage, they scan it once and carefully tuck it away to be forgotten (Applebee in Nystrand 1982).

This characterization is overgeneralized—almost no student evidences all of these characteristics. Unfortunately, the characterization is accurate to the extent that most students suffer from some combination of these problems, and most teachers have seen the results in their classes. The situation frustrates the students because they think they are doing what they are supposed to do, and it militates against teachers as we try to teach students to be knowledgeable in our disciplines and to become avid, able learners who seek and create intellectual relationships. In short, as long as students are busy coloring textbooks with yellow magic markers in preparation for multiple-choice exams and writing gobbledygook in imitation of the psycho-babble that surrounds them, we can hardly expect to welcome them into the collaborative, intellectual adventure that, for many of us, characterizes the academy (Bruffee in Olson 1984).

Sometimes, when this situation is misunderstood, professors view students as a recalcitrant bunch who obstinately refuse to recognize our great efforts and our fine motives: They just refuse to think. These lazy, careless, shiftless social butterflies seem to take joy in making our lives difficult. Indeed, if it weren't for the students, the whole system would run more smoothly. And of course, it also causes students to view us as a powerful medieval group—the keepers of knowledge whose job it is to make things difficult for them, to control them, to put them through a series of tests that, once overcome, make them employable on the day shift.

Almost certainly, neither students nor professors consciously want to be a part of such an invidious system. But given that fact, what is the nature of the language experience most of our students have had before they come to us, how does it influence their language and thinking abilities and the language experiences they have as college students, and in what ways do all these factors contribute to the present state of affairs?

These lines from John Ashbery's poem "What Is Poetry?" (*Houseboat Days* 47) offer a beginning point:

> In School
> All the thoughts got combed out:
> What was left was like a field.

Notice that the poet does not say "all the facts or knowledge got *forced* out"—he says the *thoughts* got *combed* out. To force the thoughts out would suggest an overt, explicit violence, but we do not operate that way in schools (for the most part). This is more like a gentle combing; it sounds like it might even feel good. And a field, far from being without content, is loaded with content—dirt, weeds, worms, bugs, leaves of grass, and even, in a sense, the horizon. But in the absence of the creative act of thinking, the field is meaningless. It demands the transcendental eye (I) to discover the universe in a leaf of grass. Note, also, that in Ashbery's lines the statement is clear: The thoughts were there, and they have been actively (albeit gently) removed.

How does all this happen? First, how is it that the thoughts get combed out? What are the typical language experiences of normal students in American schools (and please keep in mind that I am describing middle- and upper-middle-class kids—kids who are intellectually able and want to go to a four-year college)?

Most of these students are able to read a little, and some are even able to write a little, when they arrive at kindergarten, and many have already been through a year or two of day care where they have experienced story-telling, word play, and other traditional educational experiences. Once they arrive in kindergarten, they often find out that things have suddenly begun to "get serious" because school is a "place to learn," as though they haven't been learning prior to this point. But things are not that bad, and the teachers generally are kind, warm, reasonably intelligent people who care about the children and truly desire to help them get off to a good start so they will be able to succeed in their future educational endeavors (like first and second grade). As most people know, these first few years typically cover everything from scissors-and-pasting skills to reading-readiness activities, learning to name and print letters (for the very few who have not already begun to do so), and probably some phonics or word-identification activities. During this time, children are introduced to flashcards, basal readers (where they find out that school sometimes includes important information like "the fat cat sat on the mat"), and workbooks. In short, much of what they experience early in school—except for the fun stuff like coloring and games (for which many don't need school in the first place) and, if they are fortunate, the warmth and interest of a caring adult (which is probably the most important thing a school can afford the young student)—either is directed at socializing them or is sheer nonsense. (The latter is why, I suspect, we have them go to kindergarten for only a half-day in most areas—we need to get them ready, break them in slowly, prepare them for the next twelve to twenty years of nonsense) (Gundlach in Nystrand 1982).

Of some of the things that will change from grade to grade, the one reading/writing activity that follows them, seemingly forever, is characterized by the workbook. Whether in the form of nicely bound books or regularly distributed ditto-sheets, these workbooks almost always share a single characteristic: Either you must fill in the blank (or does the blank fill you in?—they have lots of blanks) or you must identify the correct or incorrect answer by circling it, underlining it, or drawing an X through it. In addition to all this, students will find that learning to spell involves copying the same word five times; learning the meaning of the word involves looking it up in the dictionary and copying the definition; and learning to write involves writing a sentence or two using the word they copied five times and looked up in the dictionary. Much of what they read in the first four or five grades, they will read-to-read: That is, they will be practicing reading in order to show that they can read, which much of the time means that they will be involved in "word-perfect" oral-reading activities, grouped as Cardinals (if they are good at it) or Bluebirds (if they are not). They will learn that reading has one of two functions: Either you read orally to show that you can "bark at print" well (delighting your teachers and boring your peers), or you read silently in order to fill in all those blanks in the workbook. In surprisingly few cases does one find kids reading in order to have fun or to learn something because they are too busy reading in order to learn to read. And to the extent that they write at all, they are writing-to-write; they are practicing correct punctuation and usage and business letters—getting ready for the day shift, so to speak.

Pretty soon, however, all the fun ends and they hit sixth or seventh grade and find out just how serious the entire school enterprise genuinely is. If they didn't know it already, middle school is really different from elementary school, sort of like moving off the playground and trying out for the junior varsity team, except no one really asked them if they wanted to join. Here, they are told that the baby stuff is over and they are really going to learn something. Shortly after that they receive their new workbooks with all the blanks in them or the "all new," commercially prepared ditto-sheets with blanks, and they dutifully begin to go about filling in all the blanks. But there is a difference because now they also have real textbooks—social studies books, geography books, English books, science books. That's the good news. The bad news is that often the books are used primarily in service of the workbooks and ditto-sheets: They exist as a basis on which to rest the answers that one is going to circle, underline, X out, or use to fill in one of those endless blanks. And, of course, the workbooks enable the students to develop the expertise necessary to become excellent at the most honored system of evaluation in our schools—the multiple-choice test.

For most students, high school represents a new beginning of sorts, and at first blush it looks like things have changed because there are fewer workbooks (although there are still plenty of ditto-sheets with blanks on them). But the contents of the various disciplines have become more complex and demanding, students may have begun to develop strong interests in particular areas, and things appear to be different. I stress the word *appear* because certain essentials continue to remain the same.

It is clear to me, both from published research and from the youngsters I have talked to, that many students perceive the learning process as follows: A teacher or book defines the problem, presents them with a prototype for finding the answer or solving the problem, and success is defined by their ability to plug in the prototypical solution and/or supply the already given answer. In the best of cases, many students succeed, often with very little hostility, as they play their roles in this drama of education. To the extent that they read, they do so in order to find answers to preformed questions; to the extent that they write, they do so to evidence that they found the answers they were expected to find. With or without a workbook the language activity remains much the same; the blanks just look a little different. For the most part, these students do almost no writing and relatively little reading.

Remember, we are not discussing high school dropouts or people oppressed by poverty or racial discrimination, we are discussing the large number of students who successfully exit our high schools and enter our colleges each year. These students may have strong grades, be socially desirable, be reasonably motivated to succeed in school, and even be highly motivated to succeed in the so-called real world. Indeed, each September college teachers find them smiling nervously from their movable desks in those introductory courses: They have their new textbooks, new notebooks, new pens, and teardrop backpacks to carry everything in. Armed with these necessary accoutrements, they anxiously await the "all-new" beginning; they are prepared to write down the answers as the professor delivers them; and their major question is, "Will this be on the test?" To no one's surprise, for the most part the professors proceed, over four years, to give them those answers and then process the students and the information through the rigorous ritual of multiple-choice tests and fill-in-the-blank workbooks.

It is an ugly picture, but someone has to draw it. The major irony in all this, however, is that no one (at least not teachers I talk to) wants to be a part of the drama as I have presented it. Most high school and college teachers want to break this anti-intellectual, anti-human cycle, and some succeed. They cry out in harmony (and, I believe, in sincerity) that they want to teach their students "to think," to synthesize bodies of information, to experience the creative and dynamic relationships among ideas—indeed, to create those relationships for themselves. When they do not find students ready, able, or willing to do this, many professors blame themselves, while others—perhaps a majority—blame the high school teachers for having sent them such dunderheads in the first place. After all, why should a college professor have to clean up the mess that high school teachers created? And high school teachers blame middle school teachers, who blame the elementary school teachers. All the teachers blame the administrators, who often blame the college teachers who taught the elementary, middle, and high school teachers. When things work stereotypically, everyone blames the parents until some voice cries out and lays the blame squarely where it belongs—on the shoulders of the students. Everyone wants the kids to "think for themselves," to be creative, dynamic learners—and the kids, for some peculiar reason, resist.

The ironies inherent in all this boggle the mind. In the midst of all the blaming and acknowledging that the system is not working very well, we continue to graduate those troublemaking students who "refuse" to think and they continue to end up on someone's day shift. Doubly ironic is the fact that the system is working very well, thank you; indeed, the system works with awesome efficiency as it certifies a place for each and each in her place. The real miracle is that some students escape the program.

THE SCHOOL AND PRINT LITERACY

Over the past twenty years, I have been asking a variety of elementary, high school, and college students and faculty about their past "school" experiences in general and about whatever they can remember about language learning, reading, and writing in particular.

Almost no one remembers much of anything about oral language learning, and given the fact that language learning begins at birth, it is little surprise (that is, it seems almost certain that oral language development, some sort of symbol system, is a prerequisite for conscious memory or is so integrally a part of memory that one cannot "remember" learning it). But many adults (keep in mind that these are people who are on their way to college, are presently in college, or have finished college) remember concrete elements and moments that were part of the experience of learning to read and write, and a surprising number of them—in fact, almost all of them—remember being able to read and write before they ever went to school. (For a stunning presentation and discussion of the development of cognitive processes and print literacy in youngsters ages three through six, see Harste, Woodward, and Burke 1984.) I think it is unquestionable that they are able to remember so much because reading and writing (for them as normal language learners who learned oral language processes first) were learned as secondary processes, after "language" and memory had begun to construct themselves (or after self had begun its self-construction through language and memory?). And what is it they remember? The similarities among them are amazing.

Although for many of these respondents the processes of reading and writing share many simultaneous moments (and as I have previously suggested, the two processes are probably a single process), for the present purpose and because the surface structures with which I am working demand linearity, I will discuss learning to read first, and then learning to write.

I asked people to write and talk about the following questions: What do you remember about learning to read? How far back can you remember? Who besides yourself was involved? How did you feel about it? What follow-up experiences do you remember (that is, once you could read, what did you read? Were you asked/forced to read?)? How do you presently feel about your reading abilities (are you a good or bad reader, and what do you mean by good or bad?)? What kinds of reading do you find difficult? What kinds do you most enjoy? Because these are open-ended questions and because the respondents have the opportunity to write personal essays, many choose to focus on one set of questions rather than another, but they normally try to address most of the questions to the best of their ability.

Almost all of these people remember being able to read before they went to school; easily 90 percent of them write this, and when the other 10 percent are asked to elaborate, they almost always point out that they are not sure, but the first "teaching" of reading they remember occurred when they arrived in school. Of this overwhelming majority who learned to read before they went to school, reading is associated with fond memories of sitting on a parent's or grandparent's or babysitter's lap, word-picture/alphabet books, fairy tales, animal stories, and so on. Many of them remember particular favorites. And the learning process is nearly always the same: a warm, safe atmosphere; exciting stories; and a growing sense of the fact that the funny black marks on the page had something to do with the process. This is particularly important because so many of the respondents fondly remember the moment at which they discovered that the reader (parent, babysitter) was skipping part of the story because it was late and time to go to bed, or because the loving reader had gotten sick of Snow White and the Seven Dwarfs—they remember associating what was skipped (pages and the marks on pages) as being part of the process—most important, they remember realizing that those marks meant something. After that, they remember very little (like oral language learning). Some remember memorizing, word for word, certain favorite stories and pretending to read those stories back to their parents or whomever would listen. But as nearly as I can tell from their responses, they are not really aware of when this movement changed from rehearsing whatever they had memorized to the moment at which they were genuinely interacting with the black marks on the page. I should also note that many of them clearly remember turning pages as they "read" what they had memorized, knowing that a given memorized part was on one page and not on another, so it is most difficult to decide whether this was memorization or reading. In the terms of current reading research, it is at least likely that they simply had a preponderance of nonvisual information to bring to the text and they were, indeed, reading.

After about fourth grade, we manage to standardize the school experience better than we might imagine. And the middle school and high school students I talked to seemed oppressively aware of it.

When I asked these students to write about their reading and writing experiences in school, they confirmed the sterility of the experience (they also made it clear that they would not have written the information if they had had to put their names on the papers and/or if the papers had been funneled through one of their teachers because "someone might find out what I said and that could get me in trouble"). It is unnecessary to reproduce the questionnaire here; suffice it to say that we were in a relaxed setting and I had asked them to write about why they read school assignments, what happened after they had read an assignment, what kinds of writing they were asked to do, what happened to the writing after they did it, and how they felt about the whole process.

Here is a sampling of their responses: "We read the story so that he could give us a test on it." "We took the test in order for her to make sure we had read the story." Or, most damning, "We never read much of anything because the teacher always told us what we had to know and that was all that was on the test so it was a waste of time to read the thing in the first place." Notice how clearly these responses suggest that in the students' terms, reading has a single purpose: to find out the answer that will be on the test. If the answer may be found in some other way, there is no reason to read.

And continue to keep in mind that these are good students; these students have succeeded; these are the responses of students who are almost certainly going to college. Some of them hope to become teachers.

When asked what they did after reading something for school, they said, "We take a test on it." When I clarified by saying, "No, I mean before the test and after the reading assignment, what kinds of writing activities or discussions do you engage in?" they looked at me strangely and said, "We take a test on it." Being the intrepid interviewer, I pushed harder. "Surely you sometimes write essays about whatever it is you were assigned to read, don't you?" "Of course," was the reply, and I knew that I had them now. "Okay, that's what I want to hear about," I said, knowing that I was about to find out the contradictions and truth of the matter. And they said, "Yeah, well, like we said, sometimes instead of a test we write what the teacher tells us the thing means, and then later have a test on that. Is that what you mean?"

I remember one high school student in particular because he seemed to know how silly the whole thing was, and although I believe he found me and my questions to be somewhat humorous, he finally blurted out, "Why don't they ever ask us to write or say what we really think?" I said, "That's exactly what I'm trying to get you to do now, and you've really stayed pretty silent until this moment." To which he replied, "Why do you want to know; what are you going to do with all this?" Smart kid.

It is also important to qualify this by pointing out that the students were always, in all of these discussions, able to point out teachers who were clearly different, who did conduct classroom discussions that were not simply adulterated Socratic exercises, and who asked students to speak and write what they "really think." They were also quite articulate in their praise of these teachers.

Although some college students seem more conscious of their situation and appear to recognize the absurdity of it ("These guys don't care what we think; all you need to do is psych out the teacher and give him what he wants"; "Once you figure out her system of testing, there's nothing to it") they often seem to be as accepting of the entire endeavor as their younger counterparts ("Look, all I want to do is get out of here with a degree and make some big bucks; my main goal in life is to be a yuppie").

In short, while educators debate student-centeredness and experiential approaches to teaching, and while literary critics and philosophers argue the sense and nonsense of deconstruction versus new criticism, students are being told the meaning of *Romeo and Juliet*, memorizing it, and regurgitating it. While some students are not as susceptible to such a system and work through meanings on their own, the simple fact remains that for most students, reading is not a meaning-making activity, an activity involving psychological and intellectual growth, or an activity motivated by self-interest. Rather, it is something one does in order to pass the test—if indeed one needs to do it to pass the test, because sometimes all you need to know to pass the test is what the teacher tells you and then there's no reason to read it in the first place. Little wonder, then, that they are unable to think critically about the texts we ask them to read or to synthesize information and create relationships across readings.

I, too, wish to decry the present set of circumstances, and I deeply empathize with the students who are being denied the opportunity to grow and learn through reading of all kinds and who feel they do not have an opportunity to say and write what they "really think." But I am more deeply disturbed by what I believe is the by-product of a school system that runs in this machinelike manner, producing test-takers and answer-finders—a system that, perhaps, produces students who no longer know what they really think and are unsure how to go about finding out for themselves.

If my portrayal and the statements of these various people suggest that reading is in a bad way in the schools, writing remains in even deeper trouble.

The simple fact is that Johnny and Jane cannot write because they are seldom asked to compose anything, from elementary school through graduate school: They are too busy filling in blanks and taking multiple-choice tests. In fact, if a human being were dependent on us to teach speaking and listening the way we teach reading and writing (and just about everything else), we would be a nation of deaf-mutes.

Just as I asked a broad range of people about their reading experiences, I also asked them about their writing experiences. It comes as little surprise that the responses are similar, the major difference being that most of them remember almost no writing at all (with the exception of those who have graduate degrees, and they primarily remember their theses and dissertations). Again, when they do remember writing, they remember it as an exercise, sort of like pumping academic iron in order to develop those writing muscles—something they did in order to show that they could do it rather than as an act of meaning making, becoming, and communicating. To a large extent, many of them view writing as something that English teachers "make you do because that's what English teachers do." And the overwhelming evidence is that too many English teachers, at all levels, fit the description—when they make students write, they do so because it is "good for them," and everyone should at least know how to write standard, correct English.

Unfortunately, what sometimes passes for writing in school are single-sentence responses in workbooks and filling in blanks on dittoed exercises. Even more telling is the response that I and many other teachers of composition get from our freshmen when we ask them to write personal essays, detailing their own experience in a given area and explaining how and what that experience means to them. After years of teaching freshman writing courses, telling students in advance that I want them to speak their own truths in their own language, asking them to avoid sacrificing content to form, pleading with them not to be the sports announcer whose "expression of the play should be such that it transpires in the end zone," they hand in their first set of essays pointing out in the best of "Engfish" (Macrorie 1970: 10) that "one should note that one's movement through the adolescent and difficult years of high school into the transformation of becoming a college freshman with both awe and excitement at all of the exciting stimulation that one anticipates."

I do not offer this sentence to evidence the stupidity of our students for English professors to chuckle at. This incomplete sentence (and many others like it) clearly indicates, to me at least, that we are running a costly apprenticeship system bent on producing the sports announcer and others like him. It is one thing to use gobbledygook to purposefully bilk the public or to avoid responsibility (that is willful misuse of language—sociopolitical, linguistic immorality), but it is another thing to do so because you have been taught to and because you believe it is what educated people do. (Because that means the system is amoral and irresponsible, dedicated to eradicating the possibility of choice.) Perhaps the problem is considerably worse than those with punctuation fetishes first thought.

AND MORE VOICES

The discussion becomes even more poignant, problematic, and clear when one asks successful professionals some of the same questions about their reading/writing/learning experiences, particularly those they remember from their college years. Over the past ten years, I have had the opportunity to conduct a series of faculty development workshops. Attended by college teachers from a variety of disciplines, these workshops are directed at assisting the participants in developing writing activities for students in their courses. As part of their participation, the teachers write and talk about their past experiences as learners, particularly focusing on their own memories about writing instruction. Of course, as one might expect, all of their past school experience becomes a part of the discussion. Indeed, in a group of scientists, one dedicated geologist confessed that he had failed his first calculus course, an experience that nearly caused him to withdraw from college in recognition of his failure and its implications. Although it was clear that, these many years later, he had come to terms with the failure and had come to understand that it was relatively insignificant, what was important was the discussion that his confession initiated. A physicist asked him how he had managed to pass it the second time around. The geologist said, "I realized that I had made a big mistake when I failed because I was interested and really wanted to understand this stuff, which had just caused me tremendous problems on exams, so when I took it again, I spent a lot of time memorizing the formulae and learned to plug them in where appropriate on exams. I still don't know much about calculus." The physicist turned to the group and said, "Well, there you have it. Even the best of us can be beaten by a system that rewards memorization and discourages attempts at understanding. And," he went on, "as long as the sciences continue to try to cram more and more into a given fifteen-week course, the more kids are either going to fail or become incredibly good at memorizing facts and information they have almost no control over."

Others comment more directly on their school experiences as "writers." A specialist in learning disabilities writes:

I remember being taught almost nothing about writing or having to do much in elementary school through four years of college (except for the mandatory forays into the APA style demanded by a few of my professors who required research papers). By relying primarily upon my verbal (oral) skills, I was able to emerge unscathed from the public schools because I was a good test-taker. Again I entered the arena of higher education and enrolled in a doctoral program in special education. Once more, requests for written products à la APA style began to surface. This time, however, the transition into higher production rates was facilitated by the fact that I could use a familiar style. *But something much more important really happened: My interests in the subject matter under discussion started to take hold. I now read and wrote what I wanted to write. I generated and selected the topics* [italics added].

Another comment, from a performing musician:

I do recall studying basic structures of writing a good paper, topic sentences, paragraph structure, footnotes, etc. I do recall reading short stories, writing themes about the topics of these short stories, reading examples of various styles of famous writers and attempting to write in this style or that style. I also remember that I never knew why I was doing it, and I don't really remember learning anything about my own writing. . . . Whatever my past writing experiences have been, writing is a difficult task for me. . . . [It] does not seem to be a creative outlet, but rather a tedious, laborious task with which I do not have the patience to deal. Faced with the task of writing, I either put it off until the last minute or I write, rewrite, and re-edit forever.

Again this writer re-emphasizes what so many of the participants in the workshops say: I don't remember being taught much of anything about how to write. But equally important, she also emphasizes the fact that many of us do not delight in the prospect of having to write; indeed, some of us suffer under such a prospect and run from it when possible (like our students).

One of my own favorites comes from a chemist:

Fifteen years ago, one of my daughters became the first of my children to be married. Her announcements of the impending nuptials filled me with joy. Now, for the first time, I would be able to impart my deep and extensive knowledge of the state of marriage. Shortly afterwards, I realized that I didn't know anything about the subject that would be of value to her, and limited my response to "Best Wishes." Today I am supposed to tell how I learned to write, and again I find out that I really don't know. . . . I remember I learned to read before I went to school. . . . I remember doing parsing in high school English. . . . I remember writing an undergraduate thesis in college.

I particularly like this entry because of the fatherly wisdom. But the writer also says many of the things that occur in these essays over and over: I remember doing English stuff, but I don't remember being taught anything that actually affected my writing. But in this case, the fatherly wisdom concerning marriage and children applies directly to teaching: Too often we are busy taking that opportunity that we studied so long for—the opportunity to tell students what writing is really like, or to hand them the essence of philosophy or of physics. Like my friend the chemist, I suspect that we all would like to impart our deep and extensive knowledge of the state of our disciplines. Unlike him, if we are to continue teaching, we may have to find something better to say than "Best Wishes."

Although the participants in these workshops often speak with powerful voices, it is striking to note the similarities in their experiences. For the most part, they remember being taught very little about writing; they generally have learned to write because they had to in order to attain their masters or doctorates and continue to advance professionally; they find writing difficult; many of them enjoy writing poetry and/or fiction (although they seem almost embarrassed to admit this); and they had never given the topic much thought until they had to write the paper for the workshop. Furthermore, they are generally dissatisfied with the kinds of writing they receive from their students, primarily because they believe that the students find the act of writing in school to be an artificial, unimportant activity.

This last point is best stated by the director of the Learning Center at SUC–Fredonia, Penelope Deakin, who writes:

Generally speaking, students are emphatically not writing about something which interests them or on which they have anything to say. In fact, they never even seem to consider the possibility that anyone would be interested in what they have to say. They are, instead, engaged in a desperate struggle to produce an artifact which will meet with someone's approval. They are trying to guess the rules for the production of this work as though it were some strange, separate activity which is not connected with their own minds. . . To Write A Paper has become some arcane ritual which has nothing to do with reality and certainly nothing to do with a passionate need to communicate the writer's own ideas to a reader.

Communicate? In school? Passionately? You gotta be kidding!

BUT, LIKE THE MAN SAID . . .

You pays your money and you takes your. . . . And yet there seems to very little choice for most of our students in terms of what they will experience in our high schools and colleges. By and large, high schools "prepare" these students for college. In turn, our colleges and universities, particularly at the undergraduate level, continue to offer most students the same experiences colleges have offered for the last fifty years, as we continue to demand expertise in memorization and regurgitation at the same time that we lament the inability of students to think and reason critically. In general, things do not really change much between high school and college, and that might explain, more than any other factor, why high school grades remain the best indicator of success in college. Indeed, if colleges were really different from the high schools they so often criticize, one would expect the correlation between grades and relative success in each to be somewhat less reliable. But a simple look at the facts indicates why the high school grades are such excellent indicators of success in college. What have the students had to do in their school years prior to college? They have had to memorize, fill in the blanks, regurgitate, recite, pick the correct multiple-choice answer, listen, read, remember, pass tests, and get good grades. That a group of people who are good at these activities would do well in our colleges and universities can surely surprise no one. This is what higher education is all about: not what it wants to be about, or at least not what most of the teachers want it to be about—almost certainly not what most of the students would want it to be about if they knew they had any choice—but this is what it is about. So really, you pays your money and they give you the single choice that you must choose.

"Oh but come on, get off the liberal rhetoric. None of us wants that and you know it. We want the kids to learn how to think and know something to think about. Content is always significant, but that doesn't mean that we aren't trying to teach them to be able to do something with the content." As voices go, this is often a sincere one. As such, it may represent the clearest irony that functions in our educational system. Almost none of us wants it to function as it presently does, and yet we see ourselves powerless to do much about it, so we blame students and legislators and administrators and, sometimes, ourselves. But by and large, we seem to make very little headway in doing anything about it. Perhaps we do not yet understand the nature of the problem.

A direct statement of the problem and its causes might now be in order. First, even in situations where students are required to do much reading and writing, these are not viewed as language activities focusing on meaning making and the active construing of relationships. Instead, the educational system emphasizes a computer-based metaphor of information processing and retrieval. Multiple-choice tests dominate the college scene, further emphasizing the fill-in-the-blank mentality that has been so efficiently and consistently reinforced over most of the years prior to college. When students do write, the activity is characterized as follows: (1) the writing is often entirely product-oriented—an attempt to say what you have been told to say—and has little to do with interest, passion, or the desire to communicate something; and (2) the students are not committed to what they think because they are not sure that what they think has anything to do with the assignment or that daring to write what one thinks is safe or even part of the educational game. But let's say that you get them past these first problems; let's say that you manage to provide topics that should interest them and you convince them that you want them to take some genuine intellectual risks: Why does their work still seem so poorly developed, organized, and articulated?

Students generally produce weak writing for the following reasons: Because they have done so little writing prior to college, they have developed no strategies for successful writing. For the most part, students engage in little or no prewriting rehearsal of ideas, brainstorming, free writing, or exploratory thinking-writing activities. Students most often produce papers twenty-four to forty-eight hours prior to the time they are due—which makes perfect sense if you do not know how to go about rewriting or revising in the first place. Students often confuse rewriting or revising (re-visioning) with recopying or with what a reasonably well-paid typist does: proofreading. In short, there is no such thing as rewriting or revising, and if you tell them to do it they do not generally know how to because they have never done it in the first place (Bartlett in Nystrand 1982). Finally, because many major papers are handed in at the very end of the semester (not to mention that students do not see the writing project as even vaguely related to a learning activity), they rarely even get the papers back; when they do, they are primarily concerned with the grade because the writing event has already become a part of the recent and quickly receding past.

Indeed, given the fact of much school-writing and reading, and given the ways in which many college courses operate, one can only wonder if "the rat [who] sat on the cat's mat" makes more or less sense than the assembly-line approach to higher education that typifies so many colleges and universities today. If, as Halliday suggests and as is discussed in Chapter 1 of this work, language develops primarily through social interactions that shape the linguistic structures of the individual and shape the individual's cultural world, we had best begin to examine the nature and import of such interactions as characterized by language activities in school. Even in contexts that are, at any given moment, indeterminable, if the general context of school that has been described herein characterizes the experience of many people, and if sociolinguistic and experiential contexts significantly contribute to shaping our ways of schematizing and categorizing (our ways of thinking and acting), then there appears little likelihood that most educated human beings will think of themselves as meaning makers who have any personal or intellectual power whatsoever.

3

Anxiety and Language in Society: or, Penetrating the Impenetrable

In explaining the inherent value of "un-birthdays" to Alice, that rather feisty egg, Humpty Dumpty, asserts that there are 364 un-birthdays on which one receives presents, but

"...only *one* for birthday presents, you know. There's glory for you!"

"I don't know what you mean by 'glory,' " Alice said.

Humpty Dumpty smiled contemptuously. "Of course you don't—till I tell you. I meant 'there's a nice knock-down argument for you!' "

"But 'glory' doesn't mean 'a nice knock-down argument,' " Alice objected.

"When *I* use a word," Humpty Dumpty said, in rather a scornful tone, "it means just what I choose it to mean—neither more nor less."

"The question is," said Alice, "whether you *can* make words mean so many different things."

"The question is," said Humpty Dumpty, "which is to be master—that's all."

Alice was too much puzzled to say anything; so after a minute Humpty Dumpty began again. "They've a temper, some of them—particularly verbs: they're the proudest—adjectives you can do anything with, but not verbs—however, *I* can manage the whole lot of them! Impenetrability! That's what *I* say!" (Lewis Carroll in *Through the Looking Glass*)

As any child knows, Humpty's apparently short, exciting career comes to a crashing end when he falls off his wall and not even "all the king's horses and all the king's men" can put him together again. Although it cannot be absolutely proven, it has been rumored that his assertion of individual power over meaning, the right to decide what words mean, caused that shattering fall.

LANGUAGE AND THE SOCIAL SEMIOTIC

Having already stated that contexts are never fully saturated, never fully knowable, and never entirely mutual, I am left with one set of problems. Furthermore, having asserted that language is a meaning-making activity and that the communicating and sharing of that meaning is partial, at best, I am left with another set of problems. And having itemized some of the major complexities associated with sociolinguistic positions like Halliday's and Searle's theory of speech acts, I find that I have undercut some of the points I most wish to discuss. If contexts are never fully knowable and meaning is, at best, partially shared—and if neither sociology, psychology, nor linguistics can explain the rules governing the expressing, shaping, and sharing of meaning in a sociolinguistic context—how is it possible to write (or speak) rationally about anything? Impenetrability indeed!

Fortunately the circle is not as closed nor the trap as complete as they appear. My support comes from what many might conceive as the least likely source for discussing the possibility of meaning in a constructive light. I continue to rely on Derrida's notion of dehiscence. The continued possibility for additional construction of the discussion rests firmly in the "divided opening" that "makes production, reproduction, development possible" (Derrida, "LIMITED" 1977: 197). That the deconstructionist position sees the possibility of production, reproduction, and development to be in the constant state of escaping—being literally evident primarily (only) in its absence or as it becomes absent (a single moment: the being and becoming absent)—makes the promise no less significant. Indeed, it is the nature of a constantly disappearing presence that makes the "writing" (in the broadest sense of language) all that we have and all that we are. Much like the frustrated narrator of *Tristram Shandy*, we "language" in order to "catch up" with our present, as part of an impossible attempt to avoid facing our death, with each step of the process, each moment of the writing, serving to further evidence the impossibility of the attempt and the inevitability of the death. Indeed, presence recedes farther into the past as, like the White Rabbit in *Alice in Wonderland*, we are always/already too late, too late. As Roland Barthes says in "The Death of the Author," "writing is the destruction of every voice, of every point of origin. Writing is that neutral, composite, oblique space where our subject slips away, the negative where all identity is lost, starting with the very identity of the body of writing" (Barthes 1977: 142). But there is another way of looking at this. If writing (and reading) is what we do in order to catch up with our present, avoid death, and destroy every point of origin, then it is also the assertion of our present, the recognition of being alive, and the (re)creation of our origin—even if none of these can be achieved fully.

To argue that we are not presently able to prove that rules govern the linguistic and social semiotic (and to accept the probability that, even if they do, we may never be able to describe them fully) does not necessarily leave us without possibilities. Quite the opposite. The problem is that the possibilities are tenuous, always/already in the process of escaping and disappearing; they are threatening and surrounded with menace. The problem itself necessitates the continued (im)possibility of the discussion.

Deconstruction aside for the moment, we can almost certainly agree that, even though we cannot fully know or explain contexts, sociolinguistic interactions, and/or the degrees to which surface structures of language and sociolinguistic interactions shape our schemata, we do exist within certain contexts at certain times and we are influenced by our environment. This is by no means a turn toward behavioral psychology as a system with major explanatory power. This simply asserts that human beings exist in a physical world; they interact through and within sets of identifiable behaviors; and both the physical world and the behaviors play roles in shaping the interaction between the individual and the world and the individual and other individuals.

THE SOCIAL-EDUCATIONAL TEXT

At the very beginning of this work I said that at some point we would look at education as a text with ourselves as the readers. As so often happens in the process of reading a text we also discover that we have become part of the text—we are inside and outside of it at the same time. This is one of the aspects of reading that makes literary criticism so complex, especially recent criticism about the reader's relationship to the text. It is also the reason why current literary criticism comments significantly, albeit subtly, on literacy education.

To complicate matters more, it is silly to read the text of education as anything other than a small text embedded in the larger text of modern society—again forcing a reading that places all of us immediately inside and outside of it at the same time. If one needed additional evidence for the problem of limiting contexts, the problem of reading societal texts should suffice. In an attempt to solve what appears to be an insoluble problem, I suggest that the gap between being inside and outside the social and educational texts is the dehiscence that makes construction possible. To the extent that the "reader" can do the impossible and remain conscious of being neither here nor there as well as both here and there at the same time, this reading may become possible and may also escape the unforgivable (and incredibly boring) sin of self-righteousness: Like this text and the readers who are or will be creating this text (the one I am producing right now), we are all to some degree part and parcel of the problems to be examined.

TWENTIETH-CENTURY ANXIETY: THE MACHINE AND THE FLIES

Any discussion of anxiety and the twentieth century must examine the "centers of power" that contribute to anxiety and the ways in which power affects the process of knowing. In his discussion of power and knowledge, Michel Foucault writes the following:

Power is not to be taken to be a phenomenon of one individual's consolidated and homogeneous domination over others, or that of one group or class over others. What, by contrast, should always be kept in mind is that power, if we do not take too distant a view of it, is not that which makes the difference between those who exclusively possess and retain it, and those who do not have it and submit to it. Power must be analyzed as something which circulates, or rather as something which only functions in the form of a chain. It is never localized here or there, never in anybody's hands, never appropriated as a commodity or pieces of wealth. Power is employed and exercised through a net-like organization. And not only do individuals circulate between its threads; they are always also the elements of its articulation. In other words, individuals are the vehicles of power, not its points of application. (Foucault 1980: 98)

First, consider the larger picture through a literary lens. In *The Naked and the Dead* (1948), Norman Mailer presents us with the very unpleasant and equally insightful General Cummings as a spokesman for the nature of life in the second half of the twentieth century. While lecturing the impotent Harvard intellectual Lieutenant Hearn, Cummings points out in his best fascist tone that, in the future, following World War II, moral codes and morality will be dictated by the most powerful men in society and that those who do not adjust, those who do not quietly (if not happily) accept this oppression, will be destroyed. Power will be concentrated among a "chosen" group selected by fortune of birth and a willingness to use their power to eradicate anyone who should dare oppose them. But those in power will not belong to the same "club" or meet together at conferences as much as they will, by virtue of their power and mutual desire to control others, share some unstated degree of consciousness: They will form an unincorporated repository of power. Everyone, even these powerful men (not women), will be vying for more power: The less powerful will be looking for an opportunity to destroy those above them in the hierarchy; the least powerful will be the oppressed, anxiously and often angrily serving the corporate structure. The most powerful? Those at the top of the hierarchy will live in constant threat from those immediately beneath them; constantly threatened by the loss of their power, they will use their power to attempt to control those beneath them. Power over others will become the central reason for being.

Such a concept often evokes the stereotyped belief that some anomalous "They" holds power over all of us: They do this and that; they will or will not allow us to do this and that; they can get you. But this is a romantic notion born of the desire to have someone (anyone) be in charge—if we can't have God or Satan, then let us at least have Them. But even a brief examination of world events suggests that They do not exist and that no one is actually in charge. For example, consider President Kennedy, the Bay of Pigs, and the assassination; the Civil Rights Movement, Martin Luther King, and his assassination; President Johnson, General Westmoreland, and the war in Vietnam; President Nixon, Henry Kissinger, relations with China, and Watergate; President Reagan, Admiral Poindexter, Oliver North, and the Iran-Contra Affair; the sociopolitical conditions of Nicaragua, Panama, and the Philippines; or the stock market crash of October 1987, the savings and loan crisis, and the national/international economy. Consider Beirut, Iraq, Kuwait, Israel. Who is in charge when even the "They" is part of the machine's powerful indifference? Indeed, one might well argue that some mild forms of paranoia are simply misguided attempts to find reason and purpose, to find order, where there is none.

In *Catch 22*, Joseph Heller in a hilarious and frightening novel explains the nature of twentieth-century anxiety by describing exactly what Catch-22 is—an unwritten rule covering all situations that allows authorities to ensure the obedience of everyone under their authority, a functioning principle of absurdity that entirely eliminates the importance of individual human beings except insofar as they maintain the machine and serve it as the machine demands.

There was only one catch and that was Catch-22, which specified that a concern for one's own safety in the face of dangers that were real and immediate was the process of a rational mind. Orr was crazy and could be grounded. All he had to do was ask; and as soon as he did, he would no longer be crazy and would have to fly more missions. Orr would be crazy to fly more missions and sane if he didn't, but if he was sane he had to fly them. If he flew them he was crazy and didn't have to; but if he didn't want to he was sane and had to. Yossarian was moved very deeply by the absolute simplicity of this clause of Catch-22, and let out a respectful whistle.

"That's some catch, that Catch-22," he observed.

"It's the best there is," Doc Daneeka agreed.

Yossarian saw it clearly in all its spinning reasonableness. There was an elliptical precision about its perfect pairs of parts that was graceful and shocking, like good modern art, and at times Yossarian wasn't quite sure that he saw it all, just the way he was never quite sure about good modern art or about the flies Orr saw in Appleby's eyes. He had Orr's word to take for the flies in Appleby's eyes.

"Oh, they're there, all right," Orr had assured him about the flies in Appleby's eyes after Yossarian's first fight with Appleby in the officers' club, "although he probably doesn't even know it. That's why he can't see things as they really are."

"How come he doesn't know it?" inquired Yossarian.

"Because he's got flies in his eyes," Orr explained with exaggerated patience. "How can he see he's got flies in his eyes if he's got flies in his eyes?"

It made as much sense as anything else. (Heller 1989: 47)

The flies in General Cummings's eyes prevent him from seeing things as they really are; they prevent him from seeing that he is a part of what he describes: He is fearful of his superiors, terrified by the possibility of failure, anxious about his every move, stuck on one of the rungs of the ladder of fear, and serving the machine just like everyone else. As terrifying as Yossarian's journey is, at least he learns that he is enslaved by the machine and can fight the machine only at grave risk to his own well-being, perhaps at the cost of all possibilities for living a dignified, responsible life. He is right, of course: "That's some catch, that Catch-22."

All of this relates to our own society as we look at the sociopolitical-economic machine that drives all of the Western and many of the Eastern nations. Our society is devoted to maintaining itself without examining the nature of the human selves that compose this machinelike self. Those who serve the machine best are devoted acolytes whose job it is to maintain the illusion of order, ignoring individual human crises by reducing them to unemployment statistics, family violence statistics, welfare statistics, literacy statistics, and other imaginative "body counts" like those of Vietnam, Ethiopia, Lebanon, Nicaragua, Granada, Afghanistan, and Iraq (not to mention Miami, New York City, Los Angeles, and so on). Those who serve the machine believe that sometimes, in order to save something, one must destroy it. As part of its functioning principle, the machine puts a high premium on maintaining order through a carefully outlined class system within which exists the illusion of tremendous flexibility (e.g., go to college and be a success; if you just work hard enough you will get ahead).

Nowhere is this system more honored than in our schools. Aside from the fact that getting ahead and success are primarily determined by rising within the ranks of service to the machine, the flexibility and mobility that do exist depend almost entirely on allegiance to the rules of the institutions that form the system. (On the other hand, lest I appear to engage in the mild paranoia I mentioned earlier—looking for reason where there is none by positing a mindless machine as the culprit responsible for crushing human creativity— a disclaimer is in order. This machine is simply a cultural mindset into which we allow ourselves to be inserted. Its indifference makes it most difficult to identify and resist. It can neither be located nor named.)

Like some Europeans caught in Naziism (like Heidegger and DeMan?), like academics during the war in Vietnam, like people in all too many modern situations, we are constantly faced with the dilemma of being caught within the gears of the indifferent machine. Does one maintain one's position in the system in order to possibly change it, trying to help the machine become moral, in some sense of that word? Or does one face the paradox of trying to create morality within a machinelike system of amorality, where cost accounting and efficiency are more important than the search for truth? Do we face the subtle indifference of the machine's amorality and try to tear it apart, byte by byte, microchip by microchip? Do we pass on the rules for success, the rules of running the machine and serving it well, to our young without telling them about the catch-22 inherent in the system? "You must follow the rules in order to succeed, but success may mean that you must give up any sense of self." "You may develop a sense of self, but you will have to violate it regularly, voluntarily get those flies implanted in your eyes so that you will not have to see the self-contradictions." Or does one simply become impotent, trapped in the rationalizations that are apparently necessary to function on a daily basis within such a societal structure? Who can afford to ignore the promise of the day shift? Indeed, twentieth-century man's role is anxiety.

Consciously or unconsciously, administrators and teachers serve the larger machine by working within the subsystem called school. By virtue of this fact, we need to recognize the dilemma this creates for us as teachers and students. Anxiety may be uncomfortable, but it is less dangerous than blind complicity and ignorance.

At the same time that we engage in this self-analysis, we need to remember that if we have flies in our eyes, there is little we can do except engage endlessly in the process of trying to see the flies for what they are, perhaps occasionally seeing through or beyond them, returning over and over to the same place in order to see it for the first time. That is what teaching and learning are genuinely about, and that is also what real anxiety is about.

In the world of academia, this seemingly impossible and yet absolutely necessary process of self-questioning reveals the problem of much of what passes for knowledge and research. As Heidegger has suggested, the process of knowing and coming to know has been preempted by a system that forgets to carefully question and examine its own presuppositions; scholarship and thinking have been co-opted by the "business" of research, by the "busyness" of research. And when research becomes characterized by business and busy-ness, it becomes exactly what the machine desires it to be—an endless repetition of meaningless words and statistics that have little or no real importance except insofar as they serve the machine. This busy-ness preempts any hope for the university to be a unifying force dedicated to— perhaps even mystically centered in—nourishing the interrelationship of disciplines and humans in the process of being. Instead of busily concentrating on the birth of our own being, this research in service to the machine is simply "busy being": It depends on and celebrates the "objectification of Being" (Heidegger 1979: 1–9).

"The objectification of Being"—the objectification of human *beings* and humans *being*—this is what the self-questioning and analysis of the system reveal. But to a large extent, the system as represented by schools is too easy a metaphor. Everything about the teaching-learning complex is dictated by the overriding concern for objectification and order, a promise of flexibility within a tightly structured system, the promise of upward mobility at the cost of allegiance to rules over which one appears to have little power. As

part of the larger system, even when colleges and universities devote themselves to questioning the system, they are subsumed by the very thing they
purport to question. Research is owned by the military-industrial complex.
A secretary of education, whose loyalty is first and foremost politically dictated, defines the nature of the sciences and humanities through the governmental checkbook that gives him or her control over some of the finest
minds in the country (who wittingly or unwittingly give him that control);
and colleges offer courses on cross-country skiing that include, as an interesting aside, learning how to shoot an M16. Lock and load, baby; right on.
Be all that you can be. Contradictions and synthesis. And flies.

   We have plenty of body counts here, also—the most objective kind, because they are relative only to themselves. SAT scores, high school grades,
how many of which in what percentile, percentages of males versus percentages of females, percentages of minorities, percentages of A's versus
B's, and the "economics" of grading. These are the acceptable body counts,
the ones that institutions like to tout as though they had some inherent
meaning. Indeed, the academy continues to define itself in terms of the
most absurd quantifications and objectification: Here, where one might hope
for emphasis on "the search for truth," critical thinking, creativity, and
excellence in teaching, one discovers the most mundane concerns. Here,
one's quality depends on how much one has published (how many articles
and how many books—preferably books because they are longer and have
more pages), where one has published (which journal, which press—but
seldom what one has published), and how many grants one has managed to
wangle. More often than not, decisions for job hirings, reappointments, and
promotions are made by groups of people who have counted the amounts
published and have weighed (literally) the output, but who in fact have little
knowledge of the content or quality of what was published. When teaching
is considered in such decisions (and often it is given little more than passing
lip service), those involved lament that we cannot objectively measure good
teaching—although some continue to try to create objective measures of
teaching so they might enter them into the computational accounting of
individuals in the academy. Thus we are told that in the face of such soft
data on one's teaching, we can only rely on the hard data of publication.
Student evaluations of teachers are discounted because they are done by
students, and we all know how untrustworthy they are in terms of evaluating
good teaching. Scholarship, thinking, and the mutual search for truths conducted by students and teachers is just too soft for consideration, so we
ignore it in favor of what the machine understands—numbers. We also ra-
tionalize: "It may not be a perfect system, but it's the best we have." It
isn't even a humane system, let alone perfect—and the fact is that we choose
it because it allows us to serve the machine rather than deal with human
beings.

   One might expect all this objectification and quantification to at least reduce the anxiety I mentioned earlier, make it look like things are really under control, which is certainly a major purpose of objectification. But anxiety seems to rear its ugly head all over the place anyway.

I hear students say, "My parents insist that I go into engineering even though I want to go into theater arts. But they say I'll never make a living in theater and they won't pay for my schooling if I do it." Anxiety and catch-22's. Ex–secretary of education Bennett says, let's take away their money so the cost of higher education will go down and they can get a good education (*U.S. News and World Report*, Dec. 10, 1986: 10). No one suggests cutting the defense budget in order to improve our defense systems. That's crazy, isn't it? But it's those flies again.

In this system, literacy is a tool—not so much a tool that allows you to work on the machine, changing and possibly humanizing it. Instead, literacy is a tool for working within the machine, a tool that makes it easier to put and keep each willing worker in his or her place. Of course, I do not mean real literacy (meaning making); I mean school-literacy—the kind of literacy that teaches one to write what one is told in a proper form and/or to read what one is given in order to find out the correct answer or what one is supposed to do. This is the literacy that allows groups to be controlled—the literacy of submission, of the oppressed.

One might wish to argue with the picture that I have drawn. Perhaps it is possible, if not likely, that the machine may be escaped, destroyed, or changed. And even if the picture is accurate, I believe it can be altered, knowing full well that such a belief might evidence the flies clouding my own romantic vision. But if the picture is at all valid, what are its relationships and implications in terms of the overall discussion of language?

Taking at face value some of the ideas that have been presented earlier in this discussion, consider the following: If one's social semiotic is shaped through the linguistic-social interactions most common in one's existence, and if the most common institutional interaction is marked by (de)ference, predescribed problems with prescribed answers, and an emphasis on the grasping and accumulating of knowledge rather than the creating and syn-thesizing of knowledge, then the human beings who are "trained" within such a system are likely to (1) reflect it, and (2) be damned good at it. If this description of the tenor of higher education is even partially fair, then its implications are serious, if not horrifying.

TRANSCENDENTALISM AND COGNITIVE THEORY

Walt Whitman wrote a poem, "There Was a Child Went Forth," that begins like this:

> There was a child went forth every day,
> And the first object he look'd upon, that object he became,

And that object became part of him for the day or a certain part of the day,
Or for many years or stretching cycles of years.
The early lilacs became part of this child,
And grass and white and red morning-glories, and white and red clover, and
the song of the phoebe-bird,
. . . .
And the fish suspending themselves so curiously below there, and the
beautiful curious liquid,
And the water-plants with their graceful flat heads, all became part of him.

The question I wish to pose is this: If a child actually did become all that
he saw as he went forth in our school system, what would he be? Would he
see lectures and lecturers, podiums, blackboards and chalk, books, purple
syllabi, machine-gradable forms for multiple-choice tests, no. 2 pencils,
closed doors with signs about imaginary office hours, reams of hall passes?
And if this is what he sees, what will he become? If all we offer is the best
training available in order to serve the machine, how can anyone "be all that
he can be"? Perhaps we need to change the motto: Be all that the machine
needs you to be; significant rewards guaranteed.

Again, a warning and a disclaimer. Neither Whitman nor I ever intended
to suggest that the child turned into a lilac or a fish; there is absolutely no
intention here of reinforcing a behavioral argument that humanness can be
best or most reasonably described in terms of stimulus-response reinforcement psychology. Nor has there been a convenient forgetting: The discussion
remains committed to a notion of language as a creative possibility. But no
matter how creative the possibility of language genuinely is, some—and I
think a significant—degree of the creativity is going to take place in relationship to that which is outside the creator. To say that significant elements
of our behavior are shaped by our environment is not to suggest that they
are shaped entirely or only by the environment. It simply suggests that most
of us create in relationship to and through the materials available. While
genuine creativity is never wholly limited by its surroundings, few would
argue with the fact that it is significantly influenced—positively and nega-
tively—by the surroundings. More directly related to the discussion of language development, then, the question becomes this: As children go forth
in our schools and the larger society, what dominant kinds of language do
they experience and what kinds of language uses are most likely to become
"part of [them] for the day or a certain part of the day/ or for many years or
stretching cycles of years"?

In terms of language learning, it appears unquestionable that the grammatical and surface structures surrounding the infant from birth are the
structures the infant learns as she develops language competence. American
children learn American English, most children in Harlem (regardless of
color) learn what is formally termed Black English (a dialect of standard
English), French children in Montreal learn Canadian French, and children

in Paris, France, learn Parisian French. In order to produce surface structures in a grammatical form that is part of a language the learner is not immersed in from birth, the learner must consciously seek out, study, and practice those surface structures (or else immerse herself in the language/culture that she wishes to learn).

The same appears to be true of the "deep and surface structures" (if I may transfer the terms for the moment) of a culture. People clearly adopt the cultural customs they are intimately in contact with—except, of course, when they consciously attempt to avoid adopting them. This possibility of consciousness and avoidance is important because it is one of the foundations of any argument against a simple behavioral view. That is, to be influenced (even powerfully influenced) does not mean that the individual is powerless, acting in total submission to the environment; but to be unconscious of the possibility of power and to be unconscious of alternatives to a given set of conditions is almost certainly not conducive to the exercise of individual power against a larger cultural given. The less hostile that environment or culture, the more seductive the cultural/linguistic given, the more likely one is to quietly, perhaps even joyfully, submit and adapt. What, then, is the cultural given that most of our students are immersed in? What are the outside materials and experiences through which they shape their world as they "go forth"?

And what does any of this have to do with literacy?

In many ways, what follows is an academic description of learning that uses the discursive mode and the language of cognitive psychology to say much the same thing that Whitman suggests in the poem cited before. The position I am about to articulate grows primarily out of analogies with psycholinguistic descriptions of language learning and attempts to distinguish between two kinds of language situations or uses, particularly as they might affect the literacy levels of our students, and perhaps of the society at large.

In his examination of the reading process, Frank Smith relies heavily on a cognitive theory similar to (although much more fully developed than) the one proffered by Hirsch. While it remains purely a metaphorical description of that which we do not understand, his language offers some useful images and concepts. Without getting into technical explanations of terms like *long-term memory* and *nonvisual information*, let us simply accept, for the moment, that human beings carry something inside their heads comparable to a network of associations or schemata, that these schemata are language related, and that they are highly dynamic, constantly in the process of interacting and (re)arranging, constantly in the process of becoming through the possibility of meaning making that is language. That is certainly "simple" enough.

Smith says, for example, that "the system of knowledge in our heads is organized into an intricate and internally consistent working model of the world, built up through our interactions with the world and integrated into a coherent whole. We know far more than we were ever taught." He describes this intricate web as the foundation for the *"theory* of the world" in our head, which is

the basis for all our perceptions and understanding of the world, the root of all learning, the source of hopes and fears, motives and expectancies, reasoning and creativity. And this theory is all we have. If we can make sense of the world at all, it is by interpreting our interactions with the world in the light of our theory. The theory is our shield against bewilderment. (Smith 1982: 54)

Through our use of this theory we "predict" the world before us, eliminating the possibility that "anything may happen" and replacing it with "this is probably what will happen" (Smith 1982: 61). In short, we eliminate chaos and we create contexts through purposeful acts of faith based on our inherently creative natures, our needs, desires, expectations, and past experiences. We expect things to occur in certain ways and at certain times; we expect people to act in certain ways under certain conditions. And for the most part the world appears to conform pretty much to our expectations. Cars usually stop at red lights; police normally uphold the law; our homes are normally still there when we return from work.

In terms of linguistic interactions, the conventions that allow predictions to work in the world in general allow language, generally, to follow predictable (rule-governed?) patterns of both structure and meaning. We learn to predict (both in production and reception) certain grammatical-syntactical/ semantic occurrences. Of course, it should come as no surprise that this brings us back to Halliday's idea of language as social semiotic and Searle's theory of speech acts. And as we suggested earlier, the more conventional the situation, the more likely the prediction is to be correct; the more habitual or ritualized the linguistic interaction, the more likely the prediction (of what language will occur and what it will mean) will be correct. More directly (always remembering the metaphorical nature of the terminology), it is reasonable to suggest that through our creation of schemata we *project* the world as a rule-governed structure; the quality of our projection is measured by the consistency with which our projected rules operate to successfully predict reality. The important point here is not that the universe operates according to structural rules—it may or may not: Like language, the universe might reasonably be described as a reality in a constant state of flux, subject to construction and deconstruction at any given moment. The important point here is that once again we submit to a "happy fiction" insofar as we agree to believe that reality is predictable, for the most part, and we somehow have established a cognitive system that allows us to learn or create the rules that govern it (Goodman 1978). To no small extent, in issues of this kind, we are always left with Yossarian's unsettling point: It makes as much sense as anything else.

It is when our theories and predictions fail that we are surprised, startled, and bewildered. Hijackings, assassinations, the death of a child— that which is out of the ordinary is that which we seldom predict. Of course, the bewilderment, pain, and upset that accompany the loss of a loved one or events causing world turmoil can be described in much more sensitive, human terms: We are upset by a child's loss because "it doesn't seem *fair*," "such young ones *shouldn't* die," "assassinations make *no sense*," and so on. In its own way, each statement we use to lament the ugly, painful realities that are a part of our existence are all reasonable statements. But almost always, as is suggested by the italicized words, these statements indicate the assumption of a predictable order that has somehow been interrupted by the unpredictable (and, it is important to note, the undesirable). Even these events, however, are within the realm of our possible predictions; therefore, although they upset us when they do not conform to what we expect or desire, they can be understood in the sense of being related to internal schemata. They generally do not leave us entirely bewildered, perhaps because we have a category for things that "we don't predict to happen but might happen under certain circumstance." As Thomas Kuhn has convincingly pointed out, when time-honored paradigms break down, we experience not only fear and chaos, but, equally important, we create new paradigms: When the world was no longer flat, it became round; when the earth was no longer the center of the universe, theology "adapted" (Kuhn 1970).

From the point of view of phenomenology, it is reasonable to say that if something occurred that we had no way of understanding, no way of associating with or incorporating into our cognitive schemata, then we would have no way of knowing it at all. We cannot imagine the unimaginable, and we cannot know the unknowable—until, of course, we can create a way to imagine or know it. But such truisms border on the insights garnered in introductory psychology or philosophy courses, and our present concern here is the imaginable. We can reasonably imagine cognition as being characterized by internal schemata through which we act upon and interact with the world, predicting the present and the future. Although all of this is a happy fiction, we will work with it for the moment as we begin exploring the theories of the world that our students bring with them into our classrooms, how these theories are shaped, and their implications for anyone concerned with mature literacy.

Rather than worrying about what we cannot worry about, imagining the unimaginable, and/or knowing the unknowable, we might best concern ourselves with some of the more subtle problems associated with concepts like the mental "theory of the world" and prediction when they are applied to one's ability to make sense of and within a given context. Here the problem of context rears its unsaturated head again. Clearly, any set of predictions is based on more than factual knowledge about the world and how it works.

If part of the reason that I fail to predict my own plane being hijacked or my house being destroyed by fire while I am at work or the death of my child is that these things do not normally happen to me and I have no reason to make such predictions, the other part of the reason is that we do not want such things to occur. In short, our predictions about what is likely to happen are enormously influenced by what we expect to occur, and that itself is enormously influenced by what we want, need, desire, and prefer to occur. In terms of language, we expect people to mean what we intend them to mean; we read texts—not just printed texts—as we intend, in terms of our own purposes, needs, and desires.

"Why then," one might reasonably ask, "do we not completely misunderstand one another all the time? Given the radical relativism that is being suggested here—meaning governed by prediction and prediction governed by an individual's past experiences and present purposes, needs, and desires—shared meaning appears to be impossible." It is a good question, but not a particularly new one. Of course, one answer is that we do not understand one another at all, but simply engage in an enormous individual/societal pretense because we cannot afford to face the isolation engendered by admitting the impossibility of shared meanings. Unfortunately, this threatening point of view is not easily dismissed.

But the other answer—a commonsense view that holds within it some uncommonly good sense—suggests that (1) we pretty much do fully understand one another most of the time and (2) much of the rest of the time the degree of understanding overcomes degrees of confusion or misunderstanding. The first, threatening answer leaves us at best in a state of individual, subjective isolation overcome only through a powerful act of self-delusion. The second answer allows us to read, write, speak, listen, and cross streets without getting hit by cars. Allowing, then, that the first answer may be the case, what follows is at worst an examination of the illusion that you (the reader) agree to pretend is possible. Otherwise, you would not be reading this in the first place. And there are always Yossarian's flies!

But any such theorizing, because of its inherent contradictions, invites (demands) an examination of some of the significant variables that appear to function in such an important way in sociolinguistic interactions. Consequently, in talking about the literacy of our students, it is of paramount importance to rethink much of what has already been said from the perspective of what I have just written. To the extent that students (or anyone else, for that matter) understand us and we them, what is it that we say to them, what is it that they understand by what we say to them, and to what extent are we and they aware of what we mean by what we say and what they understand? This is a complex, interesting, and important question. While it almost certainly cannot be answered in any concrete, provable sense, some important guesses may be tendered.

HAPPY FICTIONS—A RETURN TO OLD GROUND WITH A NEW VIEW

Let us begin this excursion with some formulations, some more happy fictions. For those who are irritated by the phrase *happy fictions*, I will try not to repeat it too many more times. But such fictions may be all we have when it comes to discussing language, learning, and literacy, so let us not dismiss them too easily. That they are at least happy, or that they have the potential to be so, should give us some relief.

I begin by returning to the initial stages of language learning and by differentiating between two basic uses of language, both of which intersect at various times to various degrees and, therefore, make the distinctions almost automatically artificial. Regardless of the problems inherent in labeling something as polysemous as language—especially as it functions in human interactions—the distinctions are useful at first for examining the ways in which language functions in (and perhaps influences) the lives of many of our students. I offer the following distinction: Language whose primary purpose is to effect action within an immediate or anticipatable moment, the language of getting things done (*situationally dependent* language), differs from language whose primary purpose is discursive, expressive, and/or exploratory (*expressive-exploratory* language).

In the earliest stages of learning language, most of the language the child directly experiences is centered within the immediate situation and refers to things, people, and events immediately present. When water is discussed it is usually present or is going to be made immediately present; when diapers are discussed they are usually coming off or going on; safety pins are either sticking in the baby or not; mommy and daddy are real and present; toys, pictures, names of people, foods, drinks—everything is reinforced in its immediate reality and in language. There are very few metaphysical discussions with the infant. This language that attempts to describe, ask for, and even comment on what is immediately present or what is desired to be made immediately present is the language of getting things done; it is language that depends on and refers to the immediate moment. It is not differentiated through syntax or structures, necessarily, as much as it is differentiated by the speaker-listener's involvement with (and uses of) it in the moment. It might be characterized as much by the baby's utterance of "wa-wa" as by the adult's directive to "pick up your toys." It may be standard or nonstandard, proprietary or improprietary, beautiful or ugly; as long as it is directed at the moment and at the physical reality in which speaker and listener exist, it is situationally dependent language (Britton 1970; Rosenblatt 1978; Smith 1982).

Although much of the language of the adult world consists of situational language (the language of getting things done) and is directed at immediate situations as simple as ordering something over the phone or as complex as reading manuals that give directions for building a nuclear reactor, much of the language of the college classroom is clearly (or apparently) "intentionally" different from the language of the workaday world. Again, this language (which typifies a college lecture on phenomenology or relativity, a college textbook on Marxism, or a scholarly journal in psychology, for example) may not differ from other language in syntax or structure, sometimes may not even differ too radically in vocabulary (with the exception of specialized terms of the discipline), but the intention is almost always different from situationally dependent language.

The language of the classroom is intended by the speaker/writer to express ideas, explore constructs, hypothesize, prophesy, abstract from, generalize about, consider—it is the language of the thinker. If it has any clear purpose in terms of getting something done, it is directed at the ongoing construction of self and relationships with other. This language may occur anywhere and does not depend on the immediate situation; it often involves commentary on situationally dependent language, such as an argument about the sense or quality of the directions for building the nuclear reactor or an analysis of the clinical procedures established for dealing with a particular behavior problem. Indeed, this language is emphatically not tied to the present and moves freely about the real and imagined pasts and futures that we so love to construct. It is the language of experience and becoming. And again, it need not be complex. For example, newspapers generally offer exploratory-expressive language (this may be more true of news accounts or feature articles than of editorials directed at effecting action), but they do not often analyze complex ideas in great depth or fullness. If anything, their complexity lies in absence, in that which they do not address.

Beyond the college classroom, this is the language that is necessary for the viewer-listener-reader to interact with the world (as opposed to doing whatever the world announces she must do). Facility with this use of language allows one to think about the news and come to one's own decisions, to detect irony, contradiction, deceit, and truth. It is the freely floating language that is tied to one's possibility for being human; it is the language of thought. In short, this exploratory-expressive language is at the center of the academic experience. Facility with exploratory-expressive language forms the basis for distinguishing between functional literacy and real literacy. Without it, one may understand, take, and even give orders; indeed, without it one might move well beyond any of the associations generally implied by functional literacy because one might be highly functional, effective, efficient, and powerful in a world where getting things done is highly respected and rewarded. It is at least reasonable to suggest that expertise with situational language suggests expertise in the content of the modern corporate and technological worlds. But without facility with expressive-exploratory language, one does not consider the nature of and/or reason for what is getting done. One may build the nuclear reactor, but one can hardly question the need for it or the sense of it relative to other energy forms. One may be brilliant at perceiving and even creating cause-effect relationships, but weak at estimating the value or desirability of the effects beyond their value as part of the ongoing service to the indifferent machine.

Probably there are no human beings who use language entirely of one kind or the other. It is undeniable that clear distinctions between these two uses of language are artificial, except in the most ritualized and clear-cut of circumstances. When someone says, "Lock the door before you leave," and the listener understands that the statement is directed at him in reference to a given door, the statement is clearly in the realm of getting things done and almost certainly not expressive-exploratory. In fact, even if "lock the door" is used metaphorically, as when a college president tells the admissions officer to "lock the door on new admissions," the statement is still clearly directed at getting something done in the physical world. Likewise, the statement that "the biological term *dehiscence* has been borrowed to identify the gap that allows and even necessitates the further construction of being through language, even in the face of an always/already disappearing present" is clearly exploratory-expressive and not very clearly directed at effecting immediate action or change.

But these are distinctions of relatively simplistic, ritualized linguistic interactions, especially as I am using them. They become much fuzzier when language is removed from the context where it has been purposefully interjected in order to provide an example and when it is viewed from a broader context of typical social-linguistic interactions. One might begin, for example, by questioning how language is used in the previous examples or in this entire text. While the text itself is almost certainly typical of exploratory-expressive discourse, doesn't it seem likely that it also intends to achieve some effect in the reader? I would hope so.

Also, reconsider the nature of written directions. A treatise exploring the two or three least expensive and most efficient ways of building a bomb might be intended as an exploratory discourse describing the paradoxical creativity human beings have exemplified in their continuing search for ways to destroy one another. But while the writer might intend the piece to be a philosophical commentary on the nature of man, how the piece functions beyond the writer, in the absence of the writer, depends entirely on *how the reader intends* it. If the reader is looking for an inexpensive, efficient way to build an effective bomb, what began as expressive exploratory language suddenly functions as situational language. Likewise, if the writer had written the piece in order to help terrorists build bombs, intending it purely in terms of getting something done, readers might transform it into the realm of expressive-exploratory discourse as they read it from a metaphysical/philosophical point of view or even as an example of well-written directions. The person building a bomb is concerned with the language only insofar as it contributes to getting the job done. But the individual examining the

treatise in order to generalize about the style of writing or in order to generalize about the lengths to which people will go to kill one another is viewing
the treatise from the point of view of exploratory-expressive language.

In short, the function of the language in a given situation—and therefore
its meaning—depends on the intent of the reader-listener. To the extent
that writer-speaker and reader-listener share mutual understandings of the
given situation (or, in the language that we have been using, to the extent
that their cognitive schemata are significantly similar and to the extent that
they apply a mutual set of predictive schemata), the language will essentially
be taken as intended and meaning will be shared among the participants.
For example, if one says, "John, please pass the salt," one expects to get
the salt. The last thing in the world one expects is a discourse on salt and
high blood pressure, where the salt mines that produced this salt are located,
and how the workers are treated by the government or corporation in charge.
One expects to get the salt.

Ironically, however, what appears to be a simple example of a highly
ritualized situation in which the speech act cannot possibly misfire often
provides the opportunity for an exploratory-expressive joke. Who has not
had the experience of asking, at the dinner table, "Can you reach the salt?"—
intending that the other party pass the salt—only to receive the joking
rejoinder, "Yes, I can reach it. Why?" In this case the hearer intentionally
misunderstands the speaker's intent, purposefully transforming situational
language into exploratory-expressive language in order to achieve humor,
and then usually reverses and passes the salt to the speaker before anyone
gets angry.

One might ask, at this point: What is the purpose of creating a sociolinguistic explanation of what everyone already knows? It comes as no surprise
to anyone who has studied elementary psychology, communication theory,
sociology, or linguistics to find that people understand and misunderstand
in direct relation to their own private lenses and filters based on their intents
and purposes. Rhetoric is the study of how to use language to achieve one's
own purposes and intents in terms of what one can know about the expectations and needs of one's audience. Having developed a fuzzy theory at
some length, I appear to be using it for little more than word play. However,
this is not the case.

As fuzzy as the distinctions are between situational language and exploratory-expressive language, they provide a framework for examining the kinds
of language uses and situations—and the resultant firings and misfirings—
that characterize school language in particular, and even more general uses
of language.

GOING BACKWARDS (AGAIN)

In several previous sections, we have examined language development
from the viewpoints of psycholinguistics, sociolinguistics, and philosophy.

Now we must conduct one final examination in order to piece together the parts of the puzzle.

What follows concerns "normal" language development that occurs in "normal" families. However, in this case, the word *normal* is intended with all the confusion and variety that the term generally implies. There are certainly developmental situations, environments, families, and cultures in our society that do not entirely fit the normal situation I am about to describe. But I believe that for the most part the picture that follows represents, in varying degrees, what happens to many children in the mainstream of our society and our educational system.

As I have pointed out repeatedly, before entering school most children participate in a range of language play and interaction. As the growing child uses language to explore and name her world, the adults who interact with the child encourage and reward the play of language, assisting at every turn possible, often experiencing amusement and surprise as the child appears to use language to create schemata and categories for ordering the chaos of the world around her. Although a reasonable amount of the language experiences in these early years might be labeled situationally dependent, much of it is also exploratory-expressive, with the two often overlapping and interacting in a given linguistic exchange. The parent who is reading an alphabet book to the child normally has many objectives. For some parents, a primary objective may be to give the child a head start on the academy, providing her with information about the alphabet and beginning reading skills that will later be so important in school. But, although this purpose may often accompany the activity, for most adults the activity is a moment of joy, warmth, love, and human interaction. That *A* is for *apple* may be important information—in fact, it is rather complex information if you consider that the "name" of the letter *A* bears no relationship whatsoever to the sound produced at the beginning of the word *apple*. This is pretty clearly situational language—language directed at the literal text that is present, perhaps to eventually produce a learner who can identify the letter A. But the moment is generally accompanied by exploratory-expressive language as parent and child discuss apples in general: the color red; fruit and how it grows; how good a firm, juicy apple tastes; the fun of climbing a tree to get that firm, juicy apple; but also, of course, how careful we must be when climbing trees. In many homes, it will not be unusual for Johnny Appleseed to pop into the conversation. This moves what first appeared to be a simplistic linguistic interaction into a highly complex human interaction and exploration of language, self, and other.

Moreover, it is almost certainly through interactions like this that many children learn to read before they ever get to school. Not only does reading to the child introduce her to the important fact that the marks on the page can be made to mean something and that they are somehow related to oral language, but the activity is also fun and rewarding. Reading, in these early

years, is not something one does because one is being told to or because
someone has created questions about the text so the reader can find the
answers in the text in order to prove she can read. It is something we do
because it feels good; it is part of our general linguistic, social, and intellectual
development. It represents another important part in the ongoing process
of self-construction through language. Generally speaking, both oral and
print language interactions with children prior to school may be characterized
in the same way.

Of course, there is plenty of purely situational language during these early
years, also: "pick up your toys and put them away"; "stop your damned
crying"; "please don't throw your food on the floor"; "don't touch"; and the
forever repeated "no." And, in the normal homes I am positing, one use of
language may be considerably more predominant than the other. Some
homes may be filled with the kind of situational language that characterizes
the giving of orders; these are homes in which the child is viewed as an
irritating object or animal who needs to be trained. In other homes, exploratory-expressive language may dominate; here the child is viewed as a creative, growing part of human interactions. In most homes, however, there
is a reasonable intermixture of the two.

At approximately age five (or three if the child attends a day-care center),
formal education is introduced and the child goes off to school. While there
are many different kinds of schools, it is reasonable to posit a "normal" one.
As has been previously discussed, most public schools are formally part of
a larger state structure: They are publicly financed, are supervised through
state and local agencies, operate according to specific laws, and presumably
have a defined purpose, the most obvious of which is to educate the general
public. The governmental, supervisory superstructure is important, but one
must also note that most teachers in most schools are there because they
like kids and enjoy teaching. Clearly, there are some abnormally good and
bad schools, and some teachers are probably psychopathic and/or stupid. But
the people who staff the normal school, the one we are discussing, are
reasonably intelligent, act in good faith, have honorable intentions, and
display a respectable amount of humanness.

However, because schools are what they are and because they fit into the
larger societal structure as they do, the language of schools is predominantly
situational. Whether the child is busy learning certain skills (I remember the
teacher who was worried about a kindergartner's weak scissors skills) or busy
learning content (social studies, mathematics), the point is to find out and
do what one is told (read aloud, fill in the blank, circle the correct answer,
sit still, quiet down, line up, go here, go there, do this and do that). For
the most part, schools are institutions where behavior is regulated in a variety
of ways for (presumably) both social and educational reasons, and the reg-
ulation of behavior is primarily characterized by situationally dependent lan-

guage. Much of this occurs not because teachers or students want to regulate and behave in these ways, but because such regulating and behaving characterize the larger machine of which the school is only a part.

Whereas the *A* at the beginning of *apple* once led to a joyful sociolinguistic exploration of self and other, it now generally leads to a workbook exercise. Whereas reading was a delightful activity engaged in out of self-interest, it is now something one does at certain times in order to learn how to do it (a paradox if ever there was one). Inasmuch as the purpose for reading has become situationally dependent, dedicated to getting something done, the reading materials themselves are often perverted as they no longer function in an expressive-exploratory manner. Even more ironic, school reading is often characterized by stories and language that have been purposely created, with artificially limited vocabularies, in order for the child to learn phonics rather than to have fun reading and talking about what one has read (Bettelheim and Zelan 1981). American schools are "serious" places and there is "work" to be done. There is little time for an exploratory-expressive discussion about what kind of silly rat might sit on a cat's mat because the point is neither the cat, the rat, nor the silliness. The point involves the sound we are supposed to produce when reading aloud words that have an *A* between two consonants. That warm, important, joyful activity of reading has been transformed into the activity of practicing sounds. In early reading activities in school, one reads in order to prove that one can read or in order to practice reading. All too often, the by-product is immersion in situationally dependent language at its most nonsensical and meaningless level.

Of course, one might argue that these examples of skills training from the early grades do not typify the later school experience, and to some extent that is true. But while the emphasis on basic skills diminishes over the years in many schools, the role and function of language does not change as much as one might hope or expect. The emphasis clearly moves from skills to content around the seventh or eighth grade in most schools; this content emphasis becomes serious and intense in high school as the student is prepared for the presumably even greater and more intense emphasis on content that appears to characterize higher education. But, as we have seen, neither the amount nor the complexity of content has much to do with the distinctions between exploratory-expressive and situationally dependent uses of language. Content exists in the schools as the material used to satisfy the demand of blanks that need to be filled in and multiple choices that must be circled. Content is often merely something to be grasped and then released at the appropriate time for the appropriate test.

One might also argue that, even if this is a fair description of what occurs in school, our students are in school only five hours per day, five days per week. There is no reason to assume that the dominance of situationally dependent language in school is not reversed outside of school. If exploratory-expressive language situations typified much of the home language prior to school, would it not continue to do so after the child has begun attending school? Clearly, in some homes it does. But not in most, I suspect.

Consider the environmental conditions and social life of the normal child we have posited. After he comes home from school, either he turns on the television or a computer video game and moves into a relatively private experience with the tube, or he goes out to play. No one would suggest that we genuinely know how television affects our youth, but I would suggest that the typical viewing experience is primarily a situationally dependent one. For the most part, television shows are typified by dialogue that refers directly to the situation of the actors delivering the lines. Most people (young and old alike) do not view television from a highly exploratory or analytic perspective, questioning and discussing the actions, interactions, and esthetics involved in a given show. Most people sit in relative silence as the electrons move before their eyes: Pointing out that they enjoy this, that they are entertained by this, is not intended as an elitist criticism of their intelligence. In fact, I see nothing inherently wrong with the situation. People neither need nor desire to be engaged in critical thinking every waking minute. The point, however, is that this sociolinguistic interaction does not normally break the dominant pattern of situationally dependent language. Most television shows do not invite exploratory-expressive language—or perhaps it is fairer to say that the typical viewing situation does not invite such linguistic interchange.

One might make the reasonable counterargument that television provides plenty of news shows, news analyses, and documentaries, but one would be hard put to argue that this represents the typical viewing agenda for schoolchildren. More important, not only does television occupy an enormous amount of the leisure time of the typical child (some studies suggest as much as six to eight hours per day), but socioeconomic conditions have caused television to become the national babysitter in many homes. It is no longer uncommon, in households representing the very poor as well as the upper middle class, to find that both parents work. Again intending no criticism by stating this fact (a fact that typifies my own childhood and parenting experiences), it is reasonable to expect that much after-school television viewing occurs in real isolation. And when the working parent or parents return from work, there is dinner to be prepared and eaten, lunches to prepare for the following day, television to be watched, newspapers to be read, homework to be done—everyone is pretty busy and there is not much room for exploratory-expressive rehashings of one another's day. To the extent that such rehashings take place, they often do so at the dinner table, forming fond memories for those involved. But even then, dinner generally lasts about one hour at the most, and then each is off to take care of business.

Lest anyone suggest that this focus on television or working parents represents a hidden bias, I offer this clarification. The fact that parents work or that television is viewed does not necessarily result in a lack of exploratory-expressive uses of language. Many parents, working or otherwise, consciously spend time discussing events, feelings, and even television shows with their children in the most significant ways. But by and large, we live in a society where everyone has become a little too busy for the time it takes to do something that doesn't get any*thing* done, for the time it takes to engage in reflection, examination, and sharing. Even in households where the parents might wish to engage in such activities with the kids, it is not uncommon for the kids to go out as soon as they get home from school, come home just in time for dinner, do their homework, and go to bed. And one might note that the homework that is so encouraged as being morally and intellectually good for children is most often an extension of the situationally dependent language that typified the school day.

In short, in a very busy, rushed society where material success is represented by school grades, the right college, social status, income, and so on, there appears to be little time or necessity for exploratory-expressive language. For example, creative writing in school is something that teachers may get to if there is time. Creative writing courses are seldom viewed as important as, say, computer programming courses.

One might argue, with good reason, that colleges do not emphasize situational language—just the opposite. Colleges are the places that nurture the thinkers, the places that students complain are never practical enough. And yet college English and philosophy departments advertise themselves in terms of "what you can *do* with" a degree in the humanities—like go to law school or get into business. Of course, there is nothing wrong with being able to do something, and making a living is essential in our society, but so is being able to reflect, consider, create, think, generalize, abstract, be human. Seldom does one find educational opportunities, programs, or curricula advertised in terms of their humanistic, humanizing potential. At all levels, in most of our institutions and in most of our daily interactions, situationally dependent language is employed and is most necessary for success as defined by the larger societal machine. People who delight in exploratory-expressive thinking and languaging ask too many questions and make too many demands on the indifferent machine because they are unlikely to accept orders, information, or judgments without exploring what is being said or written and expressing themselves in relation to it. Perhaps this is why the machine created publicly funded higher education—to provide a place for the thinkers to go and think without upsetting the fine-tuning of the machine.

Remember what Ashbery wrote: In school, the thoughts get combed out. This is the kind of grooming that most befits success. But what does this diatribe have to do with literacy?

Surely, colleges do not intentionally emphasize situationally dependent language over exploratory-expressive language. If nothing else, upper-level courses in mathematics, physics, history, political science, literature, philosophy, and economics—many of the courses that are part of the normal college curriculum—do not emphasize situationally dependent language. Quite the opposite, in fact. In these courses the language of the classroom discussion, of the lecturer, of the texts—even the questions on the exams— often represent exploratory-expressive language. So why is it that the college experience does not reverse what has come before? Why is it that college graduates are not fully literate (exploratory-expressive) readers, writers, speakers, listeners? Why aren't these graduates active meaning makers?

To some extent, the answer lies in the fact that schools in general, including colleges and universities, have become servants to the language of getting things done rather than the language of exploration and expression of self and other. Most of what students do with language in school is use it to prove that they can do whatever it is they have been told to do. As was clearly evidenced in the responses of high school students provided earlier, they write what they are told in order to show that they can write a properly constructed paragraph or business letter or term paper. They do not do so in order to say something. To the extent that they read, they read in order to find the answer to a predetermined question, and they do this either to prove that their "reading comprehension" is up to "grade level" (a meaningless term, if ever a term was meaningless), or to prove that they found the "correct" answer (de Beaugrande in Mandl, Stein, and Trabasso 1984: 179). They then sometimes write in order to prove that they did all this, but most of their writing involves fill-in-the-blank or short-answer activities and is seldom characterized by extended discursive effort. Even when it is an extended piece of writing (the mandatory high school or freshman composition research paper, for example), it is often done to prove that the student can do research, properly footnote, produce a bibliography, and use quotation marks correctly.

But it is not simply that fragmented skills or form have become more important than content—although this is clearly a problem in teaching writing. Content is enormously important in most schools; this is evidenced by the constant testing of facts and figures that characterizes our educational system. An equally serious problem, perhaps a central problem, is that, for the most part, in schools neither the practice of skills nor the study of form or content employs or invites the exploratory-expressive functions of language (the use of language to create, consider, think, abstract, generalize, explore, and share). From a situationally dependent perspective, the schools are doing a fine job. Students who pay attention, work hard, obey the rules, and give themselves to the experience do well on tests and get high grades. Further reinforcing the situationally dependent use of language and thought, and further emphasizing the relationship between tests, grades, and success, these students often are awarded scholarships based on the fact that their excellent performance suggests a continued excellence. That this correlation holds, that students who do well in high school normally do well in college, presents its own powerful implication: either colleges are not much different from "good" high schools or their difference is irrelevant, in some way, because they are part, parcel, and by-product of the larger educational system. From this perspective, the system is not at all unfair, and from the larger governmental perspective, the system is really a success. Generally speaking, the "right" kinds of students who do the "right" stuff in school get their high school diplomas, do well enough on the SATs, and go on to college, sometimes even the "right" college. There is usually plenty of room for them on the day shift.

But if this scenario even vaguely represents reality, it also represents a serious problem, especially insofar as we desire to create a genuinely literate public. At first look the problem may appear obvious, and the solution may appear equally obvious. By now, the scenario should be clear. For the most part, our schools do an excellent job of helping students become proficient in situational language—the language of getting things done. But they are apparently failing miserably in helping students gain facility with exploratory-expressive language—the language of becoming and being human, the language of thought. Most important, neither kind of language I refer to here has anything directly to do with the surface structure of language; that is, although one might point to superficial differences in vocabulary, rhetorical structures, sentence length, or use of active versus passive verbs, these are not the discriminating factors between situational as opposed to exploratory-expressive language. The difference lies in the ways of thinking (being) that underlie the two.

A summary may help here. Workbooks, fill-in-the-blank exercises, and multiple-choice tests are examples of situational language in the schools. In fact, most of the language of school exemplifies situational language/thinking, the language of getting through the day and of getting things done. Most of the language of the classroom is not interactive (note studies of the excessive preponderance of teacher-talk and the lack of discussion that exists in most classrooms (e.g., Atwell 1987; Delpit 1988; Goodlad 1984). Teachers talk and students (sometimes) listen; when they listen at all, they listen in order to get the answer, to find out what they must remember in order to pass the test or fill in the blank. They read in order to answer the questions at the end of the chapter or to pass the test. They write in order to evidence that they have listened to what the teacher said or to evidence that they read the chapter. All the student's language and thought is directed at getting through the day (year, years) and at achieving success (good grades, promotion), and almost none of it is directed at the construction of self, at expression of one's ideas, at the process of assimilating and/or wrestling with what is being learned.

Nothing really changes at the college level. To the extent that there is any real difference between the workbooks and fill-in-the-blank exercises of elementary and high school and the college experience, it is often characterized primarily by the fact that the blanks are simply bigger now. Now you have to fill in a whole page or several pages with predetermined answers that prove you learned the material. Ask the average college student (and the average professor) about the general requirements at any given college and you are likely to find out all you need to know. One of two answers prevails: (1) The general college requirements are good for you (them) because everyone should be well-rounded—this is the time-honored cliché that has little to do with students' reality; or the more typical answer, (2) it's a waste of time; why don't they just let you get into the major; what do I need to know all this stuff for? That last statement clarifies things considerably: What is it for? What effect will this stuff have on my material, physical situation? Imagine trying to answer these questions with descriptions of the importance of exploratory-expressive uses of language or the beauty and power inherent in the use of language as a way of being.

WILL THIS BE ON THE TEST?

Only a fool would suggest that the situation just described, an educational system bent on producing highly efficient and "knowledgeable" automatons or technologists, represents what educators, parents, or students want. Much seems to be happening in our schools, but what exactly is it, how can we know it, and if we don't like it, how can we change it? I hope the discussion that has preceded this paragraph has begun to clarify what is happening. But a closer look at the dynamics of a college classroom may reveal the problem even more fully. So far we have looked at normal families, normal children, and normal schools. Having succeeded in the use of *normal* up to this point, and recognizing the infinite abnormalities that exist within any given normal situation, let's take a look at the normal college student and college experience.

During the first two years of college, most students take courses that fill general college requirements, and, almost regardless of the rationale underlying the courses forming the core of the general college program, the student is normally expected, guided, directed, or forced to take approximately ten to twelve courses spanning the various disciplines. It is not unusual to find directives in college catalogs saying that each student must take three or four courses in each of the following areas: humanities, natural sciences, social sciences. Often, other conditions apply such as a required freshman composition course, other required introductory courses, the restriction that no more than one course may be taken in a given department in order to fulfill the requirements within a division, or the condition that students may not take courses in their major area as part of the requirements of the general college program. At some colleges these restrictions are minimal and students may pretty much pick and choose; at others, students have little or no choice as they move through specifically designated courses that form a core for all students at the college. Some colleges have taken care and interest in the creation and implementation of their general college programs, focusing on specially developed or revamped courses that emphasize cognitive and skill areas like critical thinking, mathematical-scientific thinking, oral-print-and-visual literacies, and so on. But for the most part, general college programs still look pretty much the way they did in the 1950s.

Again, while there are important exceptions, generally speaking both students and professors in these courses feel somewhat imposed upon by having to take or teach these courses. Professors are disgruntled because they believe that many of the students just "don't care" about the field or the discipline or the subject matter and are only in the course because they must fulfill a requirement. Students often feel forced into an activity they neither have chosen nor believe they will benefit from, and they often feel (sometimes rightly) that the professors "don't really care about these courses because they are being made to teach them." From this perspective, everyone would rather be in a senior seminar focusing on the essentially narrow interests of the major field of study. That is a relatively negative and typically stereotyped picture of student and professor in general college courses.

While the stereotypes do actually exist, there are many exceptions, and in this case the exceptions may be the rule. Many professors consider the introductory courses that form the general college program to be among the most important they teach. My own work in faculty development workshops involving a variety of college teachers across the full range of the curriculum suggests that most teachers consider these courses to be essential and vital because they care deeply about their disciplines and the intellectual beauty and joy that characterize them. They genuinely believe that it is important for the literate, educated public to understand the nature of physics, philosophy, literature, and mathematics. While they believe deeply in the specialized content of their disciplines, many of these teachers focus, in introductory courses, on teaching the students to become "literate" in the area: The scientists want students to have access to the scientific literature that is part of the larger society; they want the students to be able to understand information and make decisions about issues such as toxic waste, acid rain, and nuclear power. The social scientists want students to be literate enough to understand and take action on political and social issues; the humanists want students to be able to reflect, meditate, and create as readers, writers, speakers, and listeners. The teachers of these courses are often less interested in disseminating facts and information than they are interested in helping the students learn to view the world through the lens of their particular discipline and to gain conscious awareness of such viewing.

Although students do not typically share the lofty goals of the teachers, they often enter these courses with an open mind, hoping to gain something from them, and (normally) are not entirely antagonistic. Some are clearly excited about the prospect of learning. But almost all of them wonder what they will get out of the experience—that is, what good it will do later on. More specifically, even those who are somewhat interested in the area are first and foremost concerned about the grade they will achieve. Of course, we often talk about these students with contempt and disdain—Where is their love for knowledge? Where is their curiosity? What ever happened to learning for the pure joy of learning? Is it a biological developmental fact that we lose the joy of learning after about age five or six?

Anyone who has been following this discussion should be able to answer these questions. Learning for the pure joy of learning began to end the day they began school and had to start learning for the pure fact of workbooks, drill exercises, and multiple-choice tests in order to get good grades in order to move into the next grade in order to do well enough to get a scholarship and go to college in order to get a degree in order to get a job in order to make a living. No one ever mentioned making a life.

Our contempt must not be for the students. All they have done is learn what has been taught them. Steeped in an existence that emphasizes situationally dependent language devoted to getting things done, getting ahead, and getting and getting, how can anyone be surprised that they do not come to college excited about the prospect of creative, critical thinking? Of course, they can rediscover it, and what is sometimes most surprising and wonderful is that many fine students, with the assistance of many fine professors, manage to do just this. But many do not. Too many.

Consider what occurs on the first day in the normal college classroom under the best of circumstances. The professor has been preparing the course for months, sometimes years. The syllabus has been carefully prepared; it describes objectives and goals of the course and due dates for reading and writing assignments, for tests, and for whatever else may be within the structure of the course. At the first meeting, one of the most conventionalized and ritualized speech acts in academia, the teacher explains the course, usually trying to convince the students that it will be an exciting experience if only they will meet the demands halfway. Without actually saying it, many teachers try to convey to the students that regardless of what they have heard about college, this teacher actually cares, this course is designed for learners, this experience invites their genuine participation and engagement as learners. The end of this peroration is often met with nothing other than silence—everyone knows that first meetings of courses usually end early if you do not ask questions; sometimes a student wishes to clarify exactly what is due at the next class, and another wants to know if attendance is required. The situationally dependent questions, questions directed at finding out what exactly it is one has to do in this course in order to succeed, slowly but surely frustrate the professor until someone asks, "Would you please go over your grading procedure?"

In order to deal with the students who ask such questions, still more exploration and analysis are necessary. The next chapter presents a different perspective on the problem and the difficulties inherent in the situation I have described—a perspective that briefly immerses us in some currently popular ideas from the world of literary criticism. While this may, at first, appear to be an inexplicable digression, it should illuminate what has come before and suggest directions for resolving some of these problems. After all, what area of thinking should be more helpful in the consideration of mature literacy than the area of literary criticism, which is devoted to the philosophical inquiry of what happens when reader and text collide (or coincide).

4

Readers and (as) Texts

Thus is revealed the total existence of writing: a text is made of multiple writings, drawn from many cultures and entering into mutual relations of dialogue, parody, contestation, but there is one place where this multiplicity is focused and that place is the reader, not, as was hitherto said, the author. The reader is the space on which all the quotations that make up a writing are inscribed without any of them being lost; a text's unity lies not in its origin but in its destination. Yet this destination cannot any longer be personal: the reader is without history, biography, psychology; he is simply that *someone* who holds together in a single field all the traces by which the written text is constituted. . . . [We] know that to give writing its future, it is necessary to overthrow the myth: the birth of the reader must be at the cost of the death of the Author.

Roland Barthes, "The Death of the Author"

LITERACY AND THE PHOENIX

It is a fact that the death of the author has been much mourned. Many continue to argue about the death itself, asserting that, although he is seriously ill, the author will try to recover as soon as he can. This is to be expected because it is the classic way of dealing with death in our culture—either deny its occurrence, or—when denial is no longer possible—assert the possibility of resurrection and a higher state of being, or finally accept and mourn the loss as real. What is curious, however, is the kind of attention we have paid to "the birth of the reader." In our culture—in most cultures—births are celebrated, marking moments of joy, signifying the continuation and forward movement of being. But, perhaps because the birth of the reader

is so closely associated with the death of the author, we see this birth as
somehow more threatening than others. Such should not be the case, however, for it does enormous injustice to the infant. Just as all births suggest
the beginning and continuation of the species, so also, by virtue of the
impending death of all life, do they mark the death of the species. Any
conscious celebration of birth must also be a celebration of death. It is not
so much the birth of the reader that has caused the death of the author—
there has been no murder here, simply death, the death that is imminent
in all writing—it is the death of the author that has given birth to the reader.
Consequently, it makes perfect sense to proclaim, "The author is dead, long
live the reader (author?)!" That the birth of the reader appears to have taken
place without a midwife, perhaps even without a parent, suggests that the
time for nurturing has been greatly delayed. What happens to the reader
who is born into a void?

THEORIES SOMETIMES MATTER

For several years now, literary criticism has concerned itself with the reader
and the reader's relation to the text. While some, like Stanley Fish and
Wolfgang Iser, attempt to theorize the place or function of the reader in the
process of creating the text, others, like Norman Holland and David Bleich,
appear to replace the original printed text with the reader, calling forth the
reader's response as the new text still in need of interpretation. That Holland
and Bleich sometimes appear to have ordained themselves as the sole in-
terpreters of student as text is a problem I will not address here. What is of
interest, however, is that modern literary theory—far from being the im-
possibly esoteric activity of which it is so often accused—offers us a deeper,
clearer look at what occurs in terms of students reading. Whether they are
reading the educational system at large within the context of their society,
the classroom within the context of higher education, the teacher within the
context of a course, or a required text within the context of an upcoming
exam, grades, and success, they are reading. In short, current literary theory
is of major significance because it offers a way to begin to understand these
readers who have been born so recently. Only with such understanding may
we be able to parent and nurture these readers so that they can be involved
in an endeavor that moves, at least at times, beyond situationally dependent
language and motives.

In his very helpful book *On Deconstruction: Theory and Criticism after Structuralism* (1982), Jonathan Culler cites Peter Rabinowits's distinctions of readers as specific kinds of audiences: "the actual audience, the authorial
audience (which takes the work as a fictional communication from an author),
the narrative audience (which takes the work as a communication from the

narrator), and an ideal narrative audience (which interprets the narrator's communication as the narrator appears to wish)" (Culler 1982: 34).

Culler emphasizes that

one proposes these distinctions [among audiences] in order to account for what happens in reading. . . . [And] second, these "audiences" are in fact roles that readers posit and partially assume in reading. Someone who reads Swift's "A Modest Proposal" as a masterpiece of irony first postulates an audience that the narrator appears to think he is addressing: an audience entertaining specific assumptions, inclined to formulate certain objections, but likely to find the narrator's arguments cogent and compelling. The second role the reader postulates is that of an audience attending to a serious proposal for relieving famine in Ireland but finding the values and assumptions of the proposal (and of the "ideal narrative audience") singularly skewed. Finally, the reader participates in an audience that reads the work not as a narrator's proposal but as an author's ingenious construction, and appreciates its power and skill. Actual readers will combine the roles of authorial, narrative, and even ideal narrative audiences in varying proportions—without embarrassment of living in contradiction.

Furthermore, rather than assuming that the "implied reader" functions in any single role, Culler suggests that the reader's delight in the act of reading may well occur through "the interaction of contradictory engagements" (Culler 1982: 35).

This last distinction, the avoidance of positing a reader who plays a single role, is particularly significant because it describes the "mature," "sophisticated," or "educated" reader in the most constructive sense of these terms. This is the reader who does all of the above and then consciously manipulates the text for his own purposes and/or pleasure, perhaps engaging in the constructive fun of deconstructing it, regardless of other, externally imposed desires or intents deriving from the author, the genre, and/or the situation. But Culler's discussion of Rabinowits's distinctions provides an interesting basis for creating a perspective on students as readers.

For example, consider the classroom, the teacher, and the things to be taught as part of a larger text. Consider the students to be the audience (readers) of that text. The system (higher education) and/or the author/orchestrator (instructor) creates the text with the intent of affecting the audience in various ways (communicating information, causing the reader-audience to actively and consciously review past ways of thinking, belief systems, or truths). But the readers (at least some of them) do not know about the various reader-audience roles they might take (roles they must take if the author's intent is to be realized even partially); they are not yet mature or sophisticated readers. In the most traditional terms, most students are still initiates; they are in the process of moving through degrees of naiveté; they are (presumably) learning the roles they might play as they (inter)act upon (with) the text. These are the readers who should be busy being born and whom teachers are supposed to be nurturing.

The Ideal Audience

From this perspective, one might recast the student (reader-audience) as follows: First, there is the student who is part of the ideal narrative audience, the ideal reader. Note that *ideal*, in this case, ironically describes a reader who is entirely at the mercy of the narrative structure, interpreting the "narrator's communication as the narrator appears to wish." Regardless of academic background, these readers do not see their accumulated experience, their nonvisual information, all that they already know, to be immediately related to making sense of new texts. They expect the text to make its own sense because, for them, reading and learning are essentially passive experiences involving identification and reception of whatever one is told to learn. These are the readers who read the text (the course) exactly as it appears to be intended: Bound within its hard covers of course number delineations and specific classroom meetings, these readers are entirely at the mercy of the narrative, hoping to be affected as they "should be" affected, willing to read the text for what it is as well as they can. These readers do not question the text beyond the immediate experience; indeed, why do so if one is entirely in the hands of the narrator?

These readers do not recognize and experience the irony and satire of "A Modest Proposal" because they do not move outside the narrative at all. What is said within the text is what is, and that is all there is to it. These readers are not tortured by contradictions among texts, though they may be shocked by Swift's proposal. The relativism that they study in philosophy courses does not contradict the "truth" of the physics course because they are two entirely different narratives, lacking interrelationships. Even more important, contradictions found among philosophers (e.g., Sartre versus Plato) cause no problems because they are not viewed as contradictions. They are simply two different narratives. Different and equal. These are the students who repeat the plot of a novel when asked to identify and analyze the theme; these are the students who can identify the five basic points within a given chapter of a text but cannot address the importance or meaning of the five points.

For these students no logic governs the organization of a text beyond the fact that it begins at the beginning and ends at the end, both points being interrupted by an interminable middle. These students cannot see an organizational choice made by the author to be a controlling part of the reader's perspective because it has not occurred to them that another organization might affect meaning. For these students the narrative point of view in a literary work is simply a given, not an important artistic choice made by the author to give special shape to the narrative and the reader's perceptions of the work. For these readers the author is not only dead, but he never existed in the first place. These are the students for whom the school day (the school year? the entire school experience?) is essentially a series of unrelated narratives and narrators spouting stuff that they say you need to know in order to get out of there with a degree.

Insofar as these students who are part of the ideal audience are living a fragmented academic existence, they must do something to make that existence cohesive, something to make it make sense. But it is at least possible that the schematic category these students use to make sense of the experience is the category comprised of nonsensical things one does in order to move through the system successfully. These students should do very poorly in our educational system if what we really want to facilitate is the growth of well-informed, capable, thinking human beings who know how to go about the process of learning and making connections between their own experience and whatever it is they are learning. Ironically, I suspect that these students do reasonably well within the educational system as it presently exists. To the extent that such students are (1) highly motivated to master the fragments that, for them, characterize learning and (2) almost entirely unaffected by tensions created by attempts to come to terms with contradictory truths and various unknowns, they are free to move quietly through the world of lectures, multiple-choice tests, and regurgitation that characterizes many high schools and colleges.

The Narrative Audience

Second, we approach the narrative audience (readers), the students who enter the narrative of the course and read it from the point of view of its narrator (the teacher), but who measure the sense of the narrative through some amount of questioning. These readers, while still somewhat constrained by a fragmented and naive sense of learning and reading, understand that reading is not entirely a receptive process. These learners know that they have some responsibility to make sense of what is out there and that past experience and knowledge have bearing on this activity. These readers recognize the sense of the narrative structure and desire to find out what the narrator is really saying, but they are also able and willing to question the narrative and measure it against some other set of world experience. For these readers, everything one reads is not necessarily true. It is the reader's job to find out what is being said, to give some consideration to who is saying it and why, and take away from the experience whatever makes the most sense.

While these readers may not seriously question the organization of a printed text or of the course itself, they will at least recognize that an organization exists and that someone (author-teacher) has made decisions about that organization. While these readers may not discover the controlling point of view in a situation or text, they will recognize its power, to some degree, once it is pointed out.

Still, for these readers (learners) everything is not necessarily related, and it is not within the province of the reader (thinker) to relate and make connections across experience: All experience and knowledge are not brought to bear on all readings. But these readers have glimpses that suggest the possibility of interconnections among and across experience: Some things are related, and reading does not always take place simply within the confines of a given text or situation. While these readers will almost certainly not recognize (create) and work through contradictions between philosophy and physics, and while they are likely to find it difficult to recognize or create connections within a text and/or across concepts in a given course, they are able to take some initial steps toward making meaning in these more complex modes. They are likely to recognize apparent contradictions within a particular physics or philosophy course and to find the contradictions bearable and (perhaps) even worth some thought. They may recognize, on occasion, relationships between concepts and facts that are based on something more than a simple chronology of events.

These readers are not entirely at the mercy of the narrative structure that uses the label of realism to lump together and describe writers as different as Crane and Twain, although they may have serious difficulty understanding the relationships among Twain, Hemingway, Heller, and Shakespeare. And relationships between Shakespeare and Sartre may be almost unthinkable. As a text, a given course for these students is coherent and singular, but they accept and are willing to deal with the tensions created by the recognition that chapters within the text are related and that information (truth) within the text may at times be contradictory.

Furthermore, as one might expect from all that has preceded this particular discussion, these students do reasonably well in our educational system, especially if they work hard. Because they can recognize and tolerate contradictions to some extent, and because they are not committed to constantly making connections among ideas and facts, intellectual growth is not a particularly troubling experience. The world still pretty much appears to present itself as it is, and, from an educational point of view, this learner's job is to read that presentation and be ready to re-present it when called upon. That is, having engaged the process of learning to some extent, but keeping it within the province of memorizing and regurgitating answers, they perform solidly on the kinds of objective evaluative devices so cherished in most schools and colleges. While they recognize contradictions and make certain connections, they are relatively untroubled by either and try not to let them interfere with the job of memorizing and identifying correct answers.

The Authorial Audience

Third, we examine the authorial audience (readers). These readers enter the classroom with a broad base of nonvisual information (past experience with and/or knowledge about) the specific text (discipline, body of information, or content of the specific text). Just as readers of fiction read a narrative as a part of a text created by an author and re-created (or newly created) by the reader, and just as these readers recognize the whole of the narrative structure (who is seeing and saying what from what perspectives and toward what ends), so also do these student readers of the classroom/ course discourse read the instructor, textbooks, class activities, and lectures to be a part of the narrative structure through which they may learn. But unlike the actual reader, these readers do not have the same broad base of nonvisual information (conscious knowledge of, experience with) the system and purposes of higher education, the nature and variability of classrooms, instructors, textbooks, and disciplines.

For these readers each specific narrative is not automatically part of all other narratives; each text is not automatically part of all other texts. Here is an example from a literary perspective: These students might read the Romantic period as an identifiable period of literary endeavor in which authors privileged nature and are therefore related as romantics, but unrelated (except by proximity) to the Victorian period or (by chronological accident) to the Elizabethan period. These readers may read organic chemistry in relation to inorganic, but they will not necessarily (or likely) read chemistry (regardless of its focus) in relation to literature, sociology, or mathematics— except insofar as the study of such apparently unrelated material is connected by virtue of the arbitrary definition of a college education, and is forced into being primarily through the capriciousness of something called a "general college program" or "core requirements." Consequently, although these readers are able to read the specific text with considerable ability and sophistication, they do not see it in the broader perspective of thinking and knowing across disciplines. Instead of reading the specific text as part of a larger mix of intellectual/emotional experience, they read it within the context of the given discipline and perhaps even within the narrower context of the given classroom. Because these readers are primarily controlled by the author (the professor, the curriculum, the national certification test), they have less control of the text than the text has of them.

While these readers are capable of understanding the experience of the text relative to other specifically related texts, they do not move beyond the specific contexts in order to relate this specific text to all of their past experience and knowledge. Here, truth is measured primarily in terms of the narrative of the text as it coincides with, supports, relates to, or illuminates other texts within the specific context (the given course or a specific emphasis within a discipline). These readers are primarily interested in finding out what the author is saying; they read the course as "an author's ingenious construction, and appreciate its power and skill." For these readers, the experience of the text (classroom) is somewhat more fragmented than it is for the actual reader because, unlike the actual reader, these readers do not value the specific text relative to the broader text of living and experience in general. Human experience and knowledge do not form a web for these readers; rather, knowledge is still somewhat serial and cumulative, compartmentalized and related within compartments but not necessarily across compartments.

These readers, by the way, may be among the most successful college students given that higher education, in general, neither invites nor rewards the actual reader more than the authorial reader. Indeed, some might argue that actual readers are always at risk in the educational system. And it is also likely that these are the students who love physics and math but hate English because they have become authorial (reader-) audiences in one area but have remained narrative readers in the other. This is a particularly important point because it is intended as a reminder that these categories are not fixed, developmental stages that necessarily characterize or categorize the learner across all experiences. I will discuss this more later.

The Actual Audience

Fourth, consider the actual audience (reader). In these new terms, this is the student who enters the classroom with a broad base of nonvisual information about the specific text (classroom context) and its relationship to other texts (classrooms, contexts, or disciplines). In Barthes's terms, this reader has accepted the death of the author and has been growing into a mature reader. This reader knows well the system and purposes of higher education, the nature and variability of classrooms, instructors, textbooks, and disciplines. This reader knows how to read the text both for her own purposes and for the purposes defined by the cultural context. This reader is at least as much in control of the text as she is controlled by it. This reader is not limited to reading the text within the specific context of the classroom or of the given discipline; instead, she reads any given text in relation to all past texts she has experienced. This reader is comfortably aware of the fact that the professor, the lectures, the textbook, and so forth are all part of the larger text—the course. More important, this reader knows that the course itself is part of a larger text. If the professor is accepted as the narrator, then she is a narrator who must be interpreted, just as any narrator must be: Decisions must be made about her reliability, her knowledge, biases, point of view, and limitations. As with any good narrative, she deserves to be read carefully, but her truth must be measured outside the immediate text (course) against other texts and the reader's own world view.

The actual reader is, obviously, rare. To the extent that such a reader exists in a classroom, this reader might be characterized as having the self-confidence to form and venture opinions about texts and contexts; either she understands the nature and structure of the discipline being read, or she knows that it is understandable, that a structure exists and can be discovered, or at least that the people who created the text (the authors) believe that it has a structure that is knowable. Furthermore, this reader sees that any given structure of any specific text (discipline) must be measured against (known in relation to) structures of other disciplines (texts). Texts are valued in terms of their relationships to other texts; knowledge and experience are related across time and space. This reader believes that the text is true to the extent that reflective discussion, reading, thought, and engagement prove it to have truth value.

Equally important, as rare as such readers may be, it must be remembered that because of the nature of various texts and contexts, this reader may be an ideal reader at one time and a part of the narrative audience at another— a situation directly related to the amounts of nonvisual information and confidence brought to a given text. That is, the reader who reads fully and comfortably the text of the organic chemistry class may seriously misunderstand (misread) the structure and nature of a given philosophy class. An important difference, however, between this actual reader and the other readers described in this section is this: In the midst of being a part of an authorial or narrative audience, the actual reader will know the possibility of being an actual reader. This reader can choose the audience role she wishes to employ in relation to a given text.

Indeed, one might well argue that no one is, in all situations, an actual reader. These categories of readers are, after all, metaphors—attempts to describe that which cannot be said, lies designed to suggest possible truths hidden in the surface structures that often govern perception. It would be neither wise nor desirable to approach all texts as entirely open moments in which we, the actual readers, are free to create meaning and to explore connections and contradictions. As a global or constant state of mind, this would clearly be debilitating; one would have more than a little difficulty getting across a busy street. And beyond the obvious fact that the actual reader exists only at certain moments (for some of us at fewer moments than for others), it is equally important to note that the actual reader is not only a rarity among our students. It is neither false modesty nor insult to suggest that I, you, and the best of our colleagues must constantly engage in the process of becoming actual readers, settling for those happy and rare occasions in which we genuinely succeed.

While making this important distinction—that the reader categories are metaphors and that human beings seldom operate entirely within one or the other of them, but instead move back and forth among them depending on one's own needs and the demands of given situations—it is appropriate to distinguish between these categories and the positions outlined by developmental psychologists who subscribe to stages of development. In his powerful and important book, *Forms of Intellectual and Ethical Development in the College Years* (1970), William Perry presents a persuasive and complex description of human development growing out of his work with Harvard undergraduates. It is neither necessary nor possible to present a full discussion of Perry's conclusions here, but it is important to note that our reader audiences are not intended to correlate with Perry's (or anyone else's) stages of development.

To the extent that this discussion is dependent on developmental psychology, it is no more dependent on Perry's work than it is on the work of Lev Vygotsky in *Thought and Language* (1962) or that of James Moffett in *Teaching the Universe of Discourse* (1968). Indeed, given the kinds of fanatical followers that theoretical structures sometimes attract, a direct warning is appropriate. Let us, as individuals and as a profession, avoid becoming born-again developmentalists, washed in the water of someone's theory, going forward to be fishers of students that they might be bathed in the blood of the lamb as we move them from one developmental stage to another.

Of course, I do not suggest that the creators of these developmental models and stages believe that their models fully describe human beings; they know that a model or stage is not a human being any more than a dissected frog is a frog. My own experience with high school and college students, with my own colleagues, and with adults in general leads me to believe that most (all) of us spin among developmental stages, depending upon the nature of a given issue and the circumstances in which we consider or respond to the issue. We spin about within the gyre, at times struggling to find the truth while at others being firmly committed to what we know to be right and wrong; sometimes operating as dualists and at others as committed relativists; sometimes thinking in terms of concrete operations and at others in terms of formal operations. Furthermore, while this movement among stages may seem less apparent in young children, it is clearly apparent in older students, the kinds of students with whom we have been concerned.

No individual human being can be fully described by a single reader-audience category.

CERTIFICATION VERSUS EDUCATION

Given this perspective, any teacher worth his texts will be concerned with the nature of the relationships formed between readers and narrators: What elements interfere with and/or facilitate the nurturing of actual readers? For the time being, I am primarily concerned with students and teachers as they function within the educational text and read the various works within that text. As has been suggested earlier, the conscious or unconscious intentions of these readers influence (control?) the ways in which they read and the kinds of meaning they create through their readings. When teachers teach, they are most often concerned with the intellectual development of the students. It is the general intention of a teacher that the students learn the content of the material at hand and that they learn how to synthesize, manipulate, and/or use that material. But aside from this intention, teachers have another,

highly defined function, which is delineated and described by the structure
of educational systems. Teachers certify that the material has been learned
and that students have learned how to do something with it. Through the
use of tests, class discussions, reading and writing assignments, teachers
assess the degree to which students have succeeded, and they mark these
degrees of success with grades and letters of recommendation (evaluation).
Also, as has been suggested earlier, in terms of any forward movement within
the society at large, it is these marks, these bureaucratic-corporate signifiers,
that appear to take precedence over the material learned or what one is able
to do with it.

Teachers often lament this fact; they even go so far as to speak to the
problem specifically, trying to convince the students that these bureaucratic
signifiers are secondary to the project at hand (i.e., learning something and
learning how to do something with what is learned). Teachers perceive the
students as desiring to be concerned with learning but controlled by the
threat of a bad grade and/or the desire for a good grade. They know that
the speech acts of the classroom are often not directed at the intended
performative—the process of learning—but at the process of acquiring the
certificatory signifiers so cherished by the bureaucratic-corporate world.

Thus, while some students may believe that the content or ideas central
to a given course are interesting and important, their interaction with that
content and the driving motivation of that interaction are most often controlled by the signifier that will announce to the public their degree of
achievement. They believe, sometimes rightly, that the signifier of success
will have more direct influence over their immediate prospects than what they
learn and/or what they can do with what they learn. Consequently, even if
they believe that the teacher believes that learning is paramount and that
grades are not, they often treat the teacher as just another narrator, perhaps
a naive narrator, who does not genuinely understand the place of the work
within the larger text. This often translates into a statement like the following: "It doesn't matter how much I learn in here. Without high grades and
the degree, I won't get the job I want." And of course they are usually
correct. To no small degree, colleges and universities have become certificatory institutions serving the larger corporate world. Why else would anyone
be concerned with so-called grade inflation (note the unmistakable economic
basis of the metaphor)?

Thus, situationally dependent uses of language come to predominate in
higher education. In the student's past experience, much of what has been
called learning has been primarily directed at learning something and/or how
to do something in order to evidence that one learned or learned how (on
tests, in workbooks, in essays). In college, this still is (or appears to be) the
case. Consequently, the language of the discipline, of the lecture, of the
discussion, of the printed text—even though it is intended by the author
(teacher/writer) as exploratory-expressive language, language through which

the reader is expected to create meanings, abstract from, generalize about, meditate upon, and take pleasure in—becomes situationally dependent for those who choose to read it that way in the author's absence.

The evidence for such a case abounds. In the midst of the most exciting discussion or lecture of the term, someone will ask, "Do we have to know this?" or "Will this be on the test?" These are not questions born of stupidity, ignorance, or meanness. They are not intended to demoralize the teacher. These are the questions of the ideal, narrative, and sometimes authorial audiences. They simply assert the central concern and focus of situationally dependent thinking.

Here is an interesting point. At the same time that some teachers express contempt for these questions and use them to evidence the low levels of motivation and intellectual ability that students possess, the teachers also fall into the same trap and reinforce the situation. Teachers are heard to say, in many courses, "Now pay close attention to this because it will be on the test"; or "You don't really have to know this; it won't be on the test; but it is interesting to note that. . . . " Sometimes, when asked why they use one kind of test or activity rather than another, teachers will say, "This is easier to grade (objectively) than the other activity or assignment."

More evidence? It is common in many courses for a final, major project to be required, often something like a research paper or class presentation. For the time being let us examine the ways in which the research paper operates in many courses. The teacher has assigned the paper for the following reasons: (1) to give the students the opportunity to acquaint themselves with the scholarship in the area, (2) to have the students focus on one narrow topic in the discipline in order to learn how the discipline is "done," (3) to provide students with the opportunity to use that which has been learned in the course and see it in relationship to a specific area of interest, and (4) to evidence the degree of success or achievement that the students have reached in terms of the goals and objectives of the entire learning experience. Often, in support of these reasons for assigning this project, the teacher has created carefully articulated directions for completing the assignment, sometimes supplying possible topics, bibliographies, do's and don'ts of usage and form. Generally, these assignments are presented to the students early in the course, sometimes on the first day of class as part of the course syllabus. These assignments are usually to be handed in or presented toward the end of the course, often during the last week.

How do the students read the assignment? For the ideal reader, everything is relatively clear because nothing is related, and there is no reason to worry about making sense of either the assignment or the work to be done on the paper. Insofar as this reader is at the mercy of the narrative structure, he will follow directions with some care, produce a paper that is essentially correct (proper length, correct footnote and bibliography form, and so on), but the paper almost never indicates any personal commitment to the subject or to the research itself. In many ways, for this student it is just a more difficult form of the multiple-choice test: In this case, you have to actually go out and find the correct answers. While it is obvious that the students who operate in other reader categories are likely to produce better, more interesting papers depending on their engagement and willingness to confront new ideas and make more meaning of them, the research paper itself may carry some inherent pitfalls.

Given the assertion that readers do not "reside" in a given reader category, but move among them, it is safe to assume that some kinds of assignments (readings) may cause them to operate as one kind of reader rather than another. Given the relative lack of interest that students show in many of their courses in high school and in college—"Why do we have to take all this math stuff? I like history."—it is possible that the research paper in most cases drives them into or near the position of the ideal reader. Because students so often appear to have little background knowledge (in terms of complexly organized schemata, not in terms of a body of unrelated facts) relevant to a given course, they are likely to read both the assignment and the research that follows as pretty much out of their control. In a sense, it is just the "not yet written" part of the text of the course, and it makes no more or less sense than other chapters in the entire experience.

On the other hand, students who function as actual readers (or anywhere near that higher level of languaging) may find themselves in real trouble with a research paper because they are likely to make the error of becoming genuinely interested and committed. As any scholar knows, when taking on any kind of real research project, especially if one chooses an area of investigation that is still open to discovery (and what isn't?), one can hardly guarantee that the project will be finished in the given number of weeks demanded in semester or quarter systems. (We must keep in mind that the length of a semester is also part of the larger text that the students read as they read our educational system.)

Of course, in all the generalizations I am making about students there are notable, perhaps even many, exceptions; but, in general, student involvement in these research papers borders on the ludicrous because they see them as almost entirely situationally dependent activities. The first indication that something has gone seriously awry occurs about one week before the assignment is due, when one brave student asks, "Is there a paper due in this course?" This is often followed by a barrage of nervous questions as the group begins to realize the impending disaster: "*How long* does it have to be?" "*How many* sources do we have to use?" "Does a book used as a source *count* more than an article?" "Does it have to be typed?" And, of course, the most important question, the one usually not articulated but almost always present: "*Why* do we have to *do* this?" The situation is often further complicated by the fact that the paper itself is due at the end of the semester and the students have little interest in feedback on what they have written—in fact, what they have written matters little. The grade matters greatly.

Clearly, the text is being read in different ways. However one wishes to describe the speech act involved, it has seriously misfired. But the point here is not that research papers in and of themselves are inherently bad; that would be a silly assertion about almost any kind of assignment. The point is that the function and role of such an assignment in any given course must be re-examined in terms of the real students who populate our classrooms and the ways in which they read us and our constructs.

PRINT LITERACY

In terms of mature print literacy, the kind of literacy we talk about when we discuss reading, one might ask how students read a printed text when it is part of the educational enterprise. While some college students may share the guiding principle articulated by previously mentioned high schoolers—"If they are going to tell you the answers in the first place, explain what it means, there is no reason to read the book at all"—most college students know (or at least believe) that they must read the required texts for a course. What they do with and to these texts is, in itself, revealing. Keeping in mind that for the most part they read in order to find answers to test questions—regardless of the discipline of which the text is a part, they view it to be situationally dependent—they begin to underline and/or take notes.

Although there is nothing inherently wrong with this activity, its purpose suggests a serious problem. These readers are in search of items that will bring them success on tests of various sorts. Their mission is to isolate the items that must be memorized in order that they might be identified later on a multiple-choice test. Because many college courses operate in exactly the manner the students anticipate (fitting into the schemata of previous training), this often works, especially for the so-called better readers who have figured out the classroom narrator (the teacher) so well that they know which items in the text will be of greatest importance to the narrator who will make up the test. These students underline very little, carefully picking and choosing only the material that is likely to serve as fodder for tests. Other, weaker readers do not understand the narrator or the narrative. They underline everything, later facing the debilitating and self-defeating task of trying to memorize all of it. Of course, there are some mature, sophisticated readers—some of the actual readers mentioned previously. These are the students who have somehow escaped or ignored the educational programming that has preceded this moment. They are in control of the text; they are intent on making meaning. And while these readers often do very well on the multiple-choice tests (and even better on essay tests), their success is often matched by those who are good underliners and who were able to anticipate the correct answers. Furthermore, the actual readers often find themselves seriously entrapped by multiple-choice tests because they cannot identify any answer that does not demand qualification before it can be deemed acceptable. The other students, the ideal readers who underline almost everything, do not do quite as well, of course; they get C's on the tests—if they work hard.

Because everything works reasonably smoothly for these educationally successful readers, the degree and/or nature of their literacy is seldom examined, except in terms of the situationally dependent language of the system itself. That is, when it is examined, it is primarily in relation to a standardized multiple-choice test of some sort, similar to those that are already a part of the problem. Real literacy, the ability to generate meaning through interaction with a text, is almost entirely ignored in schools and in assessment at all levels. While studies and books abound on the initial processes involved in learning to read—studies on letter recognition, word recognition, phonics, syllabic approaches, whole-word approaches, picture-word approaches, schematic approaches, and so on—by and large print literacy is often dealt with in superficial ways. The word *superficial* is important here because it explains, at least in part, why the original definition of language and reading offered earlier in this book—the possibility of making meaning—is so important. If literacy is determined to be primarily concerned with letter or word recognition, if it is primarily concerned with the correct identification of phrases and sentences, if it is defined in terms of the transmission of a body of knowledge, and if success (i.e., comprehension) is evidenced through the use of standardized multiple-choice tests with answers (pre-)determined by someone other than the reader, it is small wonder that the birth of the reader has been so little celebrated or noticed. Indeed, the educational system seems devoted to aborting the birth.

Of course, for many students superficiality has long been a matter of major importance in school: Success in language activities has depended primarily on the "correctness" of the surface structures coded or decoded. Language as the possibility of making meaning falls into a void when language as a focus on surface structures, correctness, and form rather than content is highlighted. Consequently, once the student begins to evidence literacy, once the student appears to be able to read and write, there is little need for concern. In schools, tremendous attention is paid to the teaching of reading at the initial levels. It is almost as though the system suggests that once one has learned how to read, one should then, organically, become a good reader. Those who do not do so are either intellectually unable or unwilling. As a result of the focus on situationally dependent language, surface structures, and correct answers, concerns with literacy have been co-opted and misguided. Research in the teaching of reading and pedagogy have long focused primarily on the very young student in the primary grades.

Theoretical examinations of the reading process and/or the reading of actual, mature readers have most often focused on successful, adult readers. Relatively little attention has been paid to the process by which the initiate becomes a mature reader. It is time for educational systems and, more important, teachers to actively change the focus of what has come before, to delight in the birth of the reader, and to begin to help these newborns *learn to read well* after they learn how to read.

As is true of teaching anything to anyone—whether it be a skill, a process, or a body of knowledge—if meaning making through language is what we want students to be able to do, then we must involve them in the process of doing it. On the other hand, if meaning identifying is what we want them to do, we need to recognize it for what it is and stop worrying because we are doing a relatively good job at it right now.

The first part of creating a new agenda is to be clear about what good reading is. If we want to help our students read well, we need to know what *well* entails. For starters, then, what is it that they presently do well?

Both empirical studies and anecdotal classroom experiences testify clearly to the present quality and nature of literacy among young adults. In examining the findings of the 1980 National Assessment of Educational Process (NAEP) related to literacy, Anthony Petrosky observes the following:

The most significant finding from the assessment is that while students learn to read a wide range of material, they develop very few skills for examining the nature of the ideas that they take away from their reading. Though most have learned to make simple inferences . . . , they cannot return to the passage and explain the interpretations they have made. . . . Simply put, students seem not to have learned the problem-solving strategies and critical thinking skills by which to look for evidence to support their interpretations and judgments. A large proportion (75%) have mastered initial literal and inferential skills, but very few (22%) have learned to use evidence. In addition, almost none of the seventeen year olds demonstrated any knowledge or use of techniques for analyzing a passage. Hardly any of them approached a text through such conventional procedures as paragraph by paragraph . . . analysis, or by using elements of the passage to comment on such things as setting or character development or by following a theme or idea through its progression in the text. (Petrosky in Berger and Robinson 1982: 2, 16)

That these observations are made in regard to the nation's graduating high school seniors suggests a serious degree of failure in the teaching of mature literacy.

Focusing on young adults ages twenty-one through twenty-five, another NAEP study, *Literacy: Profiles of America's Young Adults*, begins by stating that while "ninety-five percent can read and understand the printed word, . . . only a very small percentage can understand complex material" (Kirsch and Jungeblut 1987: iii). Finally, findings in a major assessment project comparing the reading abilities of freshmen and juniors at the State University College of New York (Fredonia, New York) clearly suggest that both freshmen and juniors do well at identifying the central point of an article and stating the central point in their own words, but that inferential activities involving the identification and examination of underlying assumptions and relating the material to their own lives appear to pose major problems for most of these readers. Indeed, having been a part of the team creating and scoring these tests, I believe that the students have difficulty in distinguishing between literal questions about a text and questions that invite inference. Oftentimes, their answers suggest that once they have answered the literal questions ("Identify the central point of this essay") they think the inferential questions ("Identify two or three of the author's unstated assumptions") are asking the same thing as the literal questions—and therefore are hardly worth the time it takes to answer them. Given their past experiences with school and reading tests in particular and testing in general, one reasonable explanation for their response is this: Since most test questions have correct answers, once a correct answer is given, the test should be over. If the test makers continue to ask similar questions, there are two obvious possibilities: The test makers and the tests are foolish, or some kind of trick is involved.

There is, of course, another way of explaining the findings related to students' abilities as readers and critical thinkers. While it is certainly possible that they are literally unable to read inferentially and think critically about what they have read, examining a text's internal permutations and the implications that follow from a given reading, an equally likely possibility is that they simply do not understand what is being asked of them. By responding to the task as they always have, by regarding it as a situationally dependent activity in which they are supposed to find the correct answer, they see nothing more to be done. Consequently, they are not at all sure how to deal with questions that ask them to explore what a reading means beyond what it literally says. By the same token, what is particularly striking about the results of the Fredonia assessment project is this: Although students may be characterized as having certain problems in reading, writing, and reflexive thinking, their written comments clearly indicate that they know they have not been taught to do so. As their written comments suggest, they are conscious of having somehow been cheated in their educations, and they have a pretty good sense of who and what it is they wish to blame.

That these findings describe a reality surely comes as no surprise to anyone who has taught either high school or college students, especially if that teacher has attempted to engage students in discussion of a reading assignment that moves beyond rehearsal of the literal facts of the text. But few people who have genuinely attempted to teach students to become strong readers—meaning makers who are in control of the text and who are able to make meaning of it well beyond the rehearsal of literal facts—would argue that they are inherently, psychologically or intellectually, unable to read well. Insofar as they have seldom been asked to read inferentially, insofar as they have little or no practice at doing such readings, insofar as they are not quite sure what is being asked when a teacher wants them to read in such a way, and insofar as they may suspect that a trick is involved, it is small wonder that they do not take to the activity like young professionals.

The same situation holds in the area of student writing. As has already been pointed out in previous chapters, most students do little writing in school, and what writing they do is carried out to satisfy a testing demand or to evidence that they have achieved a minimal competence in the formulaic matters of usage, punctuation, and paragraphing. Ask almost anyone in or out of college what they remember about writing and you will find the answer to be either pitifully brief or emotionally wrapped in some god-awful experience through which they associate writing with a form of torture. The truth of the matter is often most clearly brought out when one asks professors in various disciplines about their writing experiences. Invariably they point out that writing became important to them in graduate school, usually associating their memory of the extended moment with a masters thesis or dissertation. Furthermore, they are quite articulate about the experience and recognize that this was the first time that what they were writing about actually mattered to them personally and professionally. This is the first time they remember writing something that they wanted to write because they had something to say. And it comes as no surprise to teachers of writing that this is also the first time that, for most of them, they genuinely cared about matters of usage, punctuation, and form because they had invested themselves in the process of languaging and making meaning.

Some might argue that movements focusing on the improvement of student writing—writing across the curriculum (WAC)—are already directly attacking the problem by emphasizing mature literacy and the use of language as a meaning-making system. To some degree this assertion is true. Certainly, most individuals in the implementation of WAC programs intend them to have such an effect. But like much curricular reform, unless the essential nature of language as a meaning-making system is understood and forms the foundation of the implementation of writing across the curriculum, it is likely for the movement to misfire and reinforce that which has come before. For example, consider the economics professor who, after changing his introductory economics course to include student writing, remarked that "All thirty-five essays said exactly the same thing, and I found myself reading them just to find out if the correct information had been included. It seemed like a waste of time because I could have evaluated their knowledge more quickly and easily with a multiple-choice test." No one in such a situation is operating in bad faith—neither the professor nor the students. But the writing activity has not escaped the process of filling in blanks. In such cases, often in college courses, the blanks have become bigger but the job remains the same: Find out what is demanded for success and give it to them.

If we are to assist students in the process of becoming mature writers and actual readers/writers, then we must engage them in the uses of language that characterize such uses of language. Demanding that everyone do more is simply not enough because it is too easy to make it more of the same. In the following chapter we will begin to examine what it is that needs to be done.

5

Readers as Authors

Dialogue and problem-posing never lull anyone to sleep. Dialogue awakens an awareness. Within dialogue and problem-posing educator-educatee and educatee-educator go forward together to develop a critical attitude. The result of this is the perception of the interplay of knowledge and all its adjuncts. This knowledge reflects the world; reflects human beings in and with the world explaining the world. Even more important it reflects having to justify their transformation of the world. . . . To reject problem-posing dialogue at any level is to maintain an unjustifiable pessimism towards human beings and to life.

Paulo Freire, *Education for Critical Consciousness*

The title of this chapter and its emphasis on the reader as author may appear somewhat confusing at first. While writing has been mentioned from time to time throughout this work, the center of the discussion has appeared to be reading. This may also seem to be the case because most discussions of literacy—especially those in the more accessible public media—tend to focus on reading ability. But, although a central concern of this book is literacy (especially as that term is applied to what we expect or hope characterizes a college graduate), the initial and underlying concern is language as the possibility of meaning making. It is in and through dialogue—written and oral—that meaning making may move from the realm of isolated subjectivity to the sharing of meanings, the creation of new meanings, and the "transformation of the world."

LONG LIVE THE AUTHOR (READER): RESURRECTIONS

Except for superficial differences, reading and writing are essentially the same. In the moment of reading, the reader is (re)writing the text that the author has previously written. Using the totality of his nonvisual information (background knowledge, past experience, cognitive schemata, mental theory of the world, or the "all" that he is), the reader makes meaning of "that which is out there" (texts) from "that which is in there" (reader).

In the moment of author(iz)ing, the moment of writing, the writer is reading (using language to make sense of) that which is in there (inside the writer) in order to externalize it through the surface structures of language (in this case, printed symbols). In the moment of externalizing the meaning, through either oral or written surface structures, the writer engages in the recursive process of reading what he is writing and writing what he is reading. The two processes are inextricably bound together: Mature literacy necessarily includes language in all of its external forms. This is particularly important because, regardless of common sense, schools often fragment language studies into separate components. Through time-honored curricular traditions, students believe that reading is a subject one studies during reading period. Writing is separate from spelling. Speech class is unrelated to English class. Grammar, usage, and punctuation are practiced in exercises unrelated to the composing process—indeed, they are often treated as the basics one must master before moving into the composing process. And too often, the composing process is almost entirely ignored.

What is perhaps most interesting about all this fragmentation—a fragmentation based on curricular decisions bearing almost no relationship whatsoever to the nature of language and/or learning processes involved in language acquisition—is this: Once the fragmentation was established, it became the theoretical foundation for literacy studies in the schools. That such an approach is completely unrelated to the nature of language and/or the ways in which people learn language causes little concern in a system devoted to evidencing successful learning in terms of grades and multiple-choice tests. Thus, any discussion of literacy that hopes to effect constructive changes in the teaching of literacy must be carefully founded in the assertion of linguistic interrelationships and the inherent relationships between thought and language.

MAKING MEANING MEANINGFUL

As Henry Giroux suggests,

a cultural politics necessitates that a discourse be developed that is attentive to the histories, dreams, and experiences that such students bring to schools. It is only beginning with these subjective forms that critical educators can develop a pedagogy that confirms and engages the contradictory forms of cultural capital that constitute how students produce meanings that legitimate particular forms of life. (1988: 106)

If we are to move toward changing the cycle that has been discussed in the last several chapters, the meaningless activities that characterize much of the reading and writing that occur in schools, there is only one place to begin. Somehow, reading and writing must become meaningful activities for us and for our students within the educational system. The words *meaningful* and *activities* in the previous sentence have equal importance for our discussion.

If language is the possibility of making meaning, then students must be given the opportunity and the responsibility of making meaning through language. If students are to become fully literate, they must be actively engaged in using language to create meaning, to make meaning of the language that others create, to examine and analyze meanings, and to share meanings with others to whatever extent is possible. While such an agenda may suggest a de-emphasis of content in favor of linguistic processes, the real effect must be just the opposite. While it is certainly possible to use language in the service of meaninglessness, it should be clear by now that this use of language is one of the primary contributors to the creation of the present problem. Thus, if students are to become literate readers-writers-listeners-speakers, they must become literate in terms of the various contents that comprise the disciplines of the academy and the world around them. There is nothing really new in that statement: You cannot write writing; you need to know something in order to make meaning; form without content defines emptiness. The statements have been made so many times that they have become clichés. The content versus process argument is an empty one, usually employed to confuse the interrelated essence of language and thought.

The new twist, however, is this. Both the content and the process of using language to make meaning of, from, and through that content must matter to the student. Remember that the one constant in the statements made by successful professionals when referring to their own reading and writing was that they specifically remember when it began to matter to them, when they were genuinely interested in writing what they were thinking, when they were no longer doing it as some sort of artificial exercise. If we want to achieve the same degrees of literacy among the students who populate our high schools and colleges, we can no longer afford to wait for the discovery to occur in the highly selective populations that make up doctoral programs. One might reasonably hope that our educational system would help learners become excited about learning prior to their entry into graduate school. This becomes even more important when one considers the fact that not everyone who goes on for an advanced degree discovers the joy of making meaning. Not all of the people who go to graduate school engage in writing that matters to them, and only a small percentage of the general population goes to graduate school anyway. Upon the briefest consideration, it begins to look as though mature literacy has been reserved for the very few.

Even this last statement, however, suggests more order than actually exists in reality. If literacy were being reserved for anyone, that would suggest some kind of conscious plan—a reassertion of a "They" that controls our lives. The likelihood, however, appears to be that some people just get lucky, discover areas of interest, and are encouraged to use language to make sense of those areas. If such a description is at all accurate, it also suggests that the problem might be more solvable than is often intimated. This is not to suggest that a solution can be easily implemented, but it does suggest that there is a solution and that it can be implemented if we decide to do so. As has been implied throughout this work, however, the solution demands giving up the time-honored rituals of standardized, multiple-choice exams, rote learning, primary emphases on form (grammar, punctuation, usage) through the use of drills and exercises, and textbooks whose primary raison d'être appears to be to supply answers for the workbooks that accompany them. Furthermore, in a system founded upon such fragmented things, the giving up may be traumatic, to say the least.

In this process of trying to help students discover for themselves that our disciplines matter, it is imperative to discard the sermonizing of old: "Given that this work (discipline) has been longest known and best understood, most honored over the ages, you too must honor it and recognize its importance." "I know this is difficult and seems boring and meaningless to you right now, but someday you'll realize that it was good for you." In some ways and like most sermons, both contain truth, but the truth is easily ignored once one is outside the pristine walls of the church (assuming, of course, one stayed awake to listen in the first place). Even more important, however, neither sermon helps the students discover that the activity matters; each simply insists that the student recognize that it matters to someone else—the priest-teacher. (There is, of course, the Protestant ethic sermon—"you must do this to get ahead"—but this has already been discussed.)

The following discussion is split into two distinct sections, but not because the distinctions are natural. They just happen to characterize the unnatural ways in which readers, writers, speakers, and listeners are treated in the academy, and they make the present discussion easier to handle. First, we will examine the ways in which the teaching of English must change; then we will see what implications this has for all of the disciplines if we wish to help students realize the power of full, actual(izing) literacy.

TEACHING ENGLISH

In most high schools and colleges, those who teach English are generally part of what is called the English department, the department whose primary job it is, presumably, to teach English. While that all seems perfectly clear, confusion enters at a gallop as soon as one asks for a definition of the thing called *English* that the department is in charge of teaching. In the high schools the department often consists of just two or three people who happen to teach English. And as we have seen, English appears to consist primarily of practicing prescriptive grammar, punctuation, usage through drills and exercises, writing according to prescribed forms, and reading for prescribed answers. When literature is the focus, it exists as a body of information, an example for a device (irony, symbolism), or in relation to historical or biographical information. For the most part, neither "language as the possibility of making meaning" nor "literature as an interactive element within that possibility" appear to exist. It is not unusual to meet members of high school English departments who feel that they have little or no control over curriculum or implementation. In colleges, except for the monolithic, chaotic structure that defines freshman composition (which, whatever it is, we make everyone take because "it is clearly good for you"), English departments are really literature departments—and most often, if truth were told, they are literary history departments. Some might argue that inroads were made against this tradition during the late 1960s and early 1970s, but even where programs in American, black, or women's studies were implemented, even in departments where journalism and film were incorporated, and always in the case of creative writing, one generally finds that the newcomers still "can't get no respect" (Graff 1987: 232–33).

Clearly, as long as English departments regard themselves as places where a "thing" is studied (or as explication factories or basic skills practice areas), language as the possibility of making meaning does not have much of a place. If there is to be a change in the teaching of English, it must begin with a change in the conceptualization of what English is and why we are bothering to teach/study it in the first place. It is not enough to change the name of the department to something like Department of English Language and Literature because this often simply results in the reduction of linguistics to a body of knowledge to be mastered along with that of literature. Name changes have precious little to do with anything beyond a superficial, although conceivably important, recognition that a problem exists. It is not the content of English departments that is the problem, but the concept of that content as a body of information to be mastered or of forms to be practiced. It is the purpose of English departments that must be examined.

To no small extent, it has appeared for years that English departments have seen their purposes to be relatively clearly defined: (1) The English department was responsible for teaching composition (whatever composition was, it was seldom clearly defined or agreed upon and usually appeared to be a hodgepodge emphasizing basic skills and short-story analysis); (2) The English department was responsible for introducing the masses of non-English majors to the rudiments of a literary cultural heritage, exposing them to the works of Chaucer (the "Prologue"), Shakespeare (a single play, usually a tragedy), one book of *The Faerie Queene*, excerpts from *Paradise Lost*, an eighteenth-century novel, one poem from *Songs of Innocence* and one from *Songs of Experience*, a bit of the *Prelude*, "Ozymandias," and so on; and (3) The English department was responsible for introducing undergraduates to the best readings of major works that had been published in juried journals.

The professors who toiled in these departments all traveled the same weary road: Most began in freshman composition, longed for escape to the survey courses, and eventually produced their own scholarly readings and published them in order that they might teach the advanced English majors what a given work really meant. Each in turn longed for the day when he would be rewarded with graduate courses wherein he and his assistants might produce even more and better readings. In short, the road most traveled in many of the larger universities led from nearly overwhelming teaching responsibilities involving many undergraduate students with highly varied interests to relatively light teaching loads involving fewer, mostly graduate, students whose narrow interests matched those of the professor. In many colleges and high schools, where teaching is supposed to be the priority, the road seems to lead to heavier and heavier teaching loads.

That such a purpose or responsibility did not gain significant public approval or even minimal respect is not much of a surprise. Indeed, it often seems contradictory and ironic that those who cry out loudest against the literacy problems of high school and college students are most personally and professionally devoted to escaping the responsibility of assisting students in the process of achieving full, mature literacy. Clearly, the purpose of English departments and the teaching of English need to be re-examined and redefined.

RE-EXAMINING AND REDEFINING

It is the purpose of English departments to create curricula and structures through which students will actively engage in the possibility of creating, examining, and sharing meaning through language. It cannot be the purpose of English teachers concerned with the development of literacy to avoid teaching the many in order to teach the few who, like themselves, want to escape to the isolation of graduate school instruction and scholarship. Within such a conceptualization, moreover, there is room for many foci: the canon as it exists; a revised canon (which will need to be regularly revised); linguistics; journalism; film; women's, black, Hispanic, Asian, and American studies—all of these are welcome within the framework. But regardless of the content of English, the essential point is that English is an activity: English is what one does in order to make meaning of the chaotic wash of experience that surrounds all of us. As such, it is the implementation and acting out of an act of faith—a belief in the possibility of meaning.

More simply, it is not so much deciding what English is that causes difficulty: It is a language. What matters is our purpose for teaching/studying it and the ways in which we fulfill that purpose.

TEACHING WRITING

Possibly one of the least respected jobs in the average English department, including some of the most reputable English departments in the country, is the teaching of writing. Although much is said emphasizing the importance of the teaching of writing—presumably because print literacy is such an important skill for the educated person—one need examine the enterprise only briefly to see that the teaching of writing is not treated as an important endeavor. At large universities, freshman composition is taught by graduate assistants; usually they are students working on advanced degrees in English who must teach these courses in order to pay for their graduate experience and gain the degree that will eventually allow them to escape the drudgery of teaching composition. That these teachers are sometimes excellent is a fortunate accident; and they are, often, still young enough to believe that someone has rewarded them with the chance to teach anything.

At smaller universities and colleges, the situation is less easy to characterize. Some institutions believe that the activity is important and they still try to staff these courses with some of the best teachers in the departments. But more often than not, freshman composition courses are staffed either (1) by people who have advanced degrees in English but who are not expected to receive tenure, and who therefore are given enormous student loads in writing courses (guaranteeing that they will never have the time or energy to produce the mandatory publishing record for achieving tenure), or (2) by adjunct faculty—a pleasant-sounding title for people who are radically underpaid to do a difficult, exhausting job. Again, that some of these people work hard and do well has little to do with the message encoded in their treatment or in the treatment of the course.

The message is this: Freshman composition is something one tries to escape from teaching; those who cannot escape, teach freshman composition. In the past, this denigrating outlook resulted almost entirely from the fact that the elite of the profession felt that composition was drudge-work that drudges should teach to drudges so that the elite might eventually teach the high culture bound within the great texts and turn the drudges into well-rounded college graduates. While it would be grossly unfair to suggest that such an attitude characterizes everyone in the profession, this kind of elitism still exists in many English departments.

In many cases under the present system, many teachers want to escape the freshman composition courses because they involve so much work. If you are teaching a writing course, especially if you are teaching it well, current research in pedagogy demands that the class be structured more like a workshop than like a traditional classroom. One is expected to create many and varied writing assignments, teach students to peer-edit one another's work, respond to the student writing regularly and clearly, direct students toward constructive change, confer with them individually or in small groups at regular intervals, encourage rewriting and respond to that, and find creative ways to grade so that students will feel free to explore and articulate what they have to say (write). The list goes on, but it is a good list. An enormous amount of fine work has been done over the last twenty years examining the nature of the writing process in young adults and the kinds of activities that assist them in becoming better writers (and, I would argue, better readers).

But the result has most often been that those who implement the good ideas suffer the most. Because the task is not shared among most members of a given English department, because the importance of good writing is honored more in the mandate than in the budget, because the literary heritage is more important than teaching students to use language to create the possibility of meaning, those who teach freshman composition well tend to be rewarded with more freshman composition courses, more students, more weekends spent reading and commenting on student papers, less time for conferencing with students, and little expectation for respect and less hope for tenure. The irony in all of this is that a careful examination of freshman composition courses and how they are taught does not reveal that writing is being taught badly—often quite the opposite. When one searches throughout the research and the academy to find out what has actually changed in the teaching of literacy, one finds that writing has received an enormous amount of constructive attention, which has resulted in better teaching. What is startling, however, is that these ideas still have not become a part of the mainstream teaching of literature and literacy in general. What is equally startling is that this single course, freshman composition, still bears the brunt of the responsibility for "fixing" all those illiterate kids who come to college.

What elementary school teacher has not heard the high school teachers lament, "If only those elementary school teachers were doing their jobs, we wouldn't have this problem"? What high school teacher has not heard the college professors hiss, "What the hell do they teach them in high school? They certainly don't teach them how to read and write!"? What professor of English has not heard a colleague in some other department contemptuously utter, "If you people were doing your job, these kids would know how to write correctly, and the rest of us wouldn't have to bother with this trivial stuff." (Remember Pat Buchanan and the agenda of not teaching kids to think, but teaching them to think correctly?) Even someone with Harry Truman's knowledge that "the buck stops here" must be amazed at how well educators pass it whenever they can.

Of course, one might respond with the apparently obvious comments. With all the good research and good teaching in the area of freshman composition, why hasn't the problem been solved? Ironically, the answer is this:

One of the problems has been solved. As good teachers of writing know and have known for some years now, it is possible to teach students to improve their writing to the extent that most of them can produce clear, readable exposition, including a reasonable degree of mastery of the proprieties of usage and punctuation. What it takes to accomplish this radical and much-to-be-desired state of written literacy is simple to describe and possible to implement, but apparently too expensive for the system to bother about.

There are ten ingredients:

1. Teachers assist children in the production of their own stories.
2. Students begin to peer-edit and publish their work.
3. Students begin to share their cultural heritage through their stories.
4. Teachers and children establish a community of meaning makers.
5. Students write in a variety of modes for a variety of reasons.
6. Students begin to develop a conscious understanding of their own reasons for reading and writing.
7. Students begin to gain proficiency with the conventions of standard English.
8. Students and teachers transform classrooms.
9. Teachers introduce new and challenging content areas.
10. Steps one through nine create a demand for changes in teacher preparation.

1. Starting as early as kindergarten (in terms of formal schooling), children should be "writing" their stories. At this early age, of course, this may mean individual or collective story-telling in the classroom with the teacher acting as scribe. Once these stories of the children's real and imagined experiences have been written, the teacher (or an aide) transcribes them to ditto and distributes them to the children to "read." The children may not yet be very competent at decoding the print symbols, but this is how competence might be effectively and enjoyably achieved. Indeed, we do the same thing in the process of learning oral language: While the infant is in the early stages of developing oral language, parents and others around the child speak and interpret for the child, until the child begins to master the surface structures. Why would we not do the same for those who are learning to read and write? Note also that instead of practicing reading and writing, the kids are actually doing it. Not only are they learning that their oral surface structures are related to print surface structures, they are also learning that their experiences are the basis for reading and writing, that language production at the oral level can result in printed forms of language, and that the printed forms of language can be recreated through the process of reading.

2. As the children begin to progress through the elementary grades this process is repeated, but significant variations are also introduced. As the children are becoming confident and familiar with the relationships between

oral and print language, and as they are experiencing the fun of rehearsing and fictionalizing their own experiences through language (as they are becoming accustomed to taking on the role of author), they are simultaneously experiencing the process of reading one another's stories and the works of professional authors (at first as the teacher reads orally to them, and eventually as they begin to read for themselves). They regularly peer-edit one another's writing. They publish their polished writing(s) to share with one another. At all moments in the process, reading, writing, listening, and speaking are inextricably bound together, each feeding and feeding upon the other. Again, just as in the development of oral language, as the learners become more able and confident with the surface structures of print and the activities of reading and writing, less and less is done for them as they begin to use the surface structures on their own.

3. At no point in this process are reading and writing treated as part of a testing system (i.e., you read to get the answers and you write to show that you got the answers). At all points in the process, what has been written and read provides the beginning of the deconstructive cycle, but in the most positive sense that we can hope exists. That is, each moment of composing and reading, each attempt to realize the possibility of meaning through language, becomes the beginning point for more examination of the meaning that has been made, more refinements, revisions, and entirely new creations of meaning. As the children produce their realities over and over again through language, so also do they discuss and examine those realities, negotiating common ground and communal understandings to whatever extent this is possible. If there is a possibility for a shared cultural heritage, it will be brought into being through these ongoing processes and no list will be necessary.

4. At no point in this process will the personal experience, feelings, and ideas of these young authors be denigrated or denied. Moreover, the opportunity to create one's realities and meanings through the personal-experience essay will be encouraged throughout the learning process from kindergarten through graduate school and beyond, if the writers choose to continue using this mode as part of their meaning-making activities. But this does not suggest that students will spend all of their school years writing "nothing but mushy personal stuff, thus contributing to the egocentric, radical subjectivism that already plagues our republic." (The quotation marks simply suggest that if somebody hasn't already said this, someone will say it as he chooses to misunderstand what I am saying here.) Because much of the writing will be made public through some form of publishing, even if it is only reproduced for classmates through the modern miracle of purple dittos, the personal experiences that are articulated will be shared, examined, and further explained. Rather than simply existing as a subjective statement of one's own experience, something that neither can nor should be questioned, these essays will become part of an ongoing dialogue intended to

help the participants develop their ability as reflexive thinkers as they become aware of the literal facts of their own experiences and the meanings that follow from those experiences.

This is a particularly important point because most writing teachers have found that many older students do a reasonably strong job of narrating their own personal experiences, often even supplying the development and detail that appear lacking in so much of their other writing. However, students who write powerful personal narratives are often unable to articulate the meaning of the experiences or the relationships that one experience has with another in their overall development as human beings. Thus, emphasis on the personal essay, examination of the experiences making up these essays, and conscious generalizing about and abstracting from those experiences are at the heart of the psychological and intellectual growth of the students. To paraphrase Stanley Fish's terms (1980), the negotiation of these student texts allows for the possibility of many texts within the class and the beginning of some sort of communal agreement on the nature of experience and reality among the learners.

5. To have people writing in a single mode with a single purpose—even if that mode is the personal essay and the purpose is to explore the meaning-making process within one's self and others—is still to limit the learner unnecessarily. Thus, as the learners advance through the grade levels they will experiment with many modes of reading and writing. They will write monologues, dialogues, poetry, exposition, letters, short plays, fiction, and even analytical essays, research papers, interviews, news reports, and so on. The point is to engage them in as many normal uses of language as possible, always keeping the linguistic interaction focused on the purposes of externalizing creative/critical thinking and communicating to self and to others through the surface structures of language.

While the content of the writing must always come from the author's experience, the experiences that contribute to the nonvisual information or mental theory of the world will come through a variety of classroom activities including viewing films; reading books, magazines, and poems; going on field trips; and engaging in ongoing creative-intellectual activities at the center of the educational experience. Unlike the present school agenda, however, these activities will be explored, discussed, written about, analyzed, fictionalized, poeticized, critiqued, and shared as part of the creation of the possibility of meaning rather than a necessary part of grade-getting.

6. Students will be engaged in real writing because they will have purposes for their work that move far beyond the arbitrary, situational motives that exist when writing is done primarily for a grade. Students will write to get something "outside of their heads" so they can look at it and examine it, or to "get something straight" inside their own heads (journal writing, personal essays), or to share their ideas with others in order to get something done (directions, persuasive essays, letters), or to share and explore an idea,

feeling, or concept with others (analytical/critical essays, fiction, poetry, drama) (Tchudi 1980). Students will read because the writing part of their creative-intellectual experience is real: It exists because someone in the class or a professional writer wrote something she wanted to share with them. Having had the experience of writing in order to make others understand something, and having read and discussed the work of other students because it contains living, breathing ideas and experiences, they will approach the act of reading with a new and genuine sense of purpose that has nothing to do with comprehension tests. They will read for the same reasons mature readers read, in order to enjoy an idea created by another, in order to share the self or meaning that others have externalized, and in order to gain the information that will assist them in generating new meanings. School language will function in the same normal, real ways that oral language functioned as they effortlessly and efficiently learned the language of their home and sociocultural environment. Classrooms become transformed into the space in which dialogues occur and are examined (Bakhtin 1981; Ritchie 1989; Halasek 1990).

7. Students will learn standard surface structures of usage, punctuation, and written grammar because the language they use will be real and will be used (created) for real purposes. Because they will be immersed in various language uses—including (1) the modeling and exemplification provided by the teacher as they learn to rewrite and standardize the grammar and usage of their own writing, and (2) the modeling and exemplification they experience as they read edited versions of their own work and published versions of professional authors—they will learn the acceptable standards of written language. They will become natural users of the standard forms because they are creating and experiencing them regularly, day after day, as their use of language as the creation of the possibility of meaning becomes a standard and normal part of their day at school. Punctuation, usage, and grammar will become functional parts of the literacy program as students discover that proper punctuation allows them to write more clearly, that professional writers use standard forms of punctuation in their own writing, that paragraphing is a form that derives its sense from their contents, and that various forms of usage are appropriate or inappropriate depending on the audience, situation, and desired effect. But they will not simply be involved in the drudgery of practicing correct usage and punctuation in preformed sentences with preformed problems and presupplied answers to be plugged in. They will not simply study all this "stuff" as they have in the past. Instead, they will be making changes in their own writing, seeing and employing the proprieties in terms of their functions within a given linguistic situation.

Likewise, one dialect will not be held above another as inherently superior or sacred. Students will be encouraged to speak and write in their own dialects at the same time that they examine the specific features of other American dialects. Since almost all printed material in this country follows a relatively conservative print dialect that crosses geographic and ethnic lines of oral dialect, they will be expected to become competent in the standard print dialect.

To some readers this proposal may sound simplistic—naiveté bordering on stupidity—but this is not the case. If speakers of nonstandard dialects are actively engaged in the reading and writing of standard printed texts, they will become competent users of the standard print forms, both as readers and as writers. If the teacher, from the earliest point in this scenario, is retyping their oral stories, conforming to standard usage and syntax, the children will learn this the same way they learn anything else. The important thing is that they are actively using the standard forms and not simply doing exercises on them. It is equally important to note that none of this has much to do with their oral dialects. As long as people are ghettoized and the ghettos are characterized by a given dialect, the people of that community will speak this dialect. Given the opportunity and the reason to actively interact with another dialect community, and given the slightest desire on the speaker's part to become competent in the new dialect, the change will occur quickly and naturally. But oral dialects are not at all the issue in print literacy; therefore, this is all that will be said here about the issue. And all this aside, it makes more sense to cherish the richness and diversity of dialects than to denigrate them.

8. While such changes are being implemented, the standard classroom experience must change radically. Teachers can no longer sensibly hope to hold forth from the front of the classroom "telling" students "stuff," and they can no longer fill the school day with nonsensical exercises and drills. Likewise, students can no longer move like robots from class to class as bells or buzzers direct them, waiting only to be told what to do in order to succeed. Classrooms will have to turn into workshops wherein students and teachers work together to explore, examine, and articulate that which they and others have explored, examined, and articulated. These changes also demand much greater involvement on the parts of teachers and students in that the lists generated by so-called curriculum experts or E. D. Hirsch will not be there like academic pacifiers to provide instant security for all the little suckers in the system. Instead of education as pacification for certification, this change will involve all of the turmoil that is a part of genuine learning.

9. These changes do not deny (explicitly or implicitly) that in order to be able to learn certain things or advance in certain ways in many disciplines, one needs to "know some things" and "know how to do some things." Consequently, such changes bring even greater demands on teachers to create learning activities that exploit the natural curiosity and intelligence of the students in such a way as to engage them in the hard work of learning. Many teachers are already succeeding in doing this; many others need to make the effort. Of course, such changes must happen over time. No one

expects that students trained in the tradition of "Will this be on the test?" are going to suddenly become born-again creative learners; no one can see the light until someone begins shining it.

10. Teacher preparation must be changed radically to prepare teachers to create and implement new theories of instruction and workable, effective methods of instruction. These must grow out of the needs of the learners and be founded on a working knowledge of how people learn, rather than simply meeting the needs of the "mechanical system of education" under which we all presently suffer (*A Blueprint for Learning and Teaching*, 1987).

HOW WORKSHOPS WORK

For many years now, countless teachers of writing (and of other subjects and activities) have employed the workshop model as their system of teaching. So in one sense there is nothing particularly new here. In another sense this is all quite new because I am suggesting that all English courses be taught as workshops. Moreover, while many creative English teachers have been experimenting with the workshop model for years, turning it into a productive, stable approach to language learning and literacy in general, many others have not. As I have established in earlier chapters of this book, most teaching at both the high school and college levels is characterized by "an overwhelming reliance on teachers talking to students," even though research indicates that "only a fraction of students learn best through listening" (*A Blueprint* 1987: 8–9). While some may argue that teacher-talk should command the center of the learning experience—after all, it is the teachers who already know what they are talking about—such logic fails miserably upon closer examination. Perhaps it is true (or should be true) that teachers already know what they are talking about; it does not follow that having them talk about what they already know has much to do with someone else's coming to know it. If we were simply trying to find out if teachers knew their subject matters, our present system might not be a bad one. But a system whose purpose is to help learners learn must rely on active interaction among and engagement of those who are supposed to be learning.

What is particularly unique in suggesting the workshop model is this: I am not making the suggestion because I am committed to the method or because it is popular, hip, or the "in" thing. In fact, I am not even suggesting a method as much as I am suggesting an approach to learning within which many methods might be employed. I continue to believe that methodology should be created and employed by teachers as they see fit in terms of the learners with whom they work. But I am committed to workshops as a generalized approach to all teaching. It may be an unfortunate irony that even though workshops are fashionable and hip, they are still honored more in the journals than in the practice.

By now it should be obvious that all the discussion preceding this section theoretically supports the workshop as the most sensible approach to teaching anything to anyone, and particularly anything that has to do with language, literacy, and thinking. If growth in literacy is naturally a part of creative, interactive uses of language within a language community, then English classes must be structured to promote those creative, interactive moments.

I begin with a description of what the workshop model does not include. Workshops are not "touchy-feely things in which everything you do is okay because everything I do is okay and we all just feel so darn good about the whole thing that we can barely control ourselves." Workshops are not *un*structured, *un*mediated, *un*evaluated, *un*controlled. Workshops are neither product nor process oriented, one to the exclusion of the other. Workshops do not lack criteria, deadlines, responsibilities, or obligations. Workshops do not focus only on individualized learning or on communal learning, one to the exclusion of the other. Workshops do not demand the absence of texts or textbooks, lectures, legitimate authorities, guidelines, constraints, or common sense.

Rather simply, workshops are places where people work, and the purpose and direction of the work is both individually and communally structured with certain goals in mind. While the emphasis in workshops is on the equal worth of all the participants, workshops also emphasize the exploitation of expertise: That is, those who are particularly good at one thing assist those who are in the process of learning. Some have argued that under this system the weaker students benefit tremendously because they are being helped by the better students. But the strong students suffer because they are not learning more and are becoming even more proficient in their areas of strength. Consequently, the argument goes, the strong benefit the weak, but the weak—by virtue of their weakness—deny the strong an opportunity to become stronger. It is an old argument that has wended its way through political, social, and economic theories for many years.

But regardless of the sense the argument may appear to make when introduced into these other areas, it makes even less sense in the area of education. First, such an argument assumes that the good student is good at everything: That is, the weak students will remain a constant as will the good students, and therefore the good students are always giving the help and the weak are always benefiting. While such an argument may accurately describe certain extremes—some learners clearly are superior readers, writers, and thinkers, while others appear always to struggle through these language-based activities—the vast majority of learners are good at some things and weak at others, competent at one moment and incompetent at another, depending on the specific task, purpose, or subject at hand. Under these more typical circumstances, those who need help in one situation are those who give the help in another. Moving out of the area of English studies for the moment, variations in expertise become even more apparent as one finds that the student who needs assistance in revising, rethinking, and editing a piece of writing in composition class is the same student who tutors his peers in science or calculus.

In the workshop approach, everyone teaches. This provides an important argument supporting the workshop model in which students and teachers work together to promote and facilitate learning. The argument is based directly on the personal/professional experiences of teachers everywhere. What teacher has not said, "I never really understood that until I had to teach it"? Instead of recounting the inherent nonsense of the old adage, "Those who can, do; those who can't, teach," we need to rethink the teaching experience. Often, those who do—and some who do something quite well—are not conscious of what they are doing or of the nature of the activity itself. That is, they simply do it, or at least appear to do so. These are the so-called natural athletes, musicians, writers, and so on.

Assuming that these people actually exist, they are relatively few in number. (And they are not necessarily good teachers.) More typical are those who, through natural ability, become relatively good at something and then proceed to learn more about it in order to become expert. While genius may be inherent and may show itself in explosive cries of "Aha!", in my own experience, those who might qualify as geniuses or experts appear to have gained their expertise through years of hard, painstaking work and thought.

Those who teach, then, are those who understand the nature and essence of what it is they are teaching. Not only can they normally do whatever it is they teach, but they also understand it. When they say that they never really understood it until they taught it, they are also saying that through the teaching of something one comes to know it in a special sense. There may be no more powerful learning experience than that of teaching something to someone. But such an argument should not be confused: The teacher may not be an expert at doing what is being taught; however, the teacher should be an expert at understanding what is involved in that which is being taught, an expert in the process and stages involved in learning whatever is at the center of the given discipline. The teacher who teaches fiction or poetry need not be an expert in writing novels or poems; he must be an expert in teaching fiction and poetry. As learners, students can and should be actively involved in the teaching process, trying to come to know the inner workings and nature of whatever it is they are studying. The teacher should be an expert at teaching, helping the students structure and interact within various teaching/learning situations. This constitutes the genuine nature of workshops. Within such a framework no one's time is wasted and everyone's varying expertise is happily exploited.

The teacher, who is presumably expert at planning and structuring the learning situation and who has had experience in facilitating large- and small-group activities, structures the workshop and sequences the learning experiences (always, of course, being prepared to restructure and manipulate sequences when appropriate). Students, along with the teacher, participate in small- and large-group discussions, read, comment on, and often even edit one another's writing. While the teacher is ultimately responsible for establishing criteria for success or for measuring good work, both students and teacher work together to establish and understand these criteria so that the emphasis is on the quality and sense of the activities at the center of the learning experience rather than on the grades that will result.

While listening to someone can be considered a kind of work, in a workshop it is an active part of the work, mixing generously with reading, writing, discussing, examining, reviewing, rethinking, revising, criticizing, and interacting over, through, and about the language activities that are at the center of the experience. Teacher-talk is generated by student needs as perceived by students and teacher: When students have questions or should have questions, it is the teacher's job to help them find answers. If this involves lecturing, then lecturing is the appropriate activity in that setting. Reading and writing assignments are not presented as activities that exist as ends in and of themselves. Instead, the workshop activities are created to achieve the following: (1) to foster learning through the discovery of problems and questions, the examination of ideas (both in the professional literature that forms the subject focus of the class and in the work produced by the students who are responding to and/or creating the subjects under investigation); (2) to foster learning through the active interchange and examination of information and opinion; and (3) to foster learning through the introduction of new ideas, information, and experiences in and out of the classroom setting.

As might be obvious even from this generalized description, workshops are difficult for both teachers and students for several reasons. (Of course, they are also infinitely rewarding, fun, and lively). Teachers must be experts in the learning process and not simply experts in the subject matter they are teaching; they must be highly creative in the structuring and planning of workshop activities; and they must be sensitive to the appropriate times for small-group activities, individualized activities, lectures, and evaluation. As someone should have said about teaching, "It's an impossible job, but somebody's gotta do it!"

Students, for their part, must be present in class, awake, on time, and prepared. The unprepared student in a workshop is unable to participate, and the student who is unable to participate is not in the workshop. Contrary to what some critics often suggest, this approach is much more demanding of the students than the traditional lecture/discussion/test approach that is so common at many colleges and high schools. Nodding and smiling just will not do. Even students who desire only to get a decent grade and pass the course are confronted with serious problems in workshops because they are expected to be actively involved in the learning process. As is so often the case, the gain that students make here in terms of self-direction, participation in the creation of criteria for evaluation, and active participation in their own learning process comes at the great expense of the anonymity and indifference that they might previously have relied on in their "learning" experiences. To be a participant in a workshop is to be responsible to both the larger and smaller groups of students in whose learning each participates.

So if someone asks, "Is there a text in this class?" the answer is that "You can bet your subjective, relativistic bottom (dollar) that there is!" In fact, there are quite a few texts. Most of them—students, teacher, and the various linguistic productions that they are generating—are in a constant state of becoming because this classroom is a place where meaning making is the priority.

SOME EXEMPLIFICATION

By now one might reasonably wonder what the specifics of a workshop model are. For example, how does one teach *The Adventures of Huckleberry Finn*, writing, or *Hamlet* employing such a model? I strongly resist modeling a classroom method. Teaching methods are best when they are devised by those who are going to employ them with a specific group of students, and teacher preparation must begin to produce teachers who are fully professional in the sense that they need not rely only on prepackaged methods. In fact, most methods that reject literary explication as a business activity with students as the dutiful consumers of predetermined explications are worth trying. We need methods that short-circuit the "explication industry" (Graff 1987: 232–33).

But some exemplification may help. Keeping in mind that we are dealing with students who are doing or have done reasonably well in high school, whose ability to score well on standardized tests is not in question, and who are relatively used to dealing with any text as something that contains answers to prescribed questions, we already know that certain beginning points will work reasonably well. We know, for example, that we can assign the text, give a due date, and give them a quiz of some sort in order to insure that, at the very least, they have read the novel. I am not, in this discussion, going to explore the ways in which a teacher might convince an unwilling class to actually read the entire text without threats or coercive measures of some sort. For many years teachers have experimented with approaches to solving such a problem. Their approaches have included assigning the text a series of chapters at a time, following each reading assignment with a fact-based quiz; and reading parts of the text aloud to the class, followed by in-class reading time.

While such approaches may at times be necessary, they are not normally necessary with the kinds of students I have been discussing—students who have genuinely accepted the system and its rules and who wish to succeed. Nevertheless, most coercive approaches simply repeat what students have experienced so often; generally speaking, they are a part of the cause of the problem we are trying to eliminate. Consequently, any use of coercion for the sake of coercion in the learning process must be counteracted if real learning is to occur. Furthermore, any suggestions proposed here do not imply that their implementation will suddenly turn things around, producing happy, intense, mature readers and writers who are enjoying and exploring literary texts on their own. Any change will take time; and it will be both difficult and frustrating on occasion.

(But we might try getting used to this concept: Real changes take time; real learning takes time; intellectual and psychological growth may appear suddenly, but they take time. Perhaps it is long past the time for all of us to begin taking the time and giving it to the students so that they might engage in sensible learning activities.)

One way or another, the students have read the text and have processed it at some basic level of decoding: They know who the characters are and they know the basic plot. In some cases, this initial step may involve showing all or part of a film or stage production based on a given work. Or it may involve the teacher telling the students the basic elements of a given text in order to make it more accessible to them. In this scenario, this is the beginning of the learning experience. Depending on the reading abilities of the students, some teachers might choose at this point to use an entire class period (or even more) to rehearse the facts of the plot, asking fact-based questions about what happened to whom and why, making sure that whatever text "is in this class," it is more or less the same text.

While this is often the end of the literary experience in too many class-rooms, the point at which the objective test is given, it is by no means even slightly adequate. The argument that it is enough or even desirable to simply introduce or expose students to works of literature is a specious one. It conjures up images of teachers with the complete works of Shakespeare hidden under long trenchcoats about to flash the work before the students' eyes. The idea is as specious as the image is offensive. In fact, if English teachers were honest, they would have to admit that simply being introduced to a literary work or its plot is an essentially useless experience—not to mention that it invites in *Cliff Notes* as the new curriculum (Graff 1987: 231). If there is to be a genuine text in this or any class, it cannot be defined by the physical book that each student is expected to read. The text, if there is to be one, is that which is created by readers reading, by readers creating meaning as they process the print and as they interact with the book and their fellow readers. The teacher must structure and facilitate these processes and, at the same time, provide the background and direction necessary to allow the process to occur.

In a world in which many students have a muddied sense of history, often being confused about chronology and facts, the teacher may have to give information about the time period in which Huck lives, the workings of slavery, the sociopolitical attitudes regarding blacks, the differences between life upriver and downriver, the legal rights of a free black, the purposeful breakup of slave families, the geography of the areas mentioned in the novel, and so on. Some teachers might choose to present this information in the form of a lecture, others in the form of a printed handout, and others might incorporate delivery of this information during the rehearsal of the plot as part of a class discussion. I have not found most students to be particularly attentive to lectures, especially students who are not majoring in the subject under discussion and who may not yet have discovered a deep personal interest in the activity. Furthermore, most of our students already know about racism, mistreatment, outcasts, and abuse. Consequently, they might begin by creating their own dialogues, fictions, and dramas based on these topics. Then, as the student creations become part of the classroom dialogue, they might serve as both incentive and context for the additional, specific information the teacher might supply. My own preference leans heavily toward such activities with the aim of incorporating additional background information in the discussion of the novel itself. But regardless of method, the point of all this moves well beyond a history lesson and focuses on the active involvement of the learners.

At a theoretical level, as has been suggested earlier, the students need background information in order to understand anything they read. The more information they have and the more fully they understand, the richer their potential understanding of the work will be. But the background information, like the novel itself, cannot be constructively presented in a void. Remember, the point here is to help students actively, creatively make sense of the activity rather than simply come away with factual knowledge. In this scenario, they still need the factual knowledge, but the purpose is to make it part of a larger cognitive network that contributes to their growing understanding of the novel, their own private experience with the novel, the experiences other young readers have with the novel, and the various ways in which professional critics view the novel. But as always, the point is not to tell them the best or most accepted interpretation of the work. The point is to help them make their own conscious choices about the meaning of the novel and its relevance to the world of their own private experience and the experiences of others. If we take the problem of shared contexts seriously, we must directly attempt to assist students in achieving more conscious contextual understanding of the texts we ask them to read.

At the practical level, each step in this early process of first reading the novel, then rehearsing and intermixing discussions of the literal events of the novel and the appropriate background information, contributes to a growing understanding of the novel itself and fuller experiencing of the text as text. Of course, the amount of time given to these activities depends on several variables, and the decision is clearly one that can only be made by a given teacher with respect to a given group of students, their needs, and the purposes of the undertaking. The college teacher who starts with Twain's novel in order to begin a careful examination of period writers and who is working with undergraduate English majors will almost certainly make different decisions than the teacher who includes the novel as part of a survey of the American novel for non–English majors taking the course to fulfill part of their general college program requirements. The high school teacher may be primarily concerned with having the students get on the raft with Jim and Huck so that they can experience the journey that constitutes the world of Twain's novel. In such a case, student response and involvement might reasonably supersede the text itself.

With a reasonably committed group of students who have already had some experience with the time period and perhaps even with the author, much of this early activity may be unnecessary; with another group, these initial activities may take up as much as three or four hours of class time—perhaps even more. (And if that is too much time, then there isn't enough time to bother with the novel in the first place.)

The next step is to resurrect the author, but not the author of the text under discussion. In this case, rumors of his death are well founded; Twain just isn't coming back. In this step, the students become authors as they begin to write their responses to the novel. While these early essays may take whatever form the students choose—and some may choose to write relatively standard, critical essays—the students should be encouraged to experiment at this point. As was suggested earlier, students should be encouraged to explore their own creative responses to the novel and its events. But since these papers are seldom intended to be more than three or four pages in length, the writing activity also becomes a lesson in focusing on and developing one or two points fully. I always provide them with the option of creating their own topics, writing on whatever point, event, character, section, or idea from the novel most piques their interest. For students who have had little or no experience with such an open-ended task, I also provide a list of topics they might choose from or scan to see some of the possibilities. In the case of *Huckleberry Finn*, I sometimes suggest they think about what the novel might have been like if Jim had been the narrator; I suggest they rewrite a given scene from his point of view. Or they might examine their own feelings about the much-examined closing chapters of the novel and the apparent change that takes place as the nonsense of Jim's escape takes over the action of the novel. Some may wish simply to vent their rage over Jim's treatment, perhaps relating it to racially oriented events they have experienced or heard about. But whether they focus on the ironic role of religion in the novel (or in their lives), or the idea of running away from it all and gaining a new life, or setting out for the frontier, or child abuse, or alcoholic parents, simply doesn't matter at this point, particularly if they actively engage the topic.

Of course, some do not actively engage the topic. This is a real world we are discussing. But it is still only the beginning of the activity. The students understand that their papers eventually will be graded and that they are expected to work hard on the production of the paper, but they also know they will have an opportunity to rewrite the paper if they choose. Most important, they know (and eventually even come to believe) that their grade will not be based solely on their feelings or opinions as much as it will be based on their ability to focus on one or two specific points and explain themselves as fully, as concretely, and in as interesting a way as possible.

Also, in terms of this particular method, some teachers argue that if students know they will have the opportunity to rewrite, they put little effort into their initial drafts. Therefore, the method simply does not work. Most teachers, however, reject "baby and bathwater" arguments and are willing to give the idea a try. The simple fact of the method in operation is this: Some students will abuse it, but most do not. First, peer pressure is operating: They generally do not want to look like fools in front of their friends and classmates. Second, most of them quickly find out that it pays to be serious from the beginning of the activity because they learn more and have some fun doing it. Third, those who continually and purposefully choose to undermine the activity can be put together to form their own unproductive group. (We really should be more open about giving them an opportunity to see the results of their own [in]actions.)

Once these papers have been written, they become the focal point for small- and large-group discussions in the class. These discussions will generate a beginning point for an open-ended discussion of the novel and a backdrop for other discussions that will follow. Students split into small groups of three or four. Each student reads the papers of the others in the group; this is a form of peer-editing, although the purpose is not overtly to help the author produce a revision. Each reader is expected to identify, in writing, the central point of the other students' papers and very briefly explain why she agrees or disagrees and/or what additional information might help explain the central point or better persuade the reader of whatever position is being taken. Once each student in the group has produced this kind of feedback on each of the papers she is reading, the students discuss each paper in turn, sharing their feedback and exploring their ideas, feelings, responses, and/or arguments regarding the novel.

Depending on time, the size of the small groups, and class size, the immediate followup for these small-group discussions may take place during the same class meeting. I have found that groups of three are able to write their feedback and generate a discussion of each of the papers in the group relatively quickly. Once they have become accustomed to the activity and know that they are to get down to work in their groups, they finish their commentary and discussion in about forty-five minutes. In the classes I teach, which last eighty minutes, this leaves time to begin the large-group discussion. In a standard, fifty-minute class, students would have to regroup briefly at the next class and quickly review their written commentaries before beginning the large-group discussions. Whether one is limited to fifty minutes or periods of longer duration, the activity is easily adapted.

However the time is handled, the follow-up discussion of these small groups is essential to the deeper exploration of their ideas and of the novel itself. Again, to answer Stanley Fish's question, there is a text in this class; in fact, there are quite a few at this point, but they have yet to be negotiated. For those who may worry that the "rumors" of Twain's death are not at all exaggerated and that this approach is leading to the very disappearance of the novel itself, reassurance is forthcoming. It is essential to note here that this reader-response approach to a novel or any other literary work does not necessitate either the implementation of a psychoanalytic approach in which the readers and their responses are analyzed (such as the approaches of Bleich and/or Holland), nor need it replace the original text through an assertion of radical subjectivism. That it can allow such occurrences is true; but it does not necessitate them. In fact, I would argue that it is the central purpose of this approach to avoid both the psychoanalysis of the readers and/or the loss of the original text because the follow-up discussions are directed at a re-examination of the text through and in relation to the readers' various responses to and perceptions of the text.

In the first large-group discussion following the small-group examinations of the students' papers, each group reports to the entire class the central points that were raised in the papers written by the group members. While there are many possible methods to direct this discussion, I generally proceed as follows, allowing and even encouraging a certain amount of chaos. As a group reports, I write down (on paper or on the blackboard) the major foci that are being mentioned. This may, at first, appear to be an enormous task, but we did all read the same book, and while responses vary—especially at the level of opinion—the topics of interest tend to be similar. If a small group finds that another small group is reporting something very similar or directly contradictory to points raised in their own discussion, they are encouraged to raise these issues as soon as the first group finishes reporting. Consequently, while we may have planned to go around the room with each group reporting in turn, the likelihood is that the discussion jumps around all over the place. Obviously, teachers who function poorly in the midst of such activity might wish to structure it more rigidly. I find the apparent chaos constructive for the moment, but only because I know that I will structure it later.

At this point, reader responses have almost entirely subsumed the text. As certain points are made, some students may appeal to the authority of the original novel for evidence of the sense of their position, but others will have articulated responses that have only vague associations with the novel as a literary masterpiece. For example, I vividly remember a freshman whose written response to *The Stranger* by Albert Camus articulated an intimate, personal identification with the character Meursault. I was initially stunned

as her paper carefully explained that Meursault was a highly sensitive character who had been mistreated at some earlier time by his mother and, she
suggested, other lovers. I found her construction of Meursault to have almost
no identifiable basis in the text itself, but once I managed to recover from
my own initial surprise, I watched her paper become a center for one of the
most engaging and important discussions of the ideas associated with exis-
tentialism and, eventually, the Camus text, that I have ever seen occur in
a classroom. Because her written response was well articulated and sincere,
it caused others in the class—students who had responded to the novel at
an understandable distance—to engage in powerful, personal ways.

This subjectivism may not be as much of a problem as some might at first
expect. The point of this activity—the point of the reading, writing, and
discussion—is not to "teach the novel" in terms of a predefined set of
meanings or as a set of facts. As I have asserted throughout this discussion,
the point is to encourage the students to become fully literate readers, writers,
and discussants by encouraging them to move from the possibility of making
meaning to the act of making and sharing meanings. Given that the theoretical discussions preceding this chapter argue that such an act of making
meaning and the moment in which it may occur are fleeting at best, the
importance of such a classroom activity should become all the more obvious.
While some may argue that this is not enough, it is all we can hope to have.

Once this first, somewhat chaotic discussion is completed, many possibilities follow. Students might work on their own to revise their original
drafts or to write entirely new responses generated by the class discussion.
In large or small groups the students, with the guidance of the teacher, might
begin to organize the list of topics and responses generated in the previous
discussion. However the review of the original chaos occurs, it is most important that everyone begin to realize that some responses appear more
closely and directly tied to specific passages and events in the novel itself,
while others appear to be centered primarily in the reader's own past experiences, with little focus on the specifics of the text.

This approach is particularly important for several reasons: (1) It allows
students to begin to see that although their own subjective feelings and
opinions are honored, there is a public reality outside their private one and
literacy demands an ability to read the outside one as well as to articulate
the inside one. Students can begin to differentiate between purely relativistic
positions and positions negotiated by various interpreting subjects; (2) it
allows a discussion of feelings and opinions generated by the reading of the
novel, although clearly distanced from the events of the novel, without
destroying or disregarding the novel; and (3) it encourages a discussion of
the specifics of the novel itself in relation to the readers' responses, encouraging close examination of language and events in the novel to discover
major or subtle variations in the readers' various readings.

Finally, as the novel is re-centered and re-examined, the teacher has the

opportunity to provide the students with information and other interpretations of the novel that may generate even more readings and responses from
them. At this point the teacher may choose to re-emphasize certain biographical or historical information, exemplifying how such a critical approach
excludes some responses and supports others. The teacher may choose to
present contradictory "new critical" readings, inviting the students to examine these as other texts, similar at least in kind to some of the readings
they produced. As they examine the work of professional critics, they may
begin to examine and question why some readings seem better than others,
why some are more widely accepted than others, or how some appear to be
influenced by the sociohistorical environment of the critic. Finally, the teacher
may choose to teach students to use supporting and explanatory evidence
from the text in order to explain their own positions more fully—or at least
to recognize when they have not done so or when they are unable to do so
because their positions, ideas, and feelings have little to do with the ways
others experience the text.

It should be clear that what appeared to begin in subjective chaos ends
in a relatively traditional setting. It should also be clear that teachers and/
or students might view the process as a somewhat painstaking, long, and
deceitful way of arriving at the same place literary studies so often arrive in
classrooms. That is, to begin with student responses in order to end up with
the best that has been thought and said, in order to show the students how
silly their own thinking and saying has been—or in order to show them the
"real" meaning of the text—is to defeat the entire purpose of the approach.
Furthermore, the approach need not end up as it has been described here.
One might choose to begin with time-honored critical readings of a given
text and have students respond to and critique them through open-ended
writing assignments and discussions.

It is not the specific method that is important. It is the theory underlying
it that must constantly be kept in mind. All of the texts—those written by
the students and those written by professional authors, dead and alive—are
part of the deconstructing, deteriorating moment. Each moment of birth is
joined by its moment of dying; each moment of dying demands birth, rebirth,
and resurrection. A self and a consciousness that are constantly, always/
already in the process of deconstructing must engage the possibility of always/
already engaging in the process of becoming.

To the extent that teachers and students understand and accept that last
sentence, education, classrooms, teaching, learning, and literacy become
significantly more important than even the most adamant supporters might
suggest.

6

Literacy beyond the English Class

Why write?

To be surprised.

That's the answer from writers who spend their lives returning morning after morning to the lonely discipline of the writer's desk. They write to find out what they will say. Peter Taylor says, "Writing is how you discover what you think." Maxine Kumin states, "I write a poem to find out what it is I want to say. It's a burrowing inward." Ruth Prawar Jhabvala adds, "I just sit down at ten in the morning and write until one and it slowly evolves. I have no idea what's going to happen." Bernard Malamud, who has said, "Writing teaches the writer," explains: "A familiar voice asks: Who am I, and how can I say what I have to? He reads his sentences to see if they answer the question. Thus the writer may tell his fortune."

Donald Murray, *A Writer Teaches Writing*

One might reasonably paraphrase all that Murray's speakers suggest by substituting the words *read* and *reading* for *write* and *writing*. We read (listen, view) to find out what is being said. We read to discover what we and others think. Reading is a simultaneous burrowing inward and extending outward. Reading teaches the reader. Reading, writing, speaking, listening, viewing, creating—these are all variations on a single melodic strain that sings itself throughout our lives and helps us define what it means to be human.

Well, then, perhaps it is time to stop leaving matters of such importance up to some isolated, artificially fragmented discipline called English!

For years the problem of literacy has been left almost entirely up to the language arts teachers, remedial reading specialists, and English teachers in general. The problems that have been created through this narrow-minded and misguided policy are easily exemplified by an analogous situation in the teaching of foreign languages. In some of the best foreign language programs in our schools, students begin studying the foreign language as early as first grade and some continue for the rest of elementary and high school, occasionally pursuing it in college and, perhaps, spending precious time in the country whose language it is. Such students are rare, but it is important to examine their characteristics. For one reason or another, these students learn to enjoy the language they are learning, they are highly motivated to learn it, and they are readily and happily reinforced in their efforts by both parents and teachers. In almost all cases, they are already fully literate in their first language when they begin the study of the second language (fully literate for their developmental levels, that is): They know what language is because they already have language and have been using it successfully and joyfully for several years. Consequently, these learners have concepts for *word*, *phrase*, and *sentence*; they have a basis for comparison and, most important, for differentiation between surface and grammatical features of the new language and their native language. If they have the opportunity to live in the land to which the foreign language is native, they are likely to develop a high degree of fluency in the language.

It is reasonable to compare this group of learners with students who become fully literate in their native language, noting the important difference that, unlike someone learning a foreign language, the native speaker is immersed in her language from birth. As we have seen, most students who are fully literate in their native language are also characterized by a high degree of motivation to learn to read and write, an intuitive understanding of the importance of these activities, and a continuing commitment to achieve a high degree of mastery. They became fully literate because they wanted to and had the opportunity to.

But for the more typical students—those who never quite discover for themselves a reason for learning a foreign language, or for whom it is simply rote exercises related to the game of getting grades in school—learning the foreign language remains a somewhat artificial activity that fits into a set of other artificial activities typifying school in general. For these students the foreign language is something one "takes in school" and then proceeds to forget. It is an object of study, a thing to be learned, a school activity irrelevant to the reality of living—and, like English, a distinctive pain in the posterior. As such, the foreign language occupies a certain period of time Monday through Friday, it requires a certain amount of homework and study in order to get good grades, but it has precious little to do with language and meaning making. Because it is essentially an isolated, fragmented activity among other isolated, fragmented activities in the curriculum, it becomes important and significant only to the extent that the individual learner discovers a personal commitment to learning it.

It is, then, reasonable to compare these students with the kinds of learners we have been discussing throughout this book. Of course, we know that some students learn little of anything in school, whether it be mathematics, English, or history. They drop out before finishing high school, or else they grudgingly finish in order to claim a high school diploma. They are told that the diploma is very important to their later success in life, which (while probably true) is particularly confusing given the real meaning(lessness) of a high school diploma. And we know that other students, those who discover motivation and satisfaction in the learning experience in general, move through elementary and high school with relative ease and choose to go on to college and, sometimes, even professional graduate studies. But we have been discussing the "washed masses": those who have been to the river and have been baptized in the waters of education; those who have learned the rules and devoutly want to follow them; those who have mastered some part of the fragmented content that has surrounded them in their schooling; those who have found or are searching for a place in the indifferent societal machine. For these students, for the great majority of students in our schools, neither the foreign language nor English means much more (and often means much less) than other fragments in the curriculum. Indeed, some may discover joy, satisfaction, and meaning in mathematics or one of the sciences. They may go on to devote years to the mastery of an isolated discipline. It is vital to remember that we are not discussing people who are stupid or who are not highly capable. We are discussing people who are caught within the narrow confines and definitions of the educational success system. We are also discussing people who have been seriously cheated.

For this group of learners, literacy (reading, writing, viewing, speaking, and listening) as it functions in school settings is a necessary component of succeeding in school. It has little to do with meaning making. It is not empowering.

LITERACY AS EMPOWERMENT

Language, the possibility of making meaning, is the essence of being human. It is at the center of individual empowerment. Through it, instead of simply being subject to the structures and activities that define the indifferent societal system, one interacts with and participates in the creation of the system. Through it, one engages in the continual, active process of Being. Without it, one is simply another brick in the wall surrounding one's self.

One might easily propose (in fact, who would dare argue?) that anything as important and essential as this should permeate the educational landscape, should be at the center of all areas of study. At the very least, it is apparent that anything this important cannot be reasonably, safely, or wisely relegated to a single discipline (English) or area of instruction (language arts) or part of the school day (9:00 A.M. to 9:50 A.M., Monday through Friday). It should be equally apparent by now that it cannot be tested through multiple-choice exams that have nothing whatsoever to do with the nature of the activity—the making of meaning.

But facts belie the reality. In the midst of the furor over the problem of literacy; intense examination, re-evaluation, and change in general college programs; and much sincere wringing of hands and gnashing of teeth, very little has really changed. In fact, while there may be pockets of change, one is likely to find that more money and time have gone toward testing literacy than have been devoted to teaching it.

One significant exception (at least an apparent exception) has occurred in the area of writing instruction. Over the last ten years, various high schools, colleges, and universities have begun to initiate writing across the curriculum (WAC) programs (Moffett 1981; Tchudi 1986). This emphasis, often treated as a major innovation of great significance, is most important for what it reveals about the present situation. First, such an emphasis would be laughable if writing were already a vital part of most high school and/or college-level courses. But writing is not a part of most of these courses, and the WAC movement is hardly laughable. Second, the movement may be most important because of its hidden agenda, which, as Stephen Tchudi has suggested, is really to encourage more inductive thinking and more student-generated exploration in all disciplines using writing as a surface-structure tool to accomplish this end. Third, the movement reveals a need for faculty development at all levels, suggesting by implication that many teachers are not fully prepared to help students learn and are especially weak in helping students become more literate learners. Fourth, insofar as the movement variously succeeds and fails (no one reports failures, but one might guess . . .), it reveals that any emphasis on literacy across the curriculum is, at best, in its infancy in terms of implementation. Fifth, those who participate in faculty development workshops sometimes reveal the rock-bottom commitment that most teachers have to the content of their disciplines—a commitment that, under examination, often supersedes a commitment to the learner.

Overt resistance to the movement takes two fascinating and revealing forms: (1) "Students should have learned how to do all this stuff long ago. If other teachers were doing their jobs, I wouldn't have to be bothered with such mundane stuff and I could get on with the real business of telling them what my discipline is genuinely about"; and (2) "I just don't have time to work with all this student writing and give them adequate feedback. They need so much help that it's just not worth it." It is impossible to avoid the cost-accounting and busyness-business metaphors when they are so often and so clearly stated.

But, forgetting the ignorant and the lazy for the moment (I am referring to teachers, by the way), let us focus on the many who attempt to implement writing across the curriculum. Let us look at the many teachers who are bright, dedicated, and willing. What are their initial doubts and confusions? What problems do they encounter? What do they learn, and how do they cope? Most important, how does all this change affect the learners?

Two of the most common concerns of teachers who desire to implement activities that will genuinely affect the literacy of their students are as follows: (1) Many feel that they do not know enough about so-called correct English to properly assist their students; and (2) many feel that they cannot afford the time necessary to work with student writing because it will block them from covering all the material they are expected to cover in a given course. The first concern, fortunately, is relatively easy to treat.

Generally speaking, the fear that one does not know enough about correct English grows out of confusion over what might most benefit students as they move toward greater degrees of literacy and confusion over the nature of literacy itself. Clearly, these confusions grow out of the past experiences of the teachers; they remember English teachers who maintained authority and demonstrated expertise through their ability to identify and define a gerund and to itemize every usage and punctuation error in a student paper. While these present teachers still resent how their own writing was treated by such "expert" English teachers, they learned one lesson well: Teaching writing is best defined as an activity in which a teacher identifies the mistakes the writer is making, punishes or embarrasses the writer, and demands that the writer fix the mistakes and stop making them in the future. Although many college teachers are reasonably good writers themselves (having produced masters and doctoral theses and, often, scholarly articles for publication), they continue to suffer resentment and insecurity about their ability to write correctly and, therefore, their ability to help anyone else learn to write well. While many high school teachers are also strong writers, it is a simple fact of life that many others do little or no writing and have strong negative attitudes toward the entire activity. One often finds both high school and college teachers to be openly fearful and resistant to showing their writing to anyone, especially their peers. That is, while they expect and welcome workshops that teach them to teach students, they are not particularly receptive, at first, to having to do the activity themselves.

In faculty development workshops designed to encourage and help such teachers implement activities that will increase literacy across the curriculum, this initial concern generally can be dispelled. Most of these people have never had the opportunity to have their intuitions confirmed: They usually know that they have been victimized by a former "expert" English teacher, and most of them are acutely aware of the fact that they write well (or at least adequately). But the nagging guilt that they still do not know what a gerund is or are unable to diagram a compound-complex sentence causes them to believe that they will be unable to help their own students become good writers. More specifically, they have not yet become fully aware of what literacy actually is and how it can most sensibly function as part of the learning process in any discipline. Of course, they are about to find out that they are involved in a "good news–bad news" scenario. The good news is that you do not need to be a walking handbook of punctuation and usage or an expert at Reed-Kellogg diagramming in order to help students become better writers. The bad news is that helping students become more literate, better, and more confident meaning makers demands a great deal more of the teacher than the "correctness" method.

Such a realization stems from understanding that the WAC movement, at its best, is not simply aimed at achieving minimal competency in writing among college students. But the realization necessitates the recognition that any emphasis on literacy across the curriculum cannot be founded in simplistic notions of language and learning. These realizations cause the second concern to evolve: Given that improving student literacy involves a great deal more than identifying surface-level mistakes of some sort, then it will clearly take considerable amounts of class time and teacher feedback. If such is the case, if helping students increase their degree of literacy is to be treated with as much significance as the central concerns of the (history, sociology, chemistry) course itself, then how can it conceivably be done without sacrificing some (or many) of the ideas and information that form the essence of the course?

It is a good question. In fact, it is such a good question that it demands several answers, some of which are subtle and complex.

Let us begin with the two most obvious answers. First, the simple (and at least slightly deceptive) answer: You can implement writing activities that will indicate to your students the important role writing plays in your discipline and in their learning, and these writing activities can be designed so that neither you nor your students will have to neglect the important content of the course. Second, the complex answer: Of course you are right. You need to change your syllabus, reduce the so-called coverage of the course, and recognize the apparent paradox that emphasis on meaning making through language will increase student learning even though you are covering less material.

The Simple Answer

Simple answers being what they are, I intend to spend precious little time or space on the first answer. If a teacher has no choice other than to continue to cover a certain amount of material in a given course, and if not covering that material means that students will suffer, then little can be done. Courses in mathematics, physics, chemistry, statistics, accounting, and so on are often described in exactly these terms. One hears that students who do not cover *a*, *b*, and *c* in a math course will be unable to contend with *d* in the following course; or one hears that success on a national, standardized exam in physics demands a certain amount of coverage in order for the student to succeed on the exam, and a lack of success on the exam means that the student will be unable to move into advanced study in the area. Accounting I is controlled by Accounting II, and these are controlled by the CPA exam. That's what the machine is all about.

While it may be unfair to summon the tea party in *Alice in Wonderland* as a metaphor, it is irresistible: If the interior logic of moving from chair to chair is accepted, if madness itself is accepted, then just as there is no room for Alice at the party, there also is no room for genuine emphasis on literacy in courses like these. Unless, of course, like Alice, the teacher simply barges in and makes room by noting that there are plenty of chairs.

But the analogy is unfair. Teachers of these courses, who often recognize the seriousness of the limitations imposed by traditional curricula and/or national exams, are caught within the larger system and cannot easily act in isolation without serious repercussions for both themselves and their students. They can ask students to write for two or three minutes at the beginning of a class to "remember through writing" what it was that occurred at the last class, what some of the most important concepts were in the last lecture; they can ask students to write for two or three minutes at the end of a class simply to rehearse what they are most confused about or interested in as a result of the lecture, but they can hardly be expected to spend much class time having students work together in small groups as they peer-edit or discuss one another's essays about the confusions and/or ideas that resulted from last night's reading assignment.

Moreover, both at the high school and college levels, it is customary for teachers (English teachers, too, I might add) to have too many students (in particular courses and across the board) to engage in sensible writing activities. What is a teacher to do if she has 40 or 50 or 120 students in a course? Precious little writing if she wishes to survive.

English teachers often carry loads of more than 100 students, both at the high school and college level. If each student wrote four papers each semester (not a particularly heavy writing demand), and if each paper was approximately 400 words (not a very long paper), each teacher would read approximately 1,000 pages of student writing each semester. Now, for good readers, for teachers who are being paid to do a job, that might not seem like much— unless, of course, you have tried it. As teachers of writing know, each paper takes at least fifteen to twenty-five minutes to read and comment on. (Remember, the activity is relatively useless if the writer is not given something other than a grade in response, if the writer is not given directions for future revision, and especially if the piece of writing is not treated as a real communication.) Now things begin to look different, even for someone who is not particularly good at arithmetic. An English teacher who has 100 students and who assigns four papers per student and spends approximately fifteen to twenty-five minutes per student paper is engaging in the equivalent of four forty-hour weeks of work just reading and responding to those papers.

For those who have wondered what good English teachers do on weekends, review the preceding statistics. And we have not even considered the time it takes to plan the activities and classes that precede and generate the writing activities. Nor have we mentioned revision. What if they rewrite? No time! No time!

Even the simple answer is not simply simple. At best, it is frustrating for all concerned. Band-Aid measures can be applied in any course, regardless of the number of students in the course and/or the amount of material that must be covered. Students who take these activities seriously may be helped a little; at the very least they may come to see that writing can function as part of their learning processes and that their articulations of meaning are related to the course readings and to the lectures. That some students will see such activities as a waste of time indicates they have learned that education is not really about what they think or meanings they can make; it is about information they can identify on standardized, multiple-choice tests. The greatest danger, of course, is the likelihood that many students' initial feelings and impressions will be reinforced by these Band-Aid measures: Writing is something that teachers make you do because it is something that teachers make you do.

The Complex Answer

The complex answer is a lot more interesting. Teachers are either victims of their disciplines and the corporate world that has defined them, or they are in charge of (inter)actively creating their disciplines through their involvement as scholars and teachers with colleagues and students. High school teachers must be encouraged to view themselves as the professionals they are, to begin to regard themselves as teacher-scholars who have been entrusted with one of the most difficult and exciting tasks in society: introducing students to a broader world of experience and knowledge. Instead of seeing themselves as victims of social pressures, they must begin to see themselves as individuals responsible for helping to shape society. Likewise, college teachers must recognize that they are teachers as well as scholars. They must openly resist the notion that publishing is somehow more important than teaching (and they might begin by openly admitting that publishing articles and books, in and of itself, is not a genuine measure of good thinking or scholarship—the busyness metaphor is particularly apt in this area). Both high school and college teachers must examine the entire notion of coverage in a discipline. If coverage is more important than genuine learning, then let us all be honest about it. If learning and/or coming-to-know is of paramount importance, then courses and syllabi must be changed.

But first a reminder: There really is a point to all this, and the preceding chapters have attempted to underscore that point. There is little value and much potential harm in implementing writing activities across any curriculum simply because writing across the curriculum appears to be in vogue. Writing activities across the curriculum and/or in English classes can be and often are as counterproductive, anti-intellectual, and time-wasting as the energy and effort devoted to multiple-choice tests and the memorization of fragmented bits and bytes of information. There are only a few good reasons for implementing writing activities in any class, but they happen to be exceptionally good reasons.

The processes of thinking and writing that are at the center of sensible writing activities are, by definition, central to the processes of becoming and knowing.

An emphasis on the interactive processes of oral and written language (as meaning making)—an emphasis on the initial processes of generating ideas and exploring one's own knowledge and commitment to an idea or topic and a continued emphasis on the growth and development of that initial moment—results in a genuinely desirable product. As students explore a discipline through their own and others' language, as they make meaning and explore that meaning, they become more powerful learners and they become more learned.

Writing activities and emphasis on the processes of making meaning through language are not peripheral to learning in any discipline; they are central. The question is not whether writing activities or an emphasis on literacy belongs in a given course. That answer is all too obvious. The point is that an emphasis on active reading, writing, speaking, and listening is essential to the learning process. Any course that cannot spare the time for these emphases admits openly that it cannot spare the time for the learning processes of its students.

WRITING AS HEURISTIC

First and foremost, then, writing is essential to all courses and to any course only and primarily insofar as it functions heuristically, engaging the student in active exploration of self and other in direct relation to a body of knowledge or way of knowing. Much of what has preceded this chapter has explored and explained the ways in which language functions as a heuristic (*the* heuristic?) in the process of realizing the possibility of meaning. Now it is time to explore some methods and activities that teachers might implement to achieve this happy possibility. But it is my hope that they will be viewed in terms of possibilities for generating other, better activities. Ultimately, each teacher in his or her own discipline and classroom will best create and judge which activities are most appropriate for a given purpose and given groups of students. To view what follows as "the way" to do things would be to pervert the intention of all that has preceded this chapter.

Methods and Approaches

It can come as no surprise that I first urge that the personal essay be considered as one of the primary and most important writing activities to be included in all courses at all levels. And yet, what may initially appear to be a simple, perhaps even simplistic, suggestion is actually rather complicated. After all, good personal essays demand the personal commitment and involvement of the writer; they demand that the writer have some sort of personal relationship with the experience and/or ideas being written about. Consequently, it is neither wise nor helpful to assume that simply assigning a personal essay will automatically create interest and commitment where none previously existed. Assigning a personal essay in a social studies course or an introduction to philosophy course is hardly likely to result in groups of students rushing home to write, eager to explore their personal relationship to the text or the lecture.

The term *personal essay* needs to be defined and its variations explored. At its most basic level, the personal essay is a written response through which a writer begins to explore her own feelings and ideas in relationship to an experience. At this level of definition, personal essays are often ridiculed as "nothing more than a lot of mushy, touchy-feely gushing" in which writers "get away with" whatever they feel like putting down on paper. Without even engaging this particular argument—after all, what is so bad about getting what you think and feel down on paper?—it is the terrain ignored by the argument that must be explored, as well as the hidden assumptions. School-writing is almost always defined as some sort of formal essay that follows certain accepted rhetorical standards in order to be judged (i.e., graded) according to long-standing and much-honored criteria. The fact that very little writing of any kind is done in most schools and colleges matters little to the stereotype. The point is that the stereotype, the accepted notion of school-writing, effectively eliminates the kinds of writing activities that are not assigned in order to evidence that everyone has learned how to write an introductory paragraph, three paragraphs developing the point made in the introduction, and a concluding paragraph noting that the promise of the introduction has been fulfilled. In fact, standard school-writing has little, if anything, to do with real writing.

You will remember that I have defined language as the possibility of making meaning. I am now asserting that the written personal response is one important way through which students may begin to realize that possibility. Teachers who have worked extensively with the personal essays of their students know through long experience that young writers are often very good at recounting personal experiences in writing; they know that their students like to write about themselves, their experiences, and the people they know. The teachers (high school and college) also know that these students are not particularly good at commenting on or analyzing the meaning of their own experiences. When asked to do so, these young writers often respond by repeating the experience—just as young writers who are asked to discuss the theme or significance of a short story or novel are likely to rehearse the plot and retell the story. Something appears to misfire or short-circuit between the telling of the experience and the analysis of it.

In terms of cognitive learning theory, we might say that simply knowing that something happened to me is of little consequence if I do not understand it in a broader "webwork" of meaning and experience. And to make broad generalizations about experience is of little use if I do not see them in relation to my own world of being and knowing. When the personal essay is abused or misused, it tends to center the fragmented experience and to ignore broader frameworks of meaning making. When school-writing becomes the primary focus, it often results in the emptiness of overgeneralizations and pomposity. Obviously, neither kind of writing activity is particularly helpful to the student's process of learning.

But written, personal responses allow for more than the retelling of an experience, just as more formal kinds of writing allow for more than soph-omoric revelations. In fact, both kinds of writing make the most sense when they are seen in relation to each other, along a broad continuum of language use, and in relationship to a broad variety of reading and writing activities. As the reader will see in the coming sections, most of my suggestions are highly conservative—perhaps even radically conservative, if such an oxy-moron can make sense. This is a call for a conservative revolution. Fur-thermore, as with most of my suggestions, I know that many teachers have been using variations on these methods for years; rather than apologize for using other people's ideas, let me simply thank the countless good teachers who taught me some of these methods.

Reader's Notes

The following litany is recognizable by most teachers. If they have not said it aloud themselves, they have either thought it or heard others say it. It is not the litany of bad teachers; it is the litany of savvy, concerned teachers. And it goes like this: "I just don't get it. I give them a reading assignment and they come into class acting as though they had never read it but claiming that they have. I give them class time to read, and they still act as though they never read it. Many of them can pass a quiz on it, but they clearly don't understand it." And, as with many respectable litanies, the students have a response: "I spent an hour on it last night, but I didn't understand a word of it. I started to underline the important sections, but pretty soon I was underlining everything (or nothing). No matter how hard I tried to concentrate, I found myself daydreaming. The stuff just doesn't make sense!" This is no surprise. It describes what happens to all of us when we are not making connections (when we are not making meaning). Just staring at something does not necessarily give it meaning or allow its meaning to be discovered. Neither teacher nor student is happy in this state of counterproductive frustration. Unlike the child in Whitman's poem, "There was a child went forth," these students are not becoming all that they see. They are barely seeing what they look at.

In these cases, to the extent that there is such a thing as a solution, it begins with the recognition that genuine "seeing" takes time.

Reader's notes, then, are just that—notes the reader makes as she reads whatever has been assigned. Depending on the purposes and needs of the readers and of the teacher, the notes may take many forms. I tell my students they may respond to the assigned reading in any form they wish, suggesting that some may want to write questions about the text as they are reading it, perhaps finding answers as they progress; others may wish to paraphrase or quote sections of the text, briefly commenting on why a given section is particularly important, confusing, contradictory, or irritating. Some choose to write statements and questions that will become part of their class discussion at our next meeting; often these students will leave space in their notebooks to take additional notes in relation to their reader's notes as we move through a discussion of the text. Some will keep reader's notes on one side of a three-ring notebook and class notes on the facing page, creating a running commentary of sorts. Some write page-long responses to a given idea or point that strikes their fancy, their imagination, or their curiosity. Others simply outline the reading assignment.

The advantages of such a system for both students and teacher should be relatively obvious. Students must make the effort to engage the text through their own language as they paraphrase and create questions. Even those who are having a terribly difficult time understanding the reading usually find that the question-asking activity helps them to understand what it is they are confused about. At the very least, they begin to create focused questions that can be answered and explained in class or in conference with the teacher. But the key, of course, is that the students who bother to take the task seriously are using their own language to make meaning of the language in the text.

Another advantage is this: Because students must read the text more actively than many normally do; because they must write about their understandings, misunderstandings, and confusions; and because they have the opportunity to discuss what they have written (and find out that others had similar confusions and questions), they begin to see themselves as part of a learning community—not a community devoted to memory and regurgitation, but a community engaged in the active exploration of meaning. Instead of coming to class waiting to find out the pre-approved answer, they come to class ready to discover some answers for themselves. (Some students, accustomed to succeeding in the business-busyness system, sometimes find this unsettling at first.)

There are some obvious disadvantages. Many teachers are already too busy trying to prepare several different classes, teach too many students, serve on committees. If each student produced a page of response for each reading assignment, and if the teacher then attempted to give full, written responses to the student writing, the teacher would never finish grading the reader's notes. I solved this problem by telling the students that I would never be able to read and comment on each set of notes, and that the activity was not about that anyway. By reading the notes very quickly, directing students to highlight questions that they find particularly tricky or points that they think the whole class should discuss, I can see and note the level of reading involvement. I use a plus, check, minus system to mark and record the papers, with a plus going to those who clearly are puzzling through the readings, a check going to those who fulfill the minimal demands, and a minus going to those who simply do not bother.

This still demands my time as a reader and recorder of the students' writing, but I have found that it also saves time and contributes to a higher-quality learning experience in the classroom. What teacher has not had the experience of not knowing what the kids do and do not understand? Who does not respond to this lack of knowledge by giving most concepts equal time in the classroom? Through the use of reader's notes, I have found that I can ignore ideas and issues that the class appears to understand and give more time to things that many students appear to be having trouble with. Likewise, by taking my cue from the reader's notes I can make better, more focused use of individual conference time with students, focusing on the specific problems one or a few have difficulty understanding.

Creating Exams

Another use for reader's notes is in small groups of three or four students who pass their notes around and/or discuss some of the specific problems each had with the reading assignment. After a relatively brief discussion in the groups, each group might then present a summary report of the focus of their discussion. This allows students to help one another when possible, to find out that their difficulties were mutual, and to begin to develop a sense of their own power as learners and meaning makers. A particularly valuable variety of this small-group experience occurs when students are directed to create essay exams and appropriate answers in relationship to given reading assignments. I have begun to use this activity in some of my courses for several purposes, not the least of which is the creation of the actual test. Students engaged in this activity analyze and discuss their questions in small groups, try to arrive at one or two questions they feel are particularly good questions, and then share their conclusions with the whole class. Aside from achieving a most thorough review of course material, students engage the material with surprising intensity. If seeing is believing, then one has to experience the moment in which one group of students explains to another group that the question they have contrived is too broad, impossible to answer in a single class period because it involves too many of the complex ideas in the course for a writer to develop in a short period of time. Or to hear in response that there is a perfectly reasonable short answer to the question, depending on the grading criteria. This, of course, leads them to discussions of legitimate and valid criteria.

What begins with personal response writing ends, at least in my experience, with students whose command of the ideas and facts of the text far surpasses what most teachers would consider normal. The students have been empowered: They have begun to gain a sense of their own power as learners and meaning makers. Ironically, although not surprisingly, the more they explore their own rights and power, the more they respect legitimate authority (including their own). As they learn to question the truth of a text or of a teacher's statements, they also learn to respect good thinking and good sense. Most important, although the emphasis here has been on student writing, the result is that the text, the readings, and the materials of the course have been moved more directly into the center of the course and into the center of the students' experiences.

Even so, no teacher with a normal teaching load in most high schools or colleges could implement such an activity with all students in all classes at all times. One or two classes in a semester is the most I would even begin to suggest. But why should we use the same method with all the students all the time? The best of methods becomes worn out and meaningless, just another kind of drudgery, when methods are reduced to the level of automated methodology. As with all methods, this one works better for some students than for others (although I have found my own students to be strongly in favor of the method). Also, a teacher might wish to have students write reader's notes only for specific assignments, eventually putting them in the position of choosing for themselves whether or not the activity assists them in their learning process.

In terms of this last (somewhat idealistic) statement, however, I am immediately reminded of one of my own experiences. I had required reader's notes from a college class for the first half of the semester, telling them at midterm that they were no long required to do the notes, although I would be happy to collect and read them if individuals wished to continue the activity. Not surprisingly, almost all of them ceased writing the notes, and I felt that class performance generally deteriorated, particularly in relationship to assigned readings. At the end of the semester when we collectively engaged in our soul-searching evaluation of the course, the discussion of the value of reader's notes proved both surprising and interesting. With only

one exception, the class unanimously agreed that it sounded like busywork
at first but soon proved to be one of the essential elements in their learning
process within the framework of the course. Somewhat puzzled, I asked if
perhaps they were not just telling me what they thought I wanted to hear,
especially given the fact that almost none of them had continued to keep
the notes. They responded that I should have continued to require the notes
and that they would have continued to benefit from them. I replied that
they should be adult enough to continue doing something that helped them
learn. They gave me one of the most sensible answers I have ever gotten
in this kind of conversation: "Maybe we should be adult enough to keep
doing it, but we weren't. You should have made us do it."

It occurs to me that I am not adult enough to always do what is best,
especially when it involves extra work and effort—the memos I know I
should file remain guilty reminders and frustrating enemies when I am searching for the one I need; all too often a good movie or a televised football
game takes precedence over a journal article. I guess I am not sure what
"adult enough" means anymore, but I do not think it means that we need
to abandon reasonable requirements and demands, and clearly these students
felt the same way. On the other hand, neither these students nor I were
disabled by our occasional tendencies to avoid work—the point is that any
requirement must meet genuine needs; it must prove itself sensible to those
who are being required to do it. I still give the students the option at midterm.
And I have tried to get better about filing my own important papers.

The notion of requiring people to do something that is "good for them,"
a phrase that smacks of caster oil and jogging, provides a convenient transition
for introducing another major writing activity that I have found useful and
successful.

Annotated Bibliographies

I almost groan along with my students as I type the words—*annotated
bibliography*. They sound academic, stultifying, boring. They bring us perilously close to one of the most hated words in classrooms: *research*. They
call to mind the encrusted, dusty halls of libraries, people going "sshh,"
and trying to find articles in journals after someone else has neatly removed the
article with a single-edged razor blade. They remind me of the difficult time
I often have trying to stay awake in a library, the confusion I experienced
when I was younger and the library was no more than an impossible maze.

They most certainly do not call to mind phrases like personal response
essay, commitment, engagement.

Knowing this, knowing that I once felt much the same way my students
do about doing research, I approach the activity with an authoritative hand.
I simply tell them that I know they think it sounds like a lot of hateful
busywork, but that they must do it. I tell them that it will eventually make

sense to them if they give it a chance. And, as is so often the case in a classroom when we bother to treat the students like genuine human beings with rights and responsibilities, they usually take me at my word and give the activity a reasonable try. Some do so because it is a requirement, but many find that it introduces them to some interesting and contradictory worlds. But before I get ahead of myself, here is a description of the activity and how it works.

Certainly, any reader of this particular book knows what an annotated bibliography is: At the top of a note card or sheet of paper (or on the back of a napkin, if you're like me) the writer produces a standard bibliographic notation citing author, title of article/book, date, publishing company, pages, and so on. Following this, one briefly summarizes the article, sometimes quoting directly if necessary or appropriate. Good scholars even remember to file their bibliographic notations in something other than the pile on the left-hand corner of the desk or the top drawer of the desk. Most important, however, most researchers have a reason for doing the research in the first place, and most often they visualize some future use for the annotations (e.g., for use in a projected article or book or for use in classroom teaching). Furthermore, most researchers know that everything in print is not necessarily true; most admit, at least grudgingly, that some material in journal articles (not to mention popular media) barely stops short of intentional falsification. Consequently, they approach this reading with a reasonable level of careful skepticism.

Students, on the other hand, do not know what an annotated bibliography is—nor has it occurred to them that they might have any good reason for doing one. Moreover, they often feel themselves to be the victims of published scholarship, unable to hazard a guess about whether or not a particular article makes good or no sense. To the extent that they have had any experience with library research, it has usually been part of a highly artificial exercise in English class in which the research paper itself—as form and formula—held the central focus. That is, *what* they were researching and writing about did not matter as much as the fact that they produced proper bibliographic form, proper outline form, proper footnote form, and a paper devoid of errors in usage and mechanics. The point of doing the research was that the student might have at least ten different sources to allow for the inclusion of at least ten footnotes and ten bibliographic entries. Seldom does one find a student engaged in research in order to find something out (unless she is working on her own, doing something that has little or nothing to do with school). Most research is being done to prove some preformulated thesis, often in an area and about a topic of little interest to the student.

It is worth remembering some of the points made in earlier chapters, especially those made by the teachers who participate in workshops designed to explore the possibilities of writing across the curriculum. Over and over, high school and college teachers make the point that, for the most part, neither writing nor research was meaningful to them (nor did they do much of it) until they began work on a master's or doctoral thesis. With the exceptions of creative forms of writing (short stories and poetry) they produced on their own, none of it made much sense. It seems likely that, unless we radically change what has been occurring over the years, our own students will have exactly the same experience. But even at that, it is important to remember that most people do not go on to graduate school; most people do not experience the discovery of writing as a useful tool for achieving a personal/public end.

Since most of what I have just written sounds like a diatribe against research and, therefore, annotated bibliographies, some clarification may help. One of the most common attacks on student-centered or personal growth emphases in education is this: The emphasis is so much on the individual as subject and his subjective exploration of self in the world that the real world is ignored. As a result, students are encouraged to immerse themselves in the anti-intellectual world of radical relativism in which all experience and all ideas are equally right and wrong depending on what any individual happens to believe. In a much less exaggerated form, this is what E. D. Hirsch complains about and almost certainly has in mind when he identifies Rousseau and Dewey as the archvillains of modern educational philosophy.

On the other hand, the logical positivists are attacked in directly opposite terms. Foolishly lulled into the security of formal logic, believing that it bears some relationship to truth and founding themselves in the assertion that the objective world can be known and analyzed, these people ignore self, spirit, and all that is human. Fearful of all that is subjective, they dismiss subjectivity entirely and search for mathematical or scientific solutions.

Epithets being what they are—fun to hurl about but seldom very helpful—and human nature being considerably more complex than the extremes of either subjectivism or logical positivism admit, we will do best to proceed without the stereotyping. Writing provides the middle road between the extremes. And the annotated bibliography, as boring as it may first seem, works surprisingly well to provide the students with the opportunity to engage the real world, to explore and articulate their own responses to that world, and to begin the attempt to make sense of the collision that occurs when self and other meet.

The requirements are relatively simple and straightforward (as well as allowing for broad variation within almost any course or discipline). Students are required to read at least two articles per week, choosing from among appropriate journals. (Obviously, the number of required articles must vary in relationship to their age and expertise and in relationship to the complexity of the topic.) While it may seem to be babying or spoon-feeding the students to do so, I recommend that the teacher (1) list the titles of the most appropriate journals and (2) show the students where the journals are in the school library or arrange for a library tour to be conducted by one of the librarians. I am reminded of one of my own students, a senior, who came to me and said that the only articles she could find were "really old stuff" on microfiche. She was an A student, very bright and capable. But she had never known about the periodical section in the library. After I showed it to her and she had a chance to read around a little, she returned to tell me what a wonderful thing it was—"They've got stuff about everything in there!"

Experiences such as this should remind us that we do not all operate from the same experiential base. Just because you value an activity or know something or how to do something does not mean that your students do. Now, this is not a new statement and it should come as no surprise, but it is easy to forget at times. I would suggest that when we do forget it, we are no longer teachers. It is not enough to say, "They should know this or that." What they should or should not know is irrelevant if they do not know it.

So, depending on the level of experience and sophistication of any given class, a little spoon-feeding may be both necessary and desirable. I often find that students are not at all sure how to proceed on a project like this because they are neither familiar nor comfortable with libraries. I have also found that librarians are almost ecstatic to have the opportunity to assist students in their exploration of the uses of libraries. But the point of the activity moves far beyond teaching students how to find periodicals in the library.

At first I encourage them to "read around" in the journals, writing only on articles that are at least generally related to the topic of the course and that they find interesting and intelligible. Most important, I require that in addition to briefly paraphrasing or summarizing the central points of the article, they comment on the article from their own points of view as well. They are told that although I may strongly disagree with their commentary or their opinion ("I hate this kind of stuff because it's just boring and stupid!"), they will not be penalized for it in the annotated bibliographies. (Obviously, if they continue to find everything to be stupid, especially insofar as the nature of that stupidity remains unarticulated and unanalyzed, they have not engaged the material of the course.) In my own experience, however, most of them manage to move quickly beyond the stupid stage, especially as they discover that much of what is in the journals is directly relevant to their learning in the course. Slowly but surely, many of the students begin to find that they can agree or disagree with a particular article, with a position taken in an article, or with points that I make in the class discussions, and that these agreements and disagreements are based on something besides their own subjective feelings.

Also, as they begin to feel and flex these new intellectual muscles—or in Bruffee's terms, as they begin to feel that they are part of the academic, scholarly community (1984), the reader's notes begin to reflect an integration of their research and the reading assignments within the course itself. To say that such an event from the point of view of the teacher is exhilarating is a gross understatement. But this is even more exciting: The class begins to change. The discussions take on a youthful professionalism. Yes, sometimes it looks like adolescent self-righteousness as they become positive that they are right about something or as they easily dismiss a perfectly good idea because it does not mesh with their own, but that is what the classroom is for. It is here that we can quietly deflate some of the pomposity (including our own) and attempt to arrive at reasonable conclusions.

Directly in relation to this last statement, the annotated bibliographies feed into small- and large-group classroom activities. Every once in a while students will come across a particularly important article or idea, and these students are invited to briefly report the article to the class and explain the nature of its importance. Sometimes someone will find something that appears to be stupid, dangerous, or contradictory, and will be invited to present it in class. At least twice during the semester students are asked to identify one of the more important articles they have read and examine it with other students in a small group. Afterwards, the small groups report to the entire class, an activity that leads to a kind of interactive brainstorming and give and take.

Does it work this way all the time? No. Do all the students engage the activity seriously? No. Is it appropriate in all courses or all disciplines? Probably not. But is it worth trying? Unquestionably. Says who?

Again, although students are not always the best evaluators of a course (I find they often think it went better than I think it did), they are usually as good at evaluating courses and the usefulness of activities as most others who engage in the process. Of the several hundred students with whom I have tried the annotated bibliographies, less than 5 percent say it was useless or silly. I confess my surprise here because I expected them to react strongly against the activity. But again, what is interesting is this: Even though many say it was a "pain" to have to go to the library every week and "read those damn articles," the overwhelming percentage of them say that the activity was "useful," and (often) interesting." Many of them also report a conscious awareness of the fact that they have begun to learn how to judge the quality and sense of professional scholarship—they have begun to be discerning readers.

The disadvantages? As usual, the problem with student writing is that someone has to read it. And frankly, I just don't believe those teachers who say that they can't wait to get home on Friday night and read all that student writing. Sure, it's fun and exciting sometimes. But around mid-semester, when the piles of papers begin to grow higher than the snow outside and I begin to feel that all I do is read student papers—well, I get tired. So it goes, and I don't have a solution. Every profession has its drawbacks, and no one forced me into this one. But if we are genuinely dedicated to helping ourselves and our students move toward real, mature literacy, and if we understand the meaning of reading and writing across the curriculum, then we must also understand that no single teacher or course can or should be responsible for student literacy. *Across* the curriculum—that's the point. If all or even most of the teachers are engaging their students in some sensible reading and writing activities, no one teacher need be persecuted.

So again I say this: Annotated bibliographies work (sometimes), but no one can do them with all his students in a given semester in all courses. The sheer amount of paper resulting from reader's notes and annotated bibliographies will smother and crush the best and most dedicated teacher if he does not carefully plan and limit the activities to certain courses or times in the semester. As with reader's notes, I try to speed-read the annotated bibliographies, giving each as little time as possible as I award grades of plus, check, or minus. One advantage is that many students begin to annotate the same article—which is not surprising since I have sent them to specific journals—and therefore I can move through the reading very quickly. Again a good news–bad news scenario: Many of the students produce interesting, insightful annotations; it is difficult to avoid being drawn into their commentaries. The better they do, the longer it takes to read their work.

On the other hand, through my work with their reader's notes and annotated bibliographies, I learn a great deal and find that working with their writing becomes a major part of my own preparation time for teaching the course. So there is something of a trade-off. In addition, in a course in which I require reader's notes and annotated bibliographies, I am careful to keep other writing assignments to a minimum. Since the central point of these writing activities is to help students use writing heuristically, the teacher must be willing to trust in the idea. Of course, to the extent that a written product is desirable and appropriate, the bibliographies lend themselves to the writing of research reports and/or in-class presentations.

Speaking of Research Papers

I confess true bias here, but a complex one. First, for the most part I believe that much of what teachers say they want to accomplish by requiring a research paper can be accomplished through modifications of the annotated bibliography activity. Second, as research papers normally play themselves through the educational machine, they seldom achieve much of what teachers say they intend to achieve.

For example, genuine research demands considerable knowledge about the topic to be researched beforehand, if the project is expected to end in a polished, written product. Students almost never have the larger perspective in a given area to allow them to engage in research in this way. Indeed, the younger they are and the newer they are to a discipline, the more likely they are to have very little knowledge about how the discipline works or what basic knowledge constitutes the discipline. In addition, genuine research is seldom subjected to artificial deadlines. The scholar/researcher may choose to accept certain deadlines, meeting dates set by journals or book publishers, but these deadlines are normally accepted by the author after she has already begun the research project and can reasonably envision an end to it. But student deadlines are set by calendar committees, and as I have previously mentioned, unless the research project has been carefully constructed and the students are interested, they often begin their research paper about one week before it is due. (Visit a college library one week before the end of a semester for graphic evidence of this syndrome). My objections might easily be expanded, but much of this has been said before. My most important qualification, however, is this: I am not arguing against having students do research; I am arguing against forcing them into doing research on topics of no interest to them in order to produce a paper that has no real purpose beyond its isolated existence as proof that the student did a research paper. Furthermore, if we are going to have students do research, let us at least give up the notion that all research is done in libraries with books. Let their research involve interviews, experiments, and the development and testing of their own ideas. Let research projects be a part of the larger project of meaning making.

Having said that, let me now argue for the research paper. In upper-level college courses within the student's major, in high school elective courses, and on those occasions in which students come to the course with some background knowledge, expertise, and motivation, research projects may make the best of sense. By approaching the idea in the right way with the right group of students, a teacher may be able to introduce young writers to the moment described by the teachers in those faculty workshops—the moment in which the writer discovers the need to say something and the opportunity to create and/or find that which needs to be said.

This statement may be too blunt about the present state of research writing in general, but one might reasonably argue that the research paper functions in the schools in much the same way that it does among professional academicians. Students often do research papers simply because they have been required to do so, having little interest, commitment, or purpose. All too often, the results are stilted writing, artificially concocted theses and syntheses, and a triumph of form over content. In the academy, all too often people write journal articles because they must amass enough publications to be granted tenure. In some ways, the problem becomes even more pernicious and perverse because some professors avoid involving themselves in the risky areas of research: Pressure to publish causes them to feel that they cannot afford to work on something that will not result in a reasonably quick publication. Overall, some students plagiarize in order to achieve the superficial goal of producing a research paper in order to produce a research paper. Some professors ignore important ideas and qualifications in order to manage a quick publication, and although it is seldom discussed, some scholars falsify findings in order to justify their theses. But then, why not—who trained them to do research papers?

PROCESS VERSUS PRODUCT

That these two words are so often presented in opposition regarding writing and reading may be the initial irony concerning their relationship and how they should be functioning in the movement toward mature literacy. The extremes of the argument go like this: Those who favor process over product cause students to wallow in their own narrow subjectivities, putting down on paper whatever they feel like writing or saying, never taking responsibility for the quality or integrity of whatever they write or say. In real life it is the quality of the product that counts, not the process you went through to get there. At the other extreme are those who obsessively favor process-centered approaches: They claim that learning is a lifelong process; whatever is read, written, or spoken is in a constant process of revision; and any emphasis on the final product eliminates learning. As with the subjectivists and logical positivists, both positions are too extreme to make much sense, especially when they are overgeneralized to all curricula, all classrooms, all kinds of learning, or all courses.

The problem has always puzzled me, however, because all products are part of a process—both produced by a process and, normally, contributing to or functioning in other processes. Someone makes or produces something through some sort of process. Once it is produced, someone else uses it in some way as part of another process, often to produce something else. You make a bicycle (product) through the careful creation and integration (process) of components and frame. I ride it in order to enjoy myself (process) and to get in good shape (product). Students write reader's notes and annotated bibliographies (process) in order to more fully understand (product) some area of a discipline. This understanding (product) then contributes to more understanding of other areas of the discipline or other disciplines. Perhaps the only time when product orientation is genuinely a problem is when it functions primarily within the business-busyness metaphor, when it exists as part of an unexamined devotion to the machine.

The simple fact is that very few teachers (I cannot presently think of any) emphasize the process of writing in such a way as to ignore the possibility of a polished, finished product. Some may take longer to get there, but almost all do intend to get there—and they generally succeed. It would be a strange writing class indeed that did not want to publish its work at some point, whether in the form of a class magazine, through submissions to school papers or literary magazines, or at least by way of the inexpensive and essential ditto machine.

Regarding the treatment of writing in courses other than writing courses, the situation is generally quite different. In fact, part of the somewhat universal contempt one finds invoked by discussions of student writing among teachers appears to result from emphasis on the written product with little regard for the processes that contribute to good writing. Often one finds teachers with the best of intentions requiring students to write a final paper (usually research oriented, but not always) in courses that have focused on the specific knowledge of the discipline throughout the semester. Frequently, students in these courses have been primarily responsible for reading a textbook, coming to class, listening to lectures, and taking multiple-choice exams, almost to the exclusion of any writing, discussing, or small-group activities. It should come as little surprise that their final papers are weak.

As a result of teaching writing across the curriculum workshops for the past ten years, I have had the opportunity to see many of these student papers and discuss the problems with the instructors of these courses. Most typically, both I and the workshop participants agree that the papers are not bad; they just are not very good. They are boring. Often filled with facts, they are usually fragmented, lacking any clear central focus, devoid of authorial commitment, seldom expressing a personal voice, at least adequate in terms of usage and mechanics, marred by the misuse of a thesaurus, and pretty clearly something the student did in order to fulfill the requirements of the course. While students in electives and upper-level courses sometimes break through the malaise, most of these papers suggest competence operating in a state of indifferent detachment. The teacher's response, given this state of affairs, is usually to give up on the whole idea or to replace the paper with a final exam (multiple-choice). Closer examination of the papers, however, often reveals that the student may have had one or two ideas that generally interested him, but that he decided were not "intellectual enough" to be in this "kind of paper." Whereas the teachers in these workshops invariably assert that they are not looking for dry academese and would give anything to discover an excited, interested, committed authorial voice, the students I talk to believe just the opposite. Clearly, each seems to be reading a different text and each is unquestionably moving through a different context (Schwartz 1984).

Part of the solution is simple. Teachers need to be clearer about what they want students to do in these papers. But as I suggested earlier, this alone is not enough. Too often the students may decide that the teacher is truly a "good person," but still, by virtue of being a teacher, she must want written stuff that sounds intellectual (i.e., dry, stilted, empty, pompous, wordy writing). And here the emphasis on process comes in, less as a solution than as a step toward establishing the possibility of a solution.

THE PROCESS OF CREATING A PRODUCT

No longer oppositions, but as related parts within a sequence, the process of writing functions in the creation of final products. As is so often the case, any implementation of the processes that follow will take time both inside and outside of the classroom—although once students have learned to do some of the activities, much less class time will be needed. Fortunately, even though the activities take time, they continue to contribute to the students' fuller understanding of the subject matter at the same time that they contribute to generally higher degrees of literacy. If the teacher does not feel that the time expenditure is worth it, then she must also question the important of a final product—is it worth it? I will leave it up to the individual to decide what is and is not worth it.

The Big Picture

Certainly, one of the most obvious facts of student writing in any discipline is that the writer often appears to have no genuine interest in the topic she is writing about. Sometimes this is because the specific topic was assigned and the student had no choice in the matter; at other times, it results because the student has not yet discovered a personal relationship with the topic or the student feels that "disinterest is the key to good academic writing." First, then, I suggest that topics for major papers be chosen by the students. The process of choosing should be set up in a way that short-circuits the kinds of choices that result from total ignorance and a desire to just "get the whole thing over with."

As will be obvious in the scenario I am describing, students are doing a significant amount of writing—perhaps an ideal amount, perhaps too much. But this is by way of exemplification; the individual teacher must always decide which pieces of the scenario best and most sensibly fit the students' learning process within any given course and/or discipline. The point here is to empower the learner, not to oppress him.

Discovering a Topic

Student Journals. The use of student journals has been discussed in many articles and has been reasonably popular in some freshman courses for many years. Contrary to the occasional fanatical reverence for student journals, they can either be useful or a waste of time, but they seem particularly appropriate as part of an emphasis on literacy across the curriculum. If for no other reason, they are particularly useful because they can become a kind of three-ring notebook file for much that has occurred in any given course. I suggest a three-ring notebook rather than a spiral notebook because this allows the removing, entering, and rearranging of separate entries. It means, for example, that reader's notes might be handed in to the teacher, replaced in the notebook later in proximity to relevant class notes, supplemented with relevant annotated bibliographies or any other writing that appears to be particularly related to a given set of notes. (It also eliminates the tiny pieces of paper that cover my study floor—the little pieces that fall off the pages that have been torn out of spiral notebooks.)

Although creating and implementing activities designed to help students discover topics is relatively easy, I do not suggest that they will have an easy time doing it. This is especially true if very few teachers in the school are attempting to focus on improving literacy across the curriculum. In cases where you are the only one making such demands in a given course, students are likely to use their past contexts to read the situation just as you might expect. They will think you have gone slightly crazy, wonder why you want to persecute them in this way, and echo statements you have heard your colleagues make: "Why do we have to write in here? This isn't English class!" But all changes take time, and one can only hope that the sense of doing the writing will begin to make its own case as the students engage the process. The fact is that most students trust us more than we deserve and are surprisingly willing to comply with our demands.

Free-Writing. It should be obvious that the reader's notes and annotated bibliographies can play an important part in the process of discovering a topic. As students find particularly interesting articles in the library or find themselves particularly interested in parts of the assigned readings, they can begin to focus on one of these interests, perhaps directing more of the bibliographic work toward related articles. But other kinds of short writing assignments may also be used to help them. The teacher might, for example, ask students to free-write for five minutes at the beginning or end of one or two classes each week.

There are not many rules for free writing because it is intended to free the thinker-writer from conventions that may get in the way of putting ideas down on paper. My own rules are simple: During a free-writing activity, you succeed as long as you keep writing. But even with activities like this, people need guidance. I suggest that the teacher create a series of oral prompts that she can use to keep the writers involved in the process of moving thought into language. Using such a procedure, the teacher asks the students to begin writing about topic X that was at the center of the assigned reading or previous lecture. If it was racism, the prompts might go like this: "Have you ever been subjected to someone's prejudice against you because of your age, sex, race, or religion? How did you feel? Do you ever feel prejudiced against someone else? When? Who? Can you describe a specific experience? Which stereotypes make sense to you? What was the most significant point in the last lecture (or reading) regarding this issue? What examples do you see in our school? What would you like to do about this? What are your three most important questions about this issue at this moment?"

The key here is for the teacher to quietly and consistently keep the writer-thinkers thinking and writing. At the beginning of the class, students can be directed to write for five minutes on whatever they most specifically remember from the last class or from last night's reading: What was interesting, confusing, ridiculous, incomprehensible, or most sensible? If nothing else happens in this kind of writing assignment, it interrupts the "real" life of the student and suggests that what occurred in the last class is at least intended to be related to what happens in the present class meeting. Establishing a sense of continuity like this is probably worth the effort in and of itself. Or students might be asked to do a similar writing assignment at the end of a class meeting. Aside from reminding them that something is supposed to be happening in their minds and that they have not simply been plugged into an information transmission system, this gives them an opportunity to make meaning of what has been occurring and to momentarily freeze that meaning in written language. Both activities force the students into the process of monitoring their own learning process, at least at a minimal level. Likewise, these writing activities begin engaging students in the process of becoming conscious and aware of what they are (or are not) learning and thinking. In more formal terms, it begins the process of making them metacognitively aware of how and what they learn. Again, if this were the only productive aspect of the activities, one could argue that it alone would make the activities worth it. Obviously, free-writings can become the focus for small- and large-group discussions or more extended writing if teacher and students so choose. I find that students are often fascinated to review these pieces of writing several weeks later to see how their thinking is progressing.

Brainstorming. Three or four weeks into the course, by which time each student would have read at least six outside articles, class time might be given over to a brainstorming activity in which students and teacher participate in listing a broad range of interesting topics on the blackboard. Once the list is developed, the group might move into an exploration of the different topics and their possibilities for more focused research and writing. The list would then be reproduced on paper and distributed to all the students, who would begin trying to decide which topics they most wanted to pursue on their own. Shortly after this, each student is required to produce a personal essay one or two pages in length explaining what topic he has decided to pursue and why it interests him; these essays would then be discussed in small groups, re-presented to the entire class for brief discussion, and, again, reproduced as a list to be given to the entire class, identifying who has chosen what topic. While some teachers may find it inappropriate for several students to work on the same topic (and while I will not go into the complexities of group projects here), I often find it valuable for students to work together in these ways, sharing research and ideas freely. Such group work need not, of course, eliminate the possibility of each individual producing a separate and different paper, although group presentations and papers might be equally acceptable. To no small extent, these decisions must be made in terms of the purpose of the assignment and the maturity of the students.

At any rate, once the students have identified topics they will begin to focus their research on their specific topics, but they must also be reminded to identify articles that might be of help to classmates working on different or related topics. If we genuinely want students to be part of a healthy, intellectual atmosphere and to participate in the community of scholars, we might begin by trying to create such a community in our classrooms. Furthermore, as students begin to be part of such a community, as they experience literacy as an integral part of their own growing and learning, they begin to enjoy the activities more and feel themselves to be part of something real, rather than something artificially created by schools and teachers in order to arrive at grades.

Depending on the nature of the class and the material being taught, students may now move into a variety of writing activities. One of the least-used resources are the people in the schools and in the local community. The teacher or other students might help each other identify other teachers, administrators, and local residents who have experience with or expertise in a given student's subject matter. Students might be assigned to conduct interviews with such individuals, or they might simply be given the option to do so if appropriate. Again, aside from letting others in the school and in the community know that these students are engaged in "real" intellectual exploration, students begin to see their work as part of a human network, part of the larger web of meaning and meaning making.

The Creative Possibilities

Some students may choose to write fictions or simulations of sorts that incorporate the material they have been researching into a narrative framework. A student in an economics class might explain how she would adjust a specific country's economic policies as it moved from an agrarian society to an industrial one. A student in a history or social studies class might write a personal narrative explaining how it might have felt to be a South Vietnamese clerical worker in Saigon after the U.S. forces pulled out. A student might write a first-person narrative describing the experience of discovering a particular fossil or anthropological site. A budding chemist might write a short story exploring the possibly dangerous events surrounding any one of many classic experiments, stressing the *science* of science fiction. A group of students might restructure the United Nations or a given government in order to achieve world peace or a more democratic form of participation among the citizens. A business or philosophy student might restructure a major corporation from the perspective of Plato or Marx. A theatre arts student might describe the changes in direction, lighting, and costuming needed to present a modern version of *Oedipus Rex* or the changes in a specific scene of *Death of a Salesman* needed to turn the tragedy into a black comedy or television soap opera. An art student might recreate the dialogue that never occurred between Van Gogh and his New York agent as Van Gogh tries to explain the commercial appeal of "Starry Night."

The possibilities are unlimited. They invite both teachers and students to engage and explore their disciplines in new and exciting ways. Each is particularly and significantly demanding. None of the suggestions can be carried out successfully unless the author has a powerful command of the facts surrounding the topic itself. He must know about the country, the anthropological or biological discovery, the art and the artist—he must know the facts before he can produce the fiction. Perhaps even more significant, these creative approaches to writing demand that the writer understand subtleties and syntheses inherent in the subject matter. Not only is it likely that students will engage such writing activities with fervor, it is almost certain that they will not approach the activity wondering how many sources or footnotes they have to have.

Just one more note about this kind of writing, this creative "stuff." I stress it here because it is the most ignored kind of writing in schools today; often it is reserved only for the elite or the "talented." Even English teachers— whose careers depend on creative writing and creative writers—often treat it as a second-class activity. It is not unusual to hear that "John is very strong on the basics and has a good imagination, so I guess he can take the creative writing elective."

I once worked with an eighth grader who had been "turned on" to writing poetry in his English class. Previously he had pretty much viewed school as a necessary interruption that occurred between 8 A.M. and 2:30 P.M. But now he spent his own money to buy his own journal in order to organize his poetry. He wrote voraciously and, sometimes, well. When he found out that his creative work *didn't count* in his final grade, even though it had been judged to be of very high quality, he got the message loud and clear. He still writes and reads poetry and fiction, but he doesn't pay much attention in English class. I suspect he decided that *English doesn't count*. Kids are funny that way.

We need to explore the likelihood that creative writing and creative activities in general are part and parcel of the process of becoming "good at the basics." This is the kind of writing in which students invest themselves: Ask the creative writing teacher how many students fail to pick up their final papers, or how many of them simply look at a grade on a short story or poem and throw the paper away. Writers care about this kind of writing because it matters to them and they want it to matter to us. People who care about and engage in this kind of writing cannot and do not write well from ignorance—they write from a powerfully clear foundation in science, art, psychology, philosophy, sociology, history, or some other discipline. What stronger argument could possibly be made for incorporating more creative writing in all courses?

To those who would argue that this kind of assignment would be unfair to the student who is "not particularly creative" or who prefers standard expository prose forms, I note the problem. Why, then, is it fair to impose the standard expository form on the student who is not particularly good at that? Perhaps some openness and compromise is necessary for all of us. Perhaps we must constantly strive to remember that not everyone is a mirror image of ourselves, that our likes and dislikes are not repeated in all other human beings, that various kinds of thinking and approaches to problem solving are equally important and valid. Perhaps we need to remember that egocentrism is not a disease of the young; it is a fact of existence. Sometimes a fact of our own existence.

Even at this stage, however, whether students are writing semifictional pieces or research papers, even if they have discovered their own topics and achieved a sense of personal commitment to the topic, even though they have been writing and researching and discussing, they are still only at the beginning stage of producing a polished, final product. What follows here is an approach to helping them achieve that final, polished product. But, as usual, teachers must ask themselves why they want to move to the final product and whether or not it is worth it. Always keep in mind that no matter how long you polish a piece of coal, it will not become a diamond. If the student has not succeeded (at least to some extent) up to this point, additional drafts and revisions of a failed beginning are probably as hopeless as they are frustrating. It often makes more sense to start over than to continue in an impossible endeavor.

But let's agree that students are having some success and have produced their first drafts. What comes next? One of the most obvious possibilities is that the teacher might collect the drafts, comment on them by providing each writer with suggestions and directions for necessary revisions and/or additions, and give any other comments that he thinks might help the writer. When the teacher is not overwhelmed with too many students, this is a perfectly reasonable way to proceed and often proves very helpful to the individual writers. I have only one caution at this point: Sometimes an overzealous teacher tries to comment on everything in the student's paper. As a result, the commentary and feedback are overwhelming for the writer, and revision or additional writing seems fruitless and impossible. Good editorial feedback in the teaching-learning situation demands that the editor or teacher recognize the human being at the other end of the piece of writing. It is not our job to show the young writer what exceptional critiques we can produce; the feedback and commentary are intended to help the writer continue writing. Teachers must also try to avoid the trap of simply marking mistakes in usage and/or mechanics. This is an easy approach for most of us, but it is not particularly helpful for the writer at this point. I do not intend to suggest that gross errors will be acceptable in the final draft; I simply mean that this may not be the best time to emphasize the most surface parts of the surface structure of language.

Of course, the teacher may not always have the energy or time to give student drafts this kind of attention. It may even be wise to avoid doing so, all of the time, regardless of energy and time. Writers need more than a single audience. In fact, personal letters are perhaps one of the only kinds of writing intended for an audience of one, with the obvious exception of journal and diary entries. For years now, many English teachers have experimented with one version or another of an activity called peer editing or peer review. Frankly, although I use the terms, I don't much like either one because they both suggest a more formalized kind of feedback and a higher level of competence than we should reasonably expect from many students. But for our purposes I will continue to use the terms, qualifying their meaning as I explain their implementation.

At its simplest level, peer editing involves students working in small groups to read and discuss one another's writing. In its earliest stages, especially with students who have never participated in the activity before, it is essential for the teacher to move them carefully into the activity, giving clear instructions. The greatest and most immediate danger is that they will act the way (they think) teachers act: Some students will set out on their "search and destroy" missions, intensely hunting for mistakes in spelling or punctuation and paying no attention whatsoever to the content of the writing. I have found this to be easy enough to stop. I tell them that, first, I don't want them to worry about mistakes, and second, I want them to read through one another's papers completely twice and then simply discuss their own reactions to whatever is being said in the paper. Another immediate problem is that many students who have been indoctrinated by the educational system believe—or at least pretend to believe—that any activity of value must be monitored and directed by the teacher. As one student said to me, "Why do we have to do this? You're the teacher!" Again, I suggest a direct, simple answer: "That's right, I am the teacher and this is what I want you to do. You're the learner!" Authority has its privileges. But it is also a fact of my own experience that an explanation of the activity and the role I intend it to play in the students' learning process makes considerably more sense after they have engaged in some form of peer editing and can relate their experience to my explanation.

Once they have become accustomed to working at this very informal level in small groups, I begin to formalize the activity, giving them the following set of instructions. The instructions are worded as if I were addressing a class.

INSTRUCTIONS FOR PEER EDITING

Professional writers seek the informed opinion of good readers to help them revise anything they have written that they intend for public audience (i.e., an audience that might not forgive the kinds of mistakes we make in personal letters, or, more important, an audience that does not share our own knowledge about the topic). One of the most common experiences for a writer is to feel that what she has written is perfectly clear, even though another reader finds the writing confused, lacking in specificity, disorganized, or generally unclear. Sometimes, of course, the writer is correct; the reader is neither well enough informed nor interested enough to understand the writing. But many times, especially with first and second drafts (believe it or not, many writers produce two, three, and even four drafts—and still have their writing refused by editors of magazines and journals), professional writers find that reader feedback assists them in revising their work.

What I am asking you to do today is engage in the process of giving reader feedback; I am asking you to peer-edit, to give your interested, constructive response to one of your peers. I am not asking you to crucify your friend, attack his or her writing, or make indiscriminately critical remarks. Rather, I am asking you to read your partner's paper, consider it carefully, and try to think of the kinds of questions that might assist him or her in the process of revising.

More than anything else, I want you to give feedback that will help the writer rethink the piece of writing from someone else's point of view. You may wish to consider the following points as an organized way of going about this; if you feel at all unsure about how to do this activity, be sure to follow these points step by step.

1. Read the essay through from beginning to end; simply try to get an overall view of what it is about.

2. Read it through again, slowly; use your pencil to mark sections that confuse you or that seem particularly strong and clear.

3. Now, without referring back to the essay, write in your own words the ideas that you most clearly remember from reading the essay: Which two of these ideas seem, to you, to be the most important points?

4. Reread the essay again, this time examining each paragraph.

    a. Is each paragraph fully developed? (Does it have a clear central idea or reason for being a separate paragraph?)

    b. How does each paragraph relate to the paragraphs before and after it? Does the relationship need to be more clearly stated or does the paragraph need to be moved or deleted?

5. Look at what you wrote in step 3: Does each paragraph clearly develop the ideas you identified as the most important points?

    a. Should some information be deleted because it is not really relevant to the central thrust of the essay?

    b. Do you find that some points need to be made clearer or elaborated on in order for you to understand the central points?

6. Make any general comments that you think might help the writer rethink the essay (please remember that no one needs to suffer through anyone else's sarcasm or silliness).

7. If you have any assistance to offer in the way of punctuation, usage, or spelling, do so: but only do it if you are absolutely sure you are correct—no creative editing!

Finally, a note to each of you as writers: It is not up to you to defend yourself, because this is not an attack. Do not try to answer every question or solve every problem your reader (peer editor) has pointed out. Read over the feedback you have received; reread your own essay; make decisions about what kinds of changes, additions, deletions you might make. Consider visiting the writing tutors over at the learning center for more feedback.

These instructions are intended only by way of exemplification. In my own classes I tailor instructions to particular assignments; I suggest that all teachers do the same. The key is to recognize that without instructions the uninitiated student simply is not sure how to proceed. For additional explorations of the process of peer editing, the reader may wish to see Peter Elbow's *Writing without Teachers* (1973) and *Writing with Power* (1981) and Donald Murray's *A Writer Teaches Writing* (1985).

Revisions

There is a key point in relation to this entire activity, and it is the reason why the term *peer editing* sometimes causes me problems. The very word *editing* suggests a formal process involved in the revision of one draft in order to achieve a final draft. Often, both teachers and students believe that if they engage in peer editing, it must immediately and/or always result in revisions of whatever was edited. I would like to argue strongly against this lockstep notion of writing, editing, and revising. First of all, it is a simple fact that not every piece of writing should be revised—professional writers know this because they are fully aware of how many pages are thrown into the wastebasket before anything ever reaches a stage of development that makes it worthy of revision. When a professional writer is totally dissatisfied with a piece of writing, he throws it away. Even when I believe myself to have a reasonably clear focus for a piece that I am writing, I often find that the first ten or twenty pages constitute something that I have to get out of my system before I can get to what it is that I want to say. Over the past few years, as I slowly moved toward the writing of this book, I filled several floppy disks with verbiage that deserved, eventually, to meet the fate of the "delete" command.

Peer editing should not automatically lead to revision; and, I suspect, it should not often lead to revision. When a paper has gone through several stages and finally reaches the point at which the writer believes it is approaching some sort of wholeness or end, then the peer-editing activity might lead to final revision. Prior to that, revision is probably a waste of time.

What, then, is the point of the activity? The answer is directly related to all the verbiage I deleted from those floppy disks. Without the false starts, without the explorations and free writing that filled those disks, I would never have reached the point of producing this text. To be more direct, writing is a way of knowing; it is a heuristic. The process leads to the product, but the process is not necessarily the product—especially in the early stages.

In peer-editing sessions students learn a great deal that contributes to their ongoing development as writers (and readers). They learn that their readers do not necessarily know what is going on inside the writer's head. They learn that full development and exploration of an idea is necessary for the reader to share the writer's understanding and for the writer's intention to be realized. They learn that certain idiosyncratic stylistic or rhetorical devices irritate some readers while others charm the readers. They learn that not everyone sees the world or their subject in the same way, and that what may appear "obviously true" to the writer seems confused and poorly artic- ulated to the reader. They also learn that sometimes the porridge is just right. They find out that what they have to say can be meaningful to another person, that what they have written can affect a reader both emotionally and intellectually—they learn the joy of making and sharing meaning.

In addition to all these benefits, peer-editing sessions provide readers and writers with the kind of intellectual community I have mentioned earlier. Emotional and intellectual growth no longer appear to be something that the educational system pours into the students' heads. Activities like this allow students to begin to perceive that they are partners in their own growth and that they are directly responsible for that growth. Learning is not some- thing that happens to them, but something that happens through them.

An Extended Example

In an upper-level literature class I teach, I recently tried a variation of this peer-editing activity. I wanted to see (1) how it would affect the students as both readers and discussants of the texts in the course, and (2) how it would affect their writing in general. The students proceeded as follows.

For each novel or play read, each student had to produce a two- to four- page personal response in writing. The essays could focus on any particulars of special interest to the individual. They generally ranged from accounts of personal experiences directly related to something in the novel to fairly traditional essays delineating theme or exploring point of view and/or nar- rative style. I provided a handout suggesting a broad range of possible topics for students who had difficulty getting started, but the primary direction was that their essays should have a clear center or focus because short papers of this kind do not allow room for the development of more than one or two central ideas. Aside from getting them to begin matching the surface structure of written language with their thoughts, it was also my purpose to begin to teach them to produce writing whose purpose is clear and fully developed through techniques such as detail, anecdote, and allusion.

Before we began formal discussion of the novel, students broke into small groups and participated in a modified peer-editing activity. In groups of three or four students, they exchanged one another's papers, read and discussed each one, and made suggestions for additional development or asked questions about sections that seemed unclear or vague. After about forty minutes (these were eighty-minute classes), we came back together in a full circle and began discussing the major points and topics that arose in the papers and through the small-group discussions. At this point, the papers were functioning like a formalized version of reader's notes, but the large-group discussion functioned like a brainstorming session. As topics, points of interest, and disagreements arose in the large group, I listed them on the board, intending that they become the focus for the next class meeting. Before the next class meeting, I read and graded the papers, organized the list that emerged in the large-group discussion, and used it to formulate discussion questions that would constitute the following class. For the third class (and often the fourth when the novel merited fuller exploration), I created discussion questions and mini-lectures focusing on the issues that I felt were particularly important but that had not yet been discussed. Although all of these papers added together counted for only one major grade, the students appeared to treat them as a significant part of the course.

Students also had to write several major papers of five to six pages in length. These papers (which both they and I viewed as "products") involved more than a single novel or play, but again they ranged across a broad spectrum of kinds of writing. Some students wrote fairly traditional essays comparing characters or themes in several works, while others produced creative essays—constructing one-act plays involving characters from several of the works or re-creating a scene in a play, introducing a character from one of the novels into the scene. Of course, they were encouraged to reread what they had already written in the shorter papers and think about the kinds of feedback they had received in small- and large-group discussions in addition to the comments I had made on their papers. If they chose to, they could rewrite these papers.

I describe this set of activities at length because it so clearly suggests how the pieces of a *literacy across the curriculum* approach can work together. First, the shorter papers forced the students to begin thinking about the novels in terms of their own personal reactions. Second, because the papers were due when we began each novel or play, everyone was fully prepared for the initial discussions. Third, at least as important as the fact of their preparation, students came to class with a vested interest in the discussion: They had formulated opinions and wanted to discuss their papers and what they had said in them. Fourth, the energy present in the small-group discussions and the quality of the follow-up large-group discussions indicated that the students were genuinely interested in what others were writing and thinking. Fifth, because we began by focusing on their own interests, they felt a sense of participation in their own learning experience—a sense of participation, by the way, that was real. Sixth, the initial discussions and their papers allowed me to construct interesting discussion questions, focusing on contradictory opinions and "blind spots."Seventh, because the first two classes so clearly focused on their own interests, the students appeared more interested than usual to find out what I thought about many of the issues, and they were especially interested in finding out what kinds of things I thought they had ignored in their own commentaries. Eighth, because the discussions moved across a broad range of kinds of critical approaches, I was able to illustrate how reader-response approaches to literature differ from new critical approaches or historical approaches. Ninth, by their own admission students became more and more interested in the discussions of these short papers, so that they began to expend more energy and time thinking about and writing them. Tenth, both they and I felt that in addition to all the advantages I have just listed, their writing improved. This was not only apparent in their shorter papers, but their major papers also improved.

In fact, as we discussed and evaluated the activities at the end of the course, the consensus was that the shorter papers—even though they were never rewritten—contributed to the success of the longer papers.

I was, of course, particularly interested in what they had to say about all this. It is not unusual for students, especially if they enjoyed a course, to agree that assignments were interesting and helpful. What I found unusual, however, is this: These students (only a few of whom were English majors) were able to comment specifically about the changes they had made in their approach to writing over the semester. They told me how important it was to discover the central point they wish to make and to develop it fully and in an interesting way. They told me how important it was to illustrate and explain generalizations. They told me that retelling the plot of a story just did not constitute good analytical writing because it did not analyze anything. And nearly half of them felt that the activities in this course affected their writing in their other courses—again, specifically, they said they no longer handed a paper in until a friend had read it and commented on it so they could at least consider revisions prior to handing it in.

CONCLUSION

My final point is this: We have the power and possibility of helping our students to become much better readers, writers, listeners, and discussants. By incorporating sensible reading, writing, and discussion activities in our courses—especially insofar as these activities are part of many courses in the curriculum, not just a few special courses—we can significantly affect the ways in which our students read us, our courses, the texts, themselves, and education in general. No one teacher, course, or discipline should or can be responsible for literacy. No one teacher can do all these activities in all his courses, nor should he. When a reading-writing activity is directly relevant to the learning experience—and when the teaching load allows—one, some, or all of these kinds of activities should be incorporated in a course.

Improving student literacy, which is much talked and written about, is not a utopian educational goal. What I have been suggesting is not even radical. It is time for the ultimate, conservative, educational revolution. It is time to center and focus on the language of our students, of ourselves, and of our disciplines as we participate in the mutual purpose of making meaning in and of the world. To paraphrase Nicole Ambrosetti, the six-year-old literary critic I quoted in the introduction to this book, I close as follows: Just as the book does not know what it means until I read it, I also do not know what I mean until I articulate my own internal text. Our students deserve the opportunity to create and articulate *their* meanings.

Bibliography

Andersen, Elaine Slosberg. *Speaking with Style: The Sociolinguistic Skills of Children.* Boston, Mass.: Routledge, 1990.

Anderson, Richard C., Elfrieda H. Hiebert, Judith A. Scott, and Ian A. G. Wilkinson. *Becoming a Nation of Readers.* Washington, D.C.: National Institute of Education, 1985.

Applebee, Arthur N. "Writing and Learning in School Settings." *What Writers Know: The Language, Process, and Structure of Written Discourse,* ed. Martin Nystrand. New York: Academic Press, 1982. 365–81.

Applebee, Arthur N., Kay Barrow, Rexford Brown, Charles Cooper, Ina Mullis, and Anthony Petrosky. *Reading, Thinking and Writing: Results from the 1979–80 National Assessment of Reading and Literature.* Denver, Colo.: National Assessment of Educational Progress Report no. 11-L-C1, 1981.

Applebee, Arthur N., Judith A. Langer, and Ina Mullis. *Writing Trends across the Decade, 1974–1984.* Princeton, N.J.: National Assessment of Educational Progress Report no. 15-W–01, 1986.

Ashbery, John. *Houseboat Days.* New York: Viking Penguin, 1977.

Assessment Committee of the General College Program. *The GCP and Student Learning.* This report summarizes the findings of the General College Program Assessment conducted at SUC–Fredonia and funded by the Fund for the Improvement of Post-Secondary Education. It was prepared by Minda Rae Amiran with assistance from Ruth Antosh, James Bowser, George Browder, Fred Byham, Grant Cooper, Patrick Courts, Paul Davey, Leanna Dunst, Barbara Kaplan, Alan LaFlamme, Raymond McLain, and Theodore Steinberg. Fredonia, N.Y.: State University College of New York, 1989.

Atwell, Nancie. *In the Middle: Writing, Reading, and Learning with Adolescents.* Upper Montclair, N.J.: Boynton/Cook, 1987.

Austin, J. L. *How to Do Things with Words.* Cambridge, Mass.: Harvard University Press, 1975.

Bailey, Richard W., and Melanie Foscheim, eds. *Literacy for Life: The Demand for Reading and Writing.* New York: Modern Language Association, 1983.

Bakhtin, Mikhail. *The Dialogic Imagination: Four Essays by Mikhail Bakhtin*, ed. Michael Holquist, trans. Caryl Emerson and Michael Holquist. University of Texas Slavic Series 1. Austin: University of Texas Press, 1981.

Barthes, Roland. "The Death of the Author." In *Image Music Text*, ed. and trans. Stephen Heath. New York: Hill and Wang, 1977. 142–48.

Bartlett, Elsa Jaffe. "Learning to Revise: Some Component Processes." In *What Writers Know: The Language, Process, and Structure of Written Discourse*, ed. Martin Nystrand. New York: Academic Press, 1982. 345–63.

Berkeley, William. *An Official Report on Virginia, 1671.* In William Carlos Williams, *The Selected Essays of William Carlos Williams.* New York: Random House, 1931.

Bettelheim, Bruno, and Karen Zelan. *On Learning to Read: The Child's Fascination with Meaning.* New York: Random House, 1981.

Bleich, David. *Readings and Feelings: An Introduction to Subjective Criticism.* Urbana, Ill.: National Council of Teachers of English, 1975.

———. *Subjective Criticism.* Baltimore and London: Johns Hopkins University Press, 1978.

A Blueprint for Learning and Teaching. In *The New York Report: A Blueprint for Learning and Teaching.* A Report of the Commissioner's Task Force on the Teaching Profession. Reprinted by the New York State United Teachers. New York: American Federation of Teachers, 1987.

Britton, James. *Language and Learning.* Coral Gables, Fla.: University of Miami Press, 1970.

———. "Writing to Learn and Learning to Write." In *Prospect and Retrospect*, ed. Gordon Pradl. Upper Montclair, N.J.: Boynton/Cook, 1982. 46–67.

Brown, Roger. *A First Language: The Early Stages.* Cambridge, Mass.: Harvard University Press, 1973.

Bruffee, Kenneth A. "Peer Tutoring and the Conversation of Mankind." In *Writing Centers: Theory and Administration*, ed. Gary Olson. Urbana, Ill.: National Council of Teachers of English, 1984. 3–15.

Carroll, Lewis. *Alice in Wonderland*, ed. Donald J. Gray, New York: W. W. Norton, 1971.

Chomsky, Noam. "A Review of B. F. Skinner's *Verbal Behavior.*" In *Proceedings of the Third Texas Conference on Problems of Linguistic Analysis*, ed. A. A. Hill. Austin: University of Texas Press, 1958. 124–58.

———. *Language and Mind.* New York: Harcourt Brace Jovanovich, 1972.

———. *The Logical Structure of Linguistic Theory.* New York: Plenum, 1975.

Clanchy, Michael T. "Looking Back from the Invention of Printing." In *Literacy in Historical Perspective*, ed. Daniel P. Resnick. Washington, D.C.: Library of Congress, 1983. 7–22.

Cressy, David. "The Environment for Literacy Accomplishment and Context in Seventeenth-Century England and New England." In *Literacy in Historical Perspective*, ed. Daniel P. Resnick. Washington, D.C.: Library of Congress, 1983. 23–42.

Culler, Jonathan. *On Deconstruction: Theory and Criticism after Structuralism.* Ithaca, N.Y.: Cornell University Press, 1982.

D'Angelo, Frank J. "Literacy and Cognition: A Developmental Perspective." In *Literacy for Life: The Demand for Reading and Writing*, eds. Richard W. Bailey and Robin Melanie Foscheim. New York: Modern Language Association, 1983. 97–114.

de Beaugrande, Robert. "Learning to Read versus Reading to Learn: A Discourse-Processing Approach." In *Learning and Comprehension of Text*, eds. Heinz Mandl, Nancy Stein, and Tom Trabasso. Hillsdale, N.J.: Lawrence Erlbaum, 1984. 159–91.

Delpit, Lisa D. "The Silenced Dialogue: Power and Pedagogy in Educating Other People's Children." *Harvard Educational Review* 58 (August 1988): 290–98.

Derrida, Jacques. "Signature Event Context." *GLYPH 1* (1977): 171–97.

———. "LIMITED INC a b c . . ." *GLYPH 2* (1977): 162–254.

———. "Structure, Sign and Play in the Discourse of Human Sciences." In *Writing and Difference*, trans. Alan Bass. London: Routledge and Kegan Paul, 1978. 278–93.

Dixon, John. *Growth through English*. 3d. ed. London: Oxford University Press, 1975.

Donald, James. *Language, Literacy, and Schooling*. London: Open University Press, 1985.

Dunham, William Huse, and Stanley Pargellis, eds. *Complaint and Reform in England 1436–1714*. New York: Octagon, 1968.

Elbow, Peter. *Writing without Teachers*. New York: Oxford University Press, 1973.

———. *Writing with Power*. New York: Oxford University Press, 1981.

Ferguson, Charles A., and Dan I. Slobin, eds. *Studies of Child Language Development*. New York: Holt, Rinehart and Winston, 1973.

Fish, Stanley. *Is There a Text in This Class?* Cambridge, Mass.: Harvard University Press, 1980.

Foucault, Michel. *Power/Knowledge: Selected Interviews and Other Writings 1972–1977*. Ed. Colin Gordon, trans. Colin Gordon, Leo Marshall, John Mepham, and Kate Soper. New York: Pantheon, 1980.

Freire, Paulo. *Education for Critical Consciousness*. New York: Seabury Press, 1973.

Freire, Paulo, and Donaldo Macedo. *Literacy: Reading the Word and the World*. South Hadley, Mass.: Bergin and Garvey, 1987.

Gardner, Howard. *The Mind's New Science: A History of the Cognitive Revolution*. New York: Basic Books, 1985.

Giroux, Henry A. *Teachers as Intellectuals: Toward a Critical Pedagogy of Learning*. Holyoke, Mass.: Bergin and Garvey, 1988.

———. "Rethinking the Boundaries of Educational Discourse: Modernism, Postmodernism, and Feminism." *College Literature* 17/2–3 (1990): 1–50.

Goodlad, John. *A Place Called School*. New York: McGraw-Hill, 1984.

Goodman, Kenneth. *Language and Literacy: The Selected Writings of Kenneth S. Goodman*, ed. and intro. Frederick V. Gollasch. Vol. 1, *Process, Theory, Research*. Vol. 2, *Reading, Language, and the Classroom Teacher*. Boston: Routledge and Kegan Paul, 1982.

Goodman, Nelson. *Ways of Worldmaking*. Indianapolis, Ind.: Hackett, 1978.

Graff, Gerald. *Professing Literature: An Institutional History*. Chicago: University of Chicago Press, 1987.

Gundlach, Robert A. "Children as Writers." In *What Writers Know: The Language,*

Process, and Structure of Written Discourse, ed. Martin Nystrand. New York: Academic Press, 1982. 129–47.

Halasek, Kay. "Mikhail Bakhtin and 'Dialogism': What They Have to Offer Composition." *Composition Chronicle* 3 (1990): 5–8.

Halliday, M. A. K. *Learning How to Mean: Explorations in the Development of Language*. Baltimore, Md.: Edward Arnold, 1975.

———. *Language as Social Semiotic: The Social Interpretation of Language and Meaning*. Baltimore, Md.: University Park Press, 1978.

Harste, Jerome C., Virginia A. Woodward, and Carolyn L. Burke. *Language Stories and Literacy Lessons*. Portsmouth, N.H.: Heinemann Educational Books, 1984.

Heidegger, Martin. "The Age of the World View." In *Martin Heidegger and the Question of Literature: Toward a Postmodern Literary Hermeneutics*, ed. William Spanos, trans. Marjorie Grenel. Bloomington: Indiana University Press, 1979. 1–16.

Heller, Joseph. *Catch–22*. New York: Simon and Schuster, 1961.

Hirsch. E. D., Jr. *Cultural Literacy: What Every American Needs to Know*. Boston: Houghton Mifflin, 1987.

Hirsch, E. D., Jr., Joseph F. Kett, and James Trefil. *The Dictionary of Cultural Literacy: What Every American Needs to Know*. Boston: Houghton Mifflin, 1988.

Holland, Norman N. *The Dynamics of Literary Response*. New York: Oxford University Press, 1968.

———. *5 Readers Reading*. New Haven: Yale University Press, 1975.

Iser, Wolfgang. *The Act of Reading*. Baltimore, Md.:Johns Hopkins University Press, 1978.

Kirsch, Irwin S., and Ann Jungeblut. *Literacy: Profiles of America's Young Adults*. Educational Testing Service Report No. 16. Princton, N.J.: National Assessment of Education Progress, 1987.

Klare, George R. "Readability." In *Handbook of Reading Research*, eds. David P. Pearson, Rebecca Barr, Michael Kami, and Peter Mosenthal. New York: Longman, 1984. 681–744.

Kuhn, Thomas. *The Structure of Scientific Revolutions*. Chicago: University of Chicago Press, 1970.

Langer, Judith, Arthur Applebee, Ina V. Mullis, and Mary Foertsch. *Learning to Read: Instruction and Achievement in Grades, 4, 8, 12*. Princeton, N.J.: National Assessment of Educational Progress, 1988.

Macnamara, John. *Names for Things*. Cambridge, Mass.: MIT Press, 1982.

Macrorie, Ken. *Uptaught*. New York: Haydn Publishing Co., 1970.

Mailer, Norman. *The Naked and the Dead*. New York: Holt, Rinehart and Winston, 1948.

McLaren, Peter. *Life in Schools: An Introduction to Critical Pedagogy in the Foundations of Education*. New York and London: Longman, 1989.

———. "Critical Literacy: Radical and Postmodern Perspectives." In *Critical Literacy: Radical and Postmodern Perspectives*, eds. Colin Lankshear and Peter McLaren. Albany, N.Y.: SUNY Press, forthcoming.

Moffett, James. *Teaching the Universe of Discourse*. Boston: Houghton Mifflin, 1968.

———. *Active Voice: A Writing Program across the Curriculum*. Upper Montclair, N.J.: Boynton/Cook, 1981.

———. "Hidden Impediments." In *Language, Schooling, and Society*, ed. Stephen Tchudi. Upper Montclair, N.J.: Boynton/Cook, 1985. 89–100.

Murray, Donald. *A Writer Teaches Writing*. 2d ed. Boston: Houghton Mifflin, 1985.

Norris, Christoper. *Contest of Faculties: Philosophy and Theory after Deconstruction*. New York: Methuen, 1985.

Nystrand, Martin, ed. *What Writers Know: The Language, Process, and Structure of Written Discourse*. New York: Academic Press, 1982.

Olson, Gary A., ed. *Writing Centers: Theory and Administration*. Urbana, Ill.: National Council of Teachers of English, 1984.

Pearson, David P., with Rebecca Barr, Michael Kami, and Peter Mosenthal. *Handbook of Reading Research*. New York: Longman, 1984.

Perry, William. *Forms of Intellectual and Ethical Development in the College Years*. New York: Holt, Rinehart and Winston, 1970.

Petrosky, Anthony R. "Reading Achievement." In *Secondary School Reading: What Research Reveals for Classroom Practice*, eds. Allen Berger and H. Alan Robinson. Urbana, Ill.: ERIC Clearinghouse on Reading and Communication Skills and the National Conference on Research in English, 1982. 7–19.

Piattelli-Palmarini, Massimo, ed. *Language and Learning: The Debate between Jean Piaget and Noam Chomsky*. Cambridge, Mass.: Harvard University Press, 1980.

Pradl, Gordon, ed. *Prospect and Retrospect: Selected Essays of James Britton*. Upper Montclair, N.J.: Boynton/Cook, 1982.

Purves, Alan C. *The Scribal Society*. New York: Longman, 1990.

Rayner, Keith, and Alexander Pollatsek. *The Psychology of Reading*. Englewood Cliffs, N.J.: Prentice-Hall, 1989.

Resnick, Daniel P., ed. *Literacy in Historical Perspective*. Washington, D.C.: Library of Congress, 1983.

Ritchie, Joy S. "Beginning Writers: Diverse Voices and Individual Identities." *College Composition and Communication* 40 (1989): 52–74.

Ronat, Mitsou. *Language and Responsibility—Noam Chomsky*, trans. Noam Chomsky. New York: Pantheon, 1979.

Rosenblatt, Louise M. *The Reader, the Text, the Poem*. Carbondale: Southern Illinois University Press, 1978.

Saussure, Ferdinand de. *Course in General Linguistics*, eds. Charles Bailey and Albert Sechehaye in collaboration with Albert Reidlinger, trans. Wade Baskin. New York: Philosophical Library, 1959.

Schwartz, Mimi. "Response to Writing: A College-wide Perspective." *College English* 46, no. 1 (January 1984): 55–61.

Searle, John S. *Speech Acts: An Essay in the Philosophy of Language*. Cambridge, Mass.: Harvard University Press, 1969.

———. "Reiterating the Differences: A Reply to Derrida." *GLYPH 2* (1977): 198–208.

Smith, Frank. *Understanding Reading: A Psycholinguistic Analysis of Reading and Learning to Read*. 3d ed. New York: Holt, Rinehart and Winston, 1982.

Stock, Brian. *The Implications of Literacy: Written Language and Models of Interpretation in the Eleventh and Twelfth Centuries*. Princeton, N.J.: Princeton University Press, 1983.

Tchudi, Stephen N. "The Experiential Approach: Inner Worlds to Outer Worlds." In *Eight Approaches to Composition*, eds. Timothy R. Donovan and Ben W. McClelland. Urbana, Ill.: National Council of Teachers of English, 1980. 37–52.

————. *Teaching Writing in the Content Areas; College Level.*: National Education Association, 1986.

————, ed. *Language, Schooling, and Society* (Proceedings of the International Federation for the Teaching of English Seminar at Michigan State University, November 11–14, 1984). Upper Montclair, N.J.: Boynton/Cook, 1985.

Tchudi, Stephen N., and Margie C. Huerta. *Teaching Writing in the Content Areas: Middle School/Junior High School.* Washington, D.C.: National Education Association, 1983.

Tompkins, Jane, ed. *Reader-Response Criticism: From Formalism to Post Structuralism.* Baltimore and London: Johns Hopkins University Press, 1980.

Vygotsky, Lev. *Thought and Language.* Cambridge, Mass.: MIT Press, 1962.

Wardaugh, Ronald. *Reading: A Linguistic Perspective.* New York: Harcourt Brace, 1969.

Whitman, Walt. "There Was a Child Went Forth." In *Complete Poetry and Selected Prose*, ed. James Miller, Jr. Boston: Houghton Mifflin, 1958. 259.

Index

About the Author

PATRICK L. COURTS is a professor of English at the State University College of New York in Fredonia and has also taught at Michigan State University and in the Chicago public school system. He has published high school composition texts *The Creative Word 4* and *The Creative Word 6* (with Stephen Tchudi) and numerous articles on the composing process, whole language approaches to teaching reading and writing at the college level, and critical theory. His major research interests are psycholinguistics and related language processes in high school and college students, literary critical theory, philosophy of language, and learning assessment.